In heavy-wheeled carts pulled by bullocks, a train of refugees makes its way under military protection from Pakistan to India in 1947. The refugees were among millions who were uprooted in the tumultuous aftermath of World War II, when British India achieved independence—but was split into two nations divided by a chasm of religious hatred.

THE AFTERMATH: ASIA

This volume is one of a series that chronicles
in full the events of the Second World War.

WORLD WAR II · TIME-LIFE BOOKS · ALEXANDRIA, VIRGINIA

BY THE EDITORS OF TIME-LIFE BOOKS

THE AFTERMATH: ASIA

Time-Life Books Inc.
is a wholly owned subsidiary of
TIME INCORPORATED

Founder: Henry R. Luce 1898-1967

Editor-in-Chief: Henry Anatole Grunwald
President: J. Richard Munro
Chairman of the Board: Ralph P. Davidson
Executive Vice President: Clifford J. Grum
Editorial Director: Ralph Graves
Group Vice President, Books: Joan D. Manley

TIME-LIFE BOOKS INC.

Editor: George Constable
Executive Editor: George Daniels
Director of Design: Louis Klein
Board of Editors: Dale M. Brown, Thomas H. Flaherty Jr.,
Thomas A. Lewis, Martin Mann, Robert G. Mason,
Ellen Phillips, Gerry Schremp, Gerald Simons,
Rosalind Stubenberg, Kit van Tulleken
Director of Administration: David L. Harrison
Director of Research: Carolyn L. Sackett
Director of Photography: John Conrad Weiser

President: Reginald K. Brack Jr.
Executive Vice President: John Steven Maxwell
Vice Presidents: George Artandi, Stephen L. Bair,
Peter G. Barnes, Nicholas Benton, John L. Canova,
Beatrice T. Dobie, Christopher T. Linen, James L.
Mercer, Paul R. Stewart

WORLD WAR II

Editor: Thomas H. Flaherty Jr.
The Aftermath: Asia was prepared under the
supervision of Time-Life Books by the following
contributors:
Editors: Charles Osborne, Sheldon Cotler
Picture Editor: Peter D. Collins
Assistant Designer: Leonard Vigliarolo
Researchers: Martha J. Mader, Jane Furth, Kay Neil
Noble, Suad A. McCoy
Writers: Cathy Beason, Eric Schurenberg, Cinda Siler,
Bryce S. Walker
Editorial Manager: Felice Lerner
Editorial Assistants: Keith Nislow, Nicholas Goodman
Special Contributors: Valerie Moolman, Frederick
King Poole, Rafael Steinberg

Time-Life Books Editorial Staff for *The Aftermath: Asia*
Researcher: Loretta Britten
Copy Coordinators: Ann Bartunek, Elizabeth Graham,
Barbara Quarmby
Art Assistant: Robert K. Herndon
Picture Coordinator: Renée DeSandies
Editorial Assistant: Myrna E. Traylor

Editorial Operations
Design: Arnold C. Holeywell (assistant director);
Anne B. Landry (art coordinator); James J. Cox (quality
control)
Research: Jane Edwin (assistant director),
Louise D. Forstall
Copy Room: Susan Galloway Goldberg (director),
Celia Beattie
Production: Feliciano Madrid (director),
Gordon E. Buck, Peter Inchauteguiz

Correspondents: Elisabeth Kraemer (Bonn); Margot
Hapgood, Dorothy Bacon (London); Miriam Hsia,
Lucy T. Voulgaris (New York); Maria Vincenza Aloisi,
Josephine du Brusle (Paris); Ann Natanson (Rome).
Valuable assistance was also provided by: Wibo
Van de Linde, Janny Hovinga, Bert Meijer
(Amsterdam); Judy Aspinall, Lesley Coleman
(London); Carolyn Chubet, Christina Lieberman (New
York); Kazuo Ohyauchi (Tokyo).

The Consultants: COLONEL JOHN R. ELTING, USA (Ret.),
was an intelligence officer with the 8th Armored Division in World War II. A former associate professor at
West Point, he is the author of *Battles for Scandinavia*
in the Time-Life Books World War II series and of *The
Battle of Bunker's Hill, The Battles of Saratoga* and
Military History and Atlas of the Napoleonic Wars.

U. ALEXIS JOHNSON first went to the Far East in 1935 as
a U.S. Foreign Service language officer, serving in Japan, Korea, China—and Manchuria, where he was
interned when the Japanese attacked Pearl Harbor.
After being exchanged, he followed U.S. troops returning to the Philippines in 1944, and in early 1945
he became U.S. Consul in liberated Manila. After the
Japanese surrender he served on General MacArthur's
staff in Japan and Korea and was subsequently named
Consul General for all of Japan and Okinawa. He later
served as U.S. Ambassador to Thailand, Deputy Ambassador to Vietnam, Ambassador to Japan, and Ambassador to the Strategic Arms Limitations Talks with
the Soviet Union.

JAMES C. THOMSON JR., a historian of American-East
Asian relations, is Curator of the Nieman Foundation
for Journalism at Harvard University. The son of missionary educators, he spent much of his childhood in
China both before and after World War II. A graduate
of Yale University with advanced degrees from Cambridge and Harvard, he served as an East Asia policy
aide in the State Department and the White House
under Presidents Kennedy and Johnson. He is the author of *While China Faced West,* co-author of *Sentimental Imperialists: The American Experience in East
Asia* and co-editor of *American-East Asian Relations.*

FRANCIS J. GALBRAITH is a retired member of the U.S.
Foreign Service. He was a U.S. Army infantryman in
New Guinea during World War II and served after the
War in various consular posts in Indonesia. He was
Ambassador to Singapore from 1966 to 1969 and Am-
bassador to Indonesia from 1969 to 1974.

ROBERT SHERROD spent more than three years in the
Pacific theater as a correspondent for *Time* and *Life,*
covering the battles of Attu, Tarawa, Saipan, Iwo Jima
and Okinawa. He remained in Asia until 1948, reporting from most of the countries that are the subjects of this volume.

Library of Congress Cataloguing in Publication Data

The Aftermath: Asia.

(World War II)
Bibliography: p.
Includes index.
1. Asia—History—1945-   I. Time-Life
Books.   II. Series.
D535.2.A38 1983   950'.42   82-19541
ISBN 0-8094-3435-0
ISBN 0-8094-3436-9 (lib. bdg.)

For information about any Time-Life book, please write:

Reader Information
Time-Life Books
541 North Fairbanks Court
Chicago, Illinois 60611

CONTENTS

1

Alongside a railroad track near the Burmese village of Waw, 60 miles northeast of Rangoon, a small group of Japanese soldiers stood morosely in the rain. They included a staff colonel from Japanese Army headquarters in Moulmein, a lieutenant acting as his escort, an interpreter, a flag-bearer and a bugler. It was August 17, 1945, and for two days the War had been over. The Japanese were awaiting the arrival of a British party to escort them from the trackside rendez-vous to a site where they were to arrange a mutual cease-fire and the withdrawal of Japanese forces facing the British across the monsoon-swollen waters of the Sittang River. The colonel ordered his detail to smarten up their uniforms; the men took off their rain capes. The flag-bearer unfurled the Rising Sun. The bugler raised his horn to his lips, then hesitated. "Colonel," he asked, "what do I blow?"

"Blow what you like!" snapped the colonel—knowing that Japanese Army regulations contained no reference to the word *kofoku*—surrender—and certainly no bugle call appropriate to the War's unthinkable outcome.

The bugler improvised—then stopped, embarrassed. At this moment the British party, a handful of Gurkhas and two British officers, appeared from the jungle on the other side of the tracks. Soon a strange-looking train pulled up, powered by a jeep whose wheels had been fitted with flanges to roll on the rails. The train bore the group to a nearby British headquarters, where the Japanese colonel and the lieutenant, aided by the interpreter, negotiated with a British brigadier. As the talks proceeded, two Gurkhas brought mugs of coffee that had been boiled with milk. The Japanese drank the hot mixture with gusto.

Later, as the Japanese rode back toward their headquar-ters, the lieutenant asked the bugler and flag-bearer, who had waited outside the negotiating room, if they had had coffee. They indicated, rubbing their bellies, that they had.

In return for the coffee, the flag-bearer said, the Gurkhas had asked the Japanese for their flag. "But we couldn't give them our national flag, could we, Lieutenant?"

The colonel broke in before the lieutenant could reply. "You could," he said, "have given them the flag."

The Japanese Empire was vanquished. The Allies, according to plans made that summer at Potsdam and at earlier conferences, were taking steps to occupy Japan and other

"ASIA FOR THE ASIANS"

areas where the Japanese had held sway. American units led by General Douglas MacArthur, commander of American forces in the Pacific, and British troops of the Southeast Asia Command under Admiral Lord Louis Mountbatten, would be the leading players in this drama of occupation, in which Soviet and Nationalist Chinese soldiers would also participate.

Many of the lands they were to occupy lay bloodstained and scarred. The war in the Pacific had claimed an estimated 15 million lives and maimed millions of people; the damage to property, agriculture and industry was beyond calculation.

Grim though they were, these losses were an expected consequence of war—one that, in its material aspects, could be remedied in time. It was officially believed in Washington and other Western capitals that cooperation among the wartime Allies—the United States, Britain, China and the Soviet Union—would bring about full recovery and establish Asia as a peaceful, prosperous region, free of the economic and military yoke that had been imposed by the conquering Japanese.

Already, however, such optimism was under challenge. By August 1945 the Soviet Union, through its actions in Asia and Europe, was showing signs of jettisoning wartime cooperation in order to pursue political and territorial goals of its own. In China, a continuing struggle for power between Communists and Nationalists was about to flare into a massive civil war. And on the divided Korean peninsula, the sharpening rivalry between East and West established a setting ripe for confrontation.

Elsewhere in Asia, turbulence bubbled angrily through the deceptive silence that followed the collapse of Japan. In the months and years ahead, the Japanese themselves, under a relatively benign American occupation, were among the few who would be truly at peace. For millions of other Asians, who had long lived under colonial domination, World War II had unleashed forces that would prove irresistible and would permanently change the political complexion of the continent.

The upheaval came as a shock to the colonial powers of Europe. The French and the Dutch had assumed throughout the War that they would return to their respective colonies in Indochina and the East Indies after an Allied victory. British leaders were aware that the tide of events was flowing against them, but some diehards expected to retain the British Empire in India, Burma and Malaya for a few years longer at least.

Colonialists everywhere failed to recognize the deep-rooted determination of the Asian peoples to achieve independence. Despite the cruelty that the Japanese had frequently displayed toward their fellow Asians, the Japanese propaganda message—Asia for the Asians—had sunk in. Though other Asians had suffered the consequences of Japanese expansionism, many admired Japan for having made itself into a nation strong enough to present a mighty challenge to the West. Asian power, wielded by Japan, had exposed the weaknesses of Westerners; Asians had driven Occidentals out of one colonial enclave after another and subjected them to humiliation and defeat. Finally, despite the considerable technological benefits, including modern transportation and sanitation, that Europeans had introduced into Asia, Asians resented the greed of white colonial masters, as well as their lordly exercise of power and their attitudes of racial superiority. What frustrated the Asians most was the colonialists' refusal to acknowledge their legitimate urge for political and economic freedom.

The colonial peoples were not long in asserting themselves. By autumn of 1945, a strong independence movement was under way in British Burma; nationalism was forcing the British to accelerate their departure from the Indian subcontinent and from Ceylon; the East Indies were rent by struggles for power among the Indonesians and by war against the Dutch; Vietnamese leaders in Indochina were bitterly contesting the sovereignty of the French; and the United States, only a marginal member of the colonialist club, was preparing to renounce voluntarily all claim to the Philippine Islands.

The troubled future of Asia had been a recurring concern of Franklin Delano Roosevelt, America's wartime President. After his death in April 1945, the U.S. State Department drafted a memorandum for his successor, Harry S. Truman—to whom Roosevelt had confided very little while he was alive. The memorandum emphasized F.D.R.'s realization that "dynamic forces leading toward self-government are growing in Asia; that the United States—as a great democracy—cannot and must not try to retard this development but rather act in harmony with it."

The idealism of such thinking had also inspired the lofty aims of the Atlantic Charter, the summary of Allied war goals enunciated in 1941 by President Roosevelt and Britain's Prime Minister Winston Churchill; the same ideals were also written into the United Nations Charter, which affirmed the right of peoples to govern themselves. After the War, however, the high purposes behind such pronouncements increasingly came to be overshadowed by another concern—the deepening antagonism that was developing between the United States and the Soviet Union in what was soon to be universally known as the Cold War. At first the principal arena of this clash was Europe, where the two postwar superpowers competed intensely for the political allegiances of the Europeans.

Given the existence of the Cold War, American policy-makers felt compelled to keep their eyes riveted on Europe and to support non-Communist European governments in all their areas of interest, including their colonies. Thus if a colonial independence movement threatened the economy of its European master—rendering that nation more vulnerable to the encroachments of Communism— the course for Washington policymakers usually was clear: Side with the European power, or at least take a position that did not offer much aid or comfort to the nationalist movement in the colony.

In general, American Cold War policy rested on four cornerstones. They were the so-called Truman Doctrine of March 1947, in which the President promised to support "free peoples who are resisting attempted subjugation by armed minorities or by outside pressures"; the Marshall Plan, named for Secretary of State George C. Marshall, its primary sponsor, and aimed at the economic recovery of Europe with massive American aid; the North Atlantic Treaty, a defense pact establishing an alliance of 12 nations led by Britain and the United States; and lastly, aid to underdeveloped countries, as called for by Truman in his 1949 inaugural address. Some of this aid was destined for areas emerging from colonialism—under a program called Point Four because it had been proposed in the fourth major segment of Truman's speech.

Although most of these policies had their greatest direct

Colonial territories in Asia claimed by Western powers at the end of the War encompassed 3.2 million square miles inhabited by an estimated 590 million people. Portugal, the first colonizer, by 1945 retained only small holdings such as Macao, Goa and part of Timor. Beginning in the 17th Century, Great Britain and the Netherlands carved out extensive empires that contributed mightily to their national prosperity. Other Western holdings in Asia—primarily French Indochina and the American Philippines—were less profitable but were prized for reasons of national prestige or military strategy.

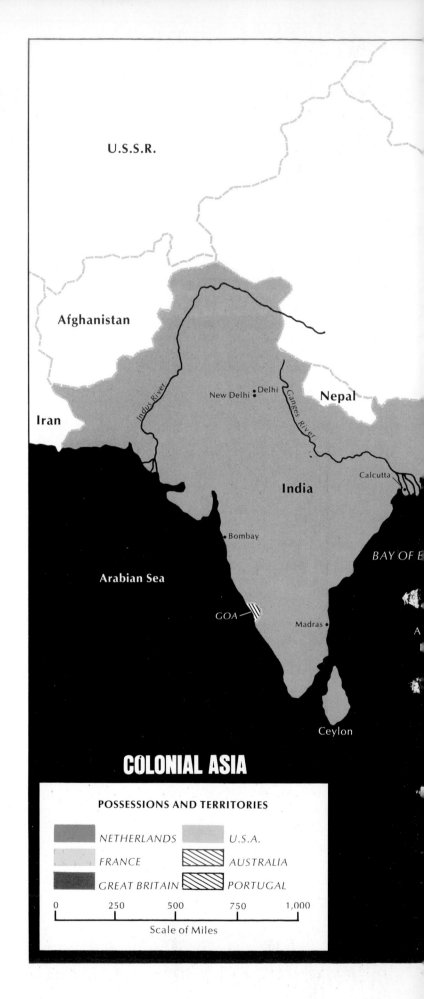

COLONIAL ASIA

POSSESSIONS AND TERRITORIES

NETHERLANDS	U.S.A.
FRANCE	AUSTRALIA
GREAT BRITAIN	PORTUGAL

0   250   500   750   1,000

Scale of Miles

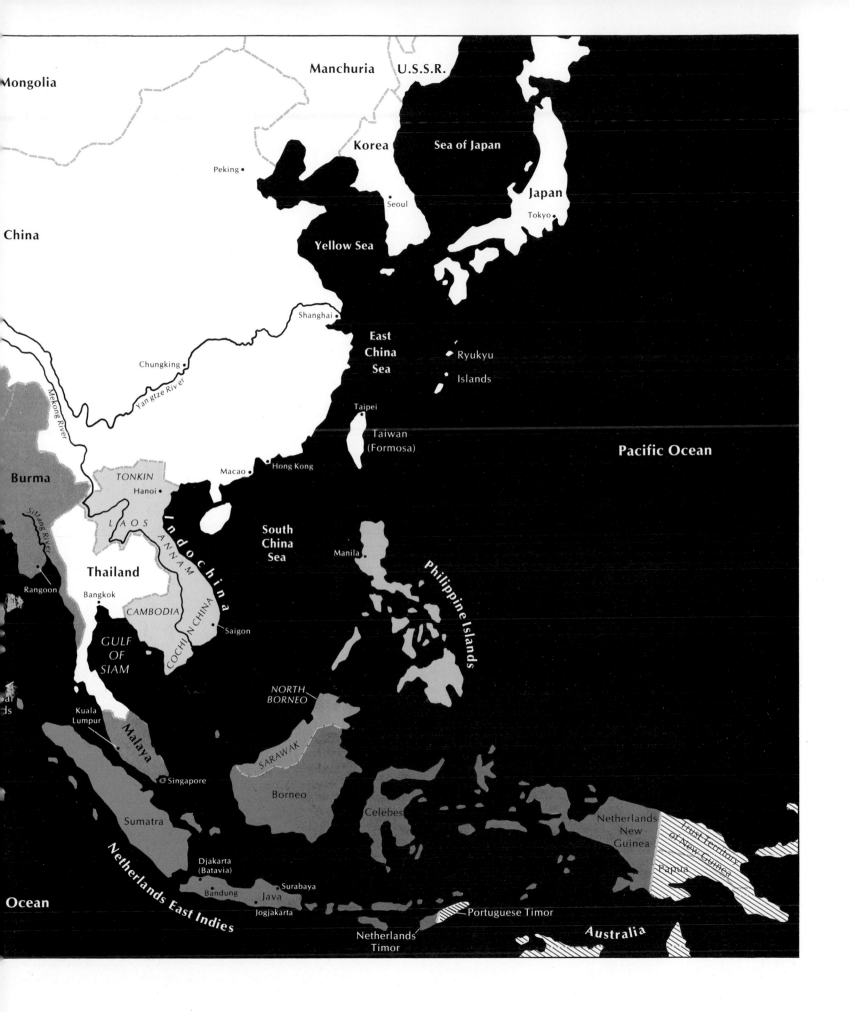

impact in Europe, the strategy behind them, aimed at containment of the U.S.S.R., was destined to have an enormous indirect effect in Asia. This was particularly true where the Soviet Union and the United States confronted each other across a hostile dividing line, as in Korea, or where a nationalist independence movement was influenced or dominated by Communists, as in Indochina.

In China, Cold War issues were more complicated. In 1945, the goal of United States leaders was to establish China as a bulwark of stability and strength on the Asian landmass, filling the power vacuum that had been left by the collapse of Japan and furnishing a solid base for the projection of American policy throughout Southeast Asia and the western Pacific.

The realization of this aim was blocked by the violent antagonism between the Chinese Communists under Mao Tse-tung and the Nationalist government of Generalissimo Chiang Kai-shek. Until 1947, it was Washington's fervent hope to bring these hostile factions together and to help them build a strong China that would be bound by ties of friendship to the United States. By the following year, however, American priorities had shifted to a policy of direct

support for Chiang against the Communists, and by 1949 it became clear that even the goal of retaining China as a friend had slipped beyond reach.

Independence came to the Philippine Islands without a revolution. It was an event that had been planned before the War by the people of the islands and their American rulers. The Americans were relative newcomers to the Philippines. Beginning in 1565, the Spanish had dominated the 7,109-island archipelago; their shipborne explorers found about 400 lushly fertile islands inhabited by no fewer than 45 strongly independent groups, who spoke a babble of 84 different dialects. The Spanish met resistance—mostly from the Moros, or Muslims, on the large islands of Luzon and Mindanao—and answered force with force, though they never completely subdued the Moros. As a source of riches, the Philippines (unlike the fabled islands of the Indies, which yielded a wealth of spices and pearls) proved to be disappointing, but the Spanish did find indigo, coconuts and sugar cane, and a little gold. The real importance of the islands (named for Spain's King Philip II) was their strategic location: They were an ideal center from which to nurture a

three-way trade between Spain, China and Spanish Mexico.

Over the years, the port of Manila on the island of Luzon grew in size and importance, and the Spanish there prospered. The islanders chafed under foreign domination, but their frequent revolts were put down. Then in 1896, Filipinos in the north rose again, and after two years of sporadic fighting they gained the upper hand. By this time Spain was embroiled in a war with the United States that had followed the blowing up of the U.S.S. *Maine* in the harbor of Havana, Cuba, another embattled Spanish colony. General Emilio Aguinaldo, a charismatic political showman and guerrilla leader, emerged as the leader of the Filipino revolutionaries. And in May 1898, an American fleet under Commodore George Dewey obliterated a weak Spanish Naval force in the Battle of Manila Bay, putting a decisive end to Spanish power in the islands.

A few weeks later, Aguinaldo proclaimed the freedom of the Philippines. A declaration of independence was signed and a national flag unfurled while, for the first time, a band played the Filipino national anthem. A few days after that, Aguinaldo had himself installed as president of the first Philippine republic.

But the United States did not recognize the new nation. The treaty that formally ended the Spanish-American War five months later transferred ownership of the Philippines from Spain to the United States in return for $20 million. The Filipinos resisted this change of masters; there followed more than four years of bitter fighting that engaged 126,000 American soldiers and cost 7,000 American casualties before the islands could be declared relatively secure.

By 1901, under an American governor general, the Philippines had begun a process of Americanization. Spanish gave way to English as the language of general use, American businesses proliferated, a system of universal compulsory primary education was established, and an unprecedented program of public health was introduced. At the same time, American democratic ideals were promoted and Filipinos were encouraged to participate in government and prepare themselves for self-rule. Talk of independence began so soon and American supervision was so benign that the revolutionary spirit of the nationalist movement began to fade. "Damn the Americans," said Manuel Luis Quezon y Malina, a leading figure in the Nacionalista Party, whose platform was independence. "Why don't they tyrannize us more?"

Though governed with a light hand, the Filipinos had little economic freedom. The prosperity of the islands became increasingly dependent upon American trade, and no effort was made by the United States to prepare the Filipinos for economic sufficiency.

A major step toward full self-government was taken on November 15, 1935, when the Philippines became a Commonwealth of the United States. Manuel Quezon was inaugurated as the first President. The U.S. Congress, in establishing the Commonwealth, provided for a 10-year period of self-government under American tutelage; during that time the Filipinos were to continue to acknowledge the authority of the United States.

One of Quezon's first acts was to secure the services of Major General Douglas MacArthur, whose father had been a troop commander and military governor in the Philippines during the Spanish-American War, and who had himself spent a year in the islands as a junior officer. MacArthur had returned to the Philippines in 1922 for almost three years as a brigadier general and had again been posted to the islands in 1935 for another tour of duty. So attuned to the islands was the general that rather than accepting a customary reassignment to the United States he took early retirement with two stars in 1937 and remained to serve as adviser to the Commonwealth armed forces.

As relations between Japan and the United States began to deteriorate alarmingly in 1941, President Roosevelt merged all the American and Filipino troops in the archipelago into a single army; he recalled MacArthur from retirement and appointed him commander of U.S. Army Forces in the Far East.

The Japanese delivered a savage air attack on Clark Field northwest of Manila on December 8, 1941, Pacific time, and two days later Lieut. General Masaharu Homma's 14th Army began a multistage invasion of the islands.

Though MacArthur had tried since 1935 to forge a respectable fighting force—with very little help from Washington—the divisions of the Philippine-American Army were undermanned and ill equipped. Retreat was inevitable. By mid-March 1942, MacArthur and Quezon had

In Saigon, the Japanese commander of a military police unit formally turns over his sword to an Indian officer of the British Army in November 1945. In the three months since the end of the War, almost all of the Japanese troops in South Vietnam had been permitted to retain their arms in order to help the British occupation forces maintain order.

made their separate ways to Australia, each vowing to return. Quezon subsequently established a government-in-exile in Washington while MacArthur took command of all Allied forces in the southwest Pacific.

In May of 1942 the Japanese Army under General Homma completed its conquest of the Philippines. When the military administrators moved in, a propaganda war had already started.

"Dear friends! Folks at home!" began the leaflets that fluttered down from Japanese planes. "You probably sincerely believe that you are defending democracy from the aggressors, but nothing could be farther from the truth." According to the leaflets, the Filipinos had been abused, exploited and neglected by the United States. "The present fighting," they said, "has been caused by America's greed to place Asia under its control." The invaders set about destroying American flags, changing American street names to Japanese, banning American films and music, tearing up American textbooks and interning American citizens.

Despite the friendly tone of their propaganda toward the Filipinos, the Japanese occupation was anything but easygoing. Politicians unwilling to collaborate and people suspected of belonging to—or sheltering—resistance groups were tortured and killed; entire villages were destroyed. Any feeling of kinship that the Filipinos might have had for their Asian conquerors was nullified by Japanese cruelty. Guerrilla bands raided Japanese outposts and disrupted communications and transportation. Filipinos everywhere laid plans for the return of the Americans.

In 1943, Japan set up a puppet government with a former judge, José P. Laurel, as president. For a while it seemed that the Japanese had won a psychological victory, for when Laurel attended a Greater East Asia Conference in Tokyo, he appeared enthusiastic about the theme of the conference: a union of nations sponsored by Japan. "One billion Orientals, one billion people of Greater East Asia!" he exclaimed. "How could they have been dominated, a great portion of them particularly by England and America?"

The Filipinos developed a remarkable attitude toward collaboration, concluding that the men who accepted positions in the puppet government did so in order to become buffers between the Japanese and the vulnerable people they controlled. Ultimately, the Japanese found that the col-

Manuel Roxas y Acuña stands in the ornate reception room of Manila's presidential palace in July 1946. Although Roxas held a minor administrative post under the Japanese occupation, he was supported by General Douglas MacArthur and by influential Filipinos in his election as President of the newly independent Philippine Republic.

Luis Taruc, leader of the anti-Japanese but Leftist guerrilla movement known as Hukbalahap, addresses followers in his brother's Manila tailor shop. Taruc was elected to the Philippine Congress in 1946 but was denied office on the grounds that he was a Communist.

laborators could not be trusted. They suspected—correctly—that some of the puppet politicians were secretly helping the underground, which included a group called the Hukbalahaps (meaning "People's Anti-Japanese Army"). The Huks, as they were called, were organized and commanded by indigenous Communists, whose primary long-term aim was to exploit the resentment of rural Filipinos against wealthy landowners. Between generally unsuccessful attacks on the Japanese, the Huks raided large estates—killing foremen and managers.

On October 20, 1944, MacArthur returned to the Philippines as commander of an American invasion force. Quezon had died in exile of tuberculosis and his Vice President, Sergio Osmeña, had succeeded him. Osmeña and another member of the government-in-exile, Carlos Romulo, a former aide to MacArthur, returned with the general.

As they advanced, the returning Americans and Filipinos found terrible evidence that the Japanese had avenged themselves on the people of the Philippines. General Tomoyuki Yamashita, commander of the retreating Japanese forces, declared Manila an open city; he evacuated his troops and deployed them in the hilly interior.

Manila, however, was not to be spared. Acting under separate Navy orders, Rear Admiral Sanji Iwabuchi made a last-ditch effort to keep the city out of American hands. A month of fighting ensued in which civilians were trapped in the combat zone and vengeful Japanese indulged in an orgy of destruction and murder. When it was over, 80 per cent of Manila lay ruined and nearly 100,000 Filipinos were dead. Entire families that until now had survived the occupation were wiped out.

One Filipino officer returned to his home to find nothing but burned-out rubble. Another found the recently bayoneted bodies of his parents, a brother and two sisters lying in the garden. Carlos Romulo's mother was crippled as a result of a savage beating. Senator Elpidio Quirino, who within a few years would become President of the Philippines, lost his wife and a son to Japanese bullets during the blood-drenched last stand.

Though Filipinos had suffered most, it was Americans who eventually prosecuted those deemed guilty. The Potsdam Proclamation had directed that "stern justice shall be meted out to all war criminals, including those who have visited cruelties upon our prisoners''; there was no doubt in the minds of the liberators of the Philippines that terrible war crimes had been committed there, and that the guilty parties had included senior Japanese officers.

Most ranking Japanese accused of war crimes, including former Prime Minister Hideki Tojo, were eventually tried in Tokyo by a tribunal of 11 civilian judges. But proceedings in the Philippines were of a different sort. One defendant was General Homma, who had been overall commander at the time of the 1942 Bataan Death March, during which 7,000 captive Filipinos and Americans died, partly as a result of brutality by their guards. Also accused was General Yamashita, overall Army commander during the 1945 destruction of Manila. The two generals were tried in Manila by courts-martial made up of U.S. Army generals who were clearly expected by General MacArthur to convict the defendants.

The courts-martial were held in the presence of Filipinos whose memories were painfully fresh. MacArthur had drawn up the charges, established the rules of evidence, and urged that the trials be concluded with dispatch.

The cases against the two officers were weak on the issue of personal involvement. Although he had been in overall command at the time, there was no evidence linking Homma directly with the Death March. In fact there were indications that orders Homma had previously given for the civilized treatment of prisoners were flouted by subordinate officers as well as by the Japanese rank and file guarding the prisoners.

Yamashita, on trial for the atrocities committed in Manila, was on record as having ordered his troops, officially at least, to ''handle the Filipinos carefully, to cooperate with them.'' In spite of the fact that he had ordered the evacuation of Manila and withdrawn his troops, and that he had not known of the atrocities until long afterward, he was made responsible for the excesses of Admiral Iwabuchi's sailors and marines. Most of them, along with the admiral, had died in the battle of Manila. Confronted with evidence of the barbaric acts, Yamashita declared: ''I positively and categorically affirm that they were against my wishes and in direct contradiction to all my expressed orders.'' He added that ''they occurred at a place and a time of which I had no knowledge whatsoever.''

To counter Yamashita's defense, the prosecution presented a film, originally made as a propaganda movie in Hollywood. The film showed a GI removing a piece of paper from the dead body of a Japanese soldier and reading its Japanese contents while the voice-over commentary translated it into English: ''Orders from Tokyo. We have discovered the secret orders to destroy Manila.''

As true evidence, the film was worthless, as Yamashita's American attorneys pointed out. ''No American who loves his country,'' said one of them, ''can read the record of the prosecution's efforts in this respect without an abiding and painful sense of shame.''

Notwithstanding the shakiness of the cases against them, Homma and Yamashita were found guilty and sentenced to death. The verdicts were appealed to the United States Supreme Court, which upheld them in a 7-to-2 decision. The dissenting justices, Wiley B. Rutledge and Frank Murphy, described the Manila proceedings as ''legalized lynching.'' MacArthur, in response, declared that ''the results are above challenge.'' President Truman refused to commute the death sentences.

On the 23rd of February, 1946, General Yamashita was hanged in the town of Los Banos, south of Manila. Eight days later General Homma, whose wife had pleaded with MacArthur for clemency, was executed in the same place by a firing squad.

Through his command of U.S. Army civil affairs units, MacArthur was still controlling the Philippines from his headquarters in Tokyo when elections were held in April 1946. Faced by formidable problems—widespread physical devastation, economic chaos and agrarian unrest fomented by the Huks—President Osmeña scarcely had time to campaign. Manuel Roxas y Acuña, a younger, more dynamic man who was supported by the landlords, the Church, the press and the civil service, was elected first President of the Republic of the Philippines, with former Senator Elpidio Quirino as his Vice President. Roxas had been captured by the Japanese and had accepted a minor administrative job in the food-distribution program under the occupation. His role as a collaborator became a campaign issue; he rebutted it and, with MacArthur's support, contended that he had only pretended to collaborate in order to prevent the abuse of his people by the Japanese.

Immediately after the votes had been counted, Roxas flew to the United States—with a stopover in Japan—on a public relations mission to seek political and economic support. General MacArthur announced to the press that "Roxas is no collaborationist. I have known him intimately for a quarter of a century and his views have been consistently anti-Japanese."

On July 4, 1946, the Commonwealth period came to an end. Throughout the islands, American flags were lowered in fulfillment of a promise made more than a decade earlier, and the new Republic of the Philippines was born amid the clamor of sirens and the pealing of church bells.

American aid poured into the Philippines in exchange for preferential trade agreements and a military-assistance pact assigning the United States a long-term lease on a number of military bases. President Roxas tried to use American rehabilitation funds for the benefit of his entire nation; but poor planning, incompetence and corrupt officials in the new government dissipated much of the money.

Shortages of practically everything, from food to electronic equipment, stimulated legitimate imports. But the same shortages led to wholesale smuggling and a flourishing black market. Inflation soared, domestic production fell, and the government's tax revenue declined at the worst possible time.

President Roxas worked hard to solve these problems, striving to institute land reform and to launch a program of industrialization. In the midst of his labors, he suffered a heart attack in 1948 and died. He was succeeded by Elpidio Quirino, under whom the blight of corruption spread. Quirino was not venal himself, but he lacked the will to control his administration. He became the victim of his associates. With their help he ran for election in 1949 under the Liberal Party banner against José Laurel, running for the Nacionalistas. Laurel, absolved of any collaborationist taint by a general amnesty granted in 1948 by President Roxas, conducted a savage campaign based on the corruption of Quirino's administration.

Quirino's supporters fought back in a manner that justified Laurel's charges, using bribery and intimidation to secure votes. In the violence that resulted, several hundred people were killed. Quirino won; but the election remained

In a rain-soaked ceremony at Manila's Luneta Park on July 4, 1946, the American flag comes down and the Philippine banner is raised in a peaceful end to 48 years of United States sovereignty in the islands.

AMERICAN ARMS FOR ASIA'S WARS

Asia's postwar conflicts were fought in large part with American arms. The Pacific theater had become a vast U.S. storage depot. Once the War ended, the United States poured millions of tons of surplus equipment into China; elsewhere in Asia the troops of European nations reclaiming their colonial possessions often owed their weapons, uniforms and transport to the U.S. stockpile.

Once the arms had been released, it was impossible to keep track of them, and sometimes they passed through several hands. In China, both the Nationalists and Communists used American weapons to wage war on each other. In Vietnam, Chinese Nationalists on occupation duty sold their American-supplied weapons to Vietnamese guerrillas; in a single week in 1945, the Chinese sold 4,000 small arms to the Vietminh and pocketed the equivalent of $1.2 million.

The American label on the means of war became an embarrassment for the United States in its relations with the emerging nations of Asia. Washington had equipped the British occupation forces in Indonesia and the Dutch marines who followed them. Both the British and the Dutch were requested to remove U.S. insignia from their gear, and Washington vigorously denied that there was any "political connotation" in its use.

But the disavowal was not convincing. Washington publicly supported the concept of self-determination, but when the Europeans rode into battle on American trucks, firing American weapons, Asian nationalists often concluded that the United States was allied with those who would deny them freedom.

An amphibious tank, manufactured in the United States and supplied to the British, rumbles ashore at Singapore in 1945 from an American-built LST.

forever suspect. Filipinos afterward said that the dead had voted once, the living at least twice, and "even the birds and bees cast ballots."

Among those repelled by such politics were the landless peasants, who in some areas represented 90 per cent of the farming population. They flocked to the support of the Huks, whose anti-Japanese army of guerrillas had transformed itself readily enough into the antilandlord People's Liberation Army. The Huks regarded all leading politicians as puppets of American imperialism. They established their own undercover "people's government," which terrorized landowners, levied taxes and made plans to overthrow the elected government.

President Quirino was having enough trouble without a popular insurrection. Widespread tax evasion kept his treasury almost empty, government social programs were slowing to a halt for lack of funds, and the people were sinking deeper into poverty. Growing bolder, the Huks—whose stronghold was Luzon—extended their operations to include not only forays against the landlords but also attacks on policemen and even ordinary citizens; travelers motoring between Manila and the airport at Clark Field, 50 miles away, were forced to make the trip under military escort.

At this point, the United States took action. In the summer of 1950, Washington granted Quirino's government a loan of $250 million in return for the government's promise to institute reforms in landownership, the tax system and basic wages. Ramon Magsaysay, a wartime resistance leader, was appointed Secretary of Defense and, with American financial and advisory support, he launched a counterattack against the Huks. Magsaysay began by reforming the Army and the constabulary—increasing their numbers, tightening discipline and punishing anyone guilty of mistreating civilians. Then he rounded up and imprisoned the Communist leaders of the Huk forces in and around Manila.

Magsaysay's tactics combined military action with aid to impoverished agricultural areas. By aggressive pursuit he managed to split the insurgents into small, uncoordinated groups; he promised amnesty to any rebel who would surrender. Farmers who had formerly been squeezed by landlords were allowed to keep more of their crops, and the government financed such projects as the digging of new artesian wells.

Within two years the back of the Huk rebellion was broken, although remnants of this movement continued to exist beneath the surface of Philippine political life. Magsaysay's success made him enormously popular, and in 1953 he was elected President of the Philippines.

An indigenous Communist uprising much like the Huk insurrection plagued the British administration of Malaya, seriously delaying the process of independence for that colony. Malaya had had no independence movement when the Japanese began their wartime advance through Asia. Indeed, Malaya, noted for its natural riches of rubber and tin, had no history as a country; stretching 450 miles south of Thailand on the Malay Peninsula, it was a loose coalition of 12 states under the British crown. Only Malacca, on the peninsula's western coast, and the islands of Penang and Singapore had a semblance of cohesion. These three states were organized as a crown colony known as the Straits Settlements, and they were administered directly by a British governor in Singapore; the governor wore a second hat as High Commissioner of the Settlements and of nine other Malay states, which were governed by local sultans—each advised by a British Resident—under the supervision of the High Commissioner. Great Britain claimed sovereignty only over the Straits Settlements; the nine other states were designated as protectorates.

Three ethnic communities—Malay, Chinese and Indian—coexisted in Malaya, a circumstance that helped to slow the growth of nationalism in the various states. Most of the Malays, who numbered 2.4 million in 1945, were not politically conscious and had no concept either of self-government or of allegiance to any future Malayan nation; loyalty was owed merely to the local sultan and to the benevolent British administration in Singapore.

Those who thought at all about nationhood feared that independence would mean domination by the Malayan Chinese. Of the 2.5 million Chinese in Malaya, 700,000 were concentrated in Singapore. Their interests were primarily economic. Prominent as merchants and entrepreneurs, many Chinese led a prosperous life and saw no reason to disturb it or to ruffle the British by political agitation. Malaya's 450,000-member Indian community, which included civil servants and businessmen as well as laborers, also had become relatively affluent under British rule; moreover, the Indians depended on the British to protect them against discrimination by the rest of the Asian population.

The dramatic fall of Singapore to the Japanese on February 15, 1942, was a devastating blow to British prestige, and one that Japan might have turned to its advantage. The people, stunned by the rapidity of the Japanese conquest, felt bereft and angry at the failure of the British to protect them. They were also terrified at the prospect of a harsh Japanese occupation.

And rightly so. In their vicious and overbearing conduct, the Japanese justified every fear—exacting a particularly terrible toll from the Chinese community. The Malays and Indians were spared, in some measure because the Japanese saw political advantage in not antagonizing them too much. The Indians were viewed as potential supporters in a future Japanese-controlled government of India, the Malays as allies in the administration of Malaya. Nevertheless, many Malayans of all races were drafted to help build a Japanese military railroad in Burma and Thailand—the infamous "Death Railway"—and thousands of them died.

The Japanese executed thousands of Malayan Chinese. Their purported reason was that they suspected the Chinese—in spite of their visibly capitalist way of life—had ties to Communism. True, some Chinese were Communists; but most of them were on their guard and escaped. They formed resistance groups under the banner of the Malayan People's Anti-Japanese Army, which eventually numbered about 7,000 men. They were trained and supported by British "stay-behind" parties, which had been organized before the defeat to recruit partisan bands and to harass the Japanese. The Malayan Communists, more closely tied to Moscow than to the Chinese Communists, accepted aid from Malaya's British colonial masters because Britain, following Hitler's attack on Russia in 1941, was an ally of the Soviet Union.

The Malayan People's Anti-Japanese Army conducted only modest operations against the Japanese; however, they did, often brutally, establish underground rule in the interior of the country. After the Japanese surrender, and before regular British forces returned to Malaya in September of 1945, the Malayan People's Army took over the administration of substantial areas of the Malay Peninsula, using the

month's interval before the British arrived to avenge themselves on local policemen and others who had collaborated with the Japanese.

Once the British got there, they required all resistance groups to disband and disarm. The guerrillas in many instances hid their weapons in the jungle. After officially demilitarizing the Communists, the British honored them as allies against the Japanese, including them in their victory parades both in the capital city, Kuala Lumpur, and in London. The Communists' response to all such gestures was to foment civil strife. They infiltrated and soon controlled Malaya's fledgling labor unions and staged strikes aimed at dis-

Following the independence ceremonies in Rangoon on January 4, 1948, Burma's Prime Minister Thakin Nu shakes hands with the departing British Governor General, Sir Hubert Rance. Unlike neighboring India, Burma had severed all ties to the British Commonwealth.

rupting the rehabilitation of the rubber plantations and the tin mines. In 1947, when the movement was in full cry, there were 300 major work stoppages.

Meanwhile, the Colonial Office in London had proposed an entirely new administrative structure for the loosely joined Malayan states. Formulated during the War without any serious consultation with the Malays themselves, the plan demonstrated how deeply colonialist attitudes still clouded the minds of some Britons in positions of authority. The plan called for the unification of all the states into a Malayan Union. State governments were to be directly subject to a central colonial government in Kuala Lumpur; the sultans would be stripped of their powers and reduced to figureheads. Only Singapore was to remain as a separate colony.

The Malays of the former protectorate states were outraged: First the British had failed to protect them from the Japanese, now they were proposing to cancel the special position that the Malays had enjoyed under the sultans. Whatever reasons the British had had for concocting the Malayan Union, its result was dramatic: a newfound spirit of nationalism among the heretofore apathetic Malays.

Protest meetings were held throughout Malaya; even in London, the scheme was harshly attacked in Parliament. So fierce was the opposition that the British were forced to backtrack before the Malayan Union was fairly launched in April of 1946. The London government set up a working group of British and Malays that included representatives of the sultans; this committee came up with a compromise plan that restored the concept of a federation, under which Malay rulers retained their old powers. The plan also ensured greater unity for Malaya as a whole by creating a central federal government. The new scheme was embodied in a draft constitution called the Federation of Malaya Agreement, which was to become effective in 1948.

The Communists, however, were pursuing separate aims. In February of 1948, the Malayan Communist Party sent delegates to a Soviet-sponsored Southeast Asian Youth Conference in Calcutta. A prime topic at the conference was the need for armed uprisings throughout the region; at subsequent meetings of the Malayan Communists, the party decided to take direct action.

Using the weapons they had hidden in the jungle in 1945, the Communists struck at their old targets—rubber estates and tin mines—killing managers and lesser employees. The surge of violence climaxed in June of 1948 with the murder of three European planters. In July, the new federal government declared an emergency.

Special measures that were taken over the next three years, such as resettlement of people from the countryside in new fortified villages, helped break up the Communists' supply and support system; but the insurrection was still very much alive in the early 1950s, effectively delaying the independence sought by Malay and non-Communist Chinese political factions.

In 1952, General Sir Gerald Templer took over the anti-terrorist campaign and conducted what many consider to be the most successful counterinsurgency operation of the 20th Century. Reinforced with troops from throughout the British Commonwealth, Templer's Malay and British forces pounced on Communist strongholds, where they captured terrorist leaders and brought them to justice. When the Communists retreated farther into the jungle, Templer ordered search-and-destroy missions carried out from forts deep in the bush; these footslogging missions, augmented by helicopterborne patrols and paratroop strikes, were supplied by air, enabling the men to operate for substantial periods away from their bases.

Once Templer's counterinsurgency forces cleared terrorists from a parcel of countryside, curfews and other emergency regulations were quickly rescinded. In such so-called "white areas," life could go back to normal, and this encouraged people in regions still plagued by terrorism to cooperate with the authorities and hasten their own return to a peaceful existence.

When Templer left Malaya in 1954, the Communists were on the defensive their popular support drastically curtailed, many of their key leaders dead or in jail. By 1957, it was deemed safe for Malaya to become independent within the British Commonwealth, although the Communists continued to fight on for years from sanctuaries across the Thai border.

Unlike Malaya, Burma even before the War was alive with independence movements. A country about the size of Texas, positioned along the western edge of the Indochinese

Peninsula, Burma consisted primarily of the vast, fertile Irrawaddy River valley and was protected from its neighbors by a horseshoe of mountain ranges. It had been a kingdom with a venerable history before it came under the domination of the British in the 19th Century. Governed as a province of India, Burma had developed into one of the most productive and prosperous regions of southeastern Asia—primarily through the export of rice, teak, petroleum and various minerals.

Despite its appearance of unity and cohesiveness, however, Burma was a politically volatile mixture of diverse groups. The majority of its population was Burman, a people who had migrated from Tibet in successive waves beginning in the Seventh Century. Different tribal minorities—among them the Shans, the Karens and the Kachins—represented about one fifth of the modern population. They had separate languages and cultural heritages and were traditionally at odds with the Burmans.

In 1937 the administration of Burma was separated from that of India; Britain granted the Burmese a measure of self-government and membership in the British Commonwealth, but without the proud dominion status that such countries as Canada and Australia enjoyed.

Not content with this limited progress—many saw it as a shameful compromise—activists in Burma organized a movement aimed at full independence. Fervently nationalistic, the movement was hostile both to foreign rule and to Western cultural influences. By 1939, the drive for economic and political freedom was rapidly approaching the flash point.

Even before the War broke out in Asia in December 1941, a group of young Burmese nationalists was trying to enlist the aid of the Japanese in toppling British rule. Burma's Prime Minister, U Saw, had gone to London to ask the British to grant his country full independence. He was informed, however, that the clauses in the new Atlantic Charter that guaranteed a people's right to choose its own government did not apply to British imperial possessions in Asia, and that Burma's postwar status would be determined by the degree of its support for Britain's war effort. From London's standpoint, U Saw was clearly not to be trusted in such matters: Indeed, on the way back to Burma, he also began negotiations with the Japanese. The British swiftly arrested him and for the rest of the War interned him in Uganda, one of their African protectorates.

As a result of groundwork already laid, the Japanese found a measure of cooperation when they invaded Burma in late December 1941. In August 1942, after the British had been driven out, they set up a compliant government under a former Prime Minister named Ba Maw, whose loathing for British rule outweighed his wariness of the Japanese. A year later, on August 1, 1943, Ba Maw became the head of what the Japanese called the independent Republic of Burma. Burma then declared war on Great Britain and the United States.

Japanese-style independence did not sit well with most Burmese—least of all with a zealous nationalist named Aung San, who was Defense Minister of the new republic. When it became clear in mid-1944 that the War was turning against the Japanese, and that one day the British would return, Aung San and a number of other Burmese leaders forged an underground called the Anti-Fascist People's Freedom League.

Allied armies swept through Burma in late 1944 and early 1945 and the Japanese evacuated Rangoon. Ba Maw's government fell and in April he fled from the capital. Aung San and his colleagues remained on the scene as spokesmen for their countrymen.

Aung San, who was only 30 years old in 1945, was a remarkable figure whom the Burmese called Bogyoke—great general. Although Winston Churchill and some other Britons stubbornly regarded him as a traitor and collaborationist because of his relationship with the Japanese early in the War, such men as Louis Mountbatten and General Sir William J. Slim, who had fought in Burma, felt otherwise. To Slim, Aung San was "a genuine patriot and a well-balanced realist." Combining these qualities with a talent for leadership, Aung San was able to weld a working political coalition out of the country's diverse groups. In doing so, he began to overcome the mutual hostility between Burmans and tribal minorities.

Aung San needed all the strength he could summon. His country was in chaos; few places in Asia outside of Japan were so badly ravaged by the War. Of equal concern was the fact that the British government, in Burma's case, was reluctant to abandon colonialism. The British wartime Governor of Burma, Sir Reginald Dorman-Smith, had seen the need for eventual dominion status, saying that he wanted to "build a contented Burma, which will have no wish whatsoever to contract out of the Empire." He had suggested as much to the Churchill government in London, stipulating a waiting period of five to seven years. The proposal was totally rejected. Instead, the British authorities proposed in May 1945 to withhold even the partial self-government that the Burmese had enjoyed before the War—at least until 1948. The British promised to restore it thereafter "as circumstances permitted."

In July of 1945 a Labor government generally more willing to relinquish colonial possessions took over in Britain. The retrogressive policy toward Burma was nonetheless continued, and tensions deepened.

On May 18, 1946, during one of a series of demonstrations protesting British rule, the police fired into a crowd at Tantabin, just outside Rangoon. The shots killed three people and wounded eight. Aung San arranged—and brought off peacefully—a public funeral for the victims. A few months later he also orchestrated a drum roll of demonstrations, including walkouts by police, postal workers, railway staff and a general work stoppage throughout the country. Subsequent negotiations led to a partial reversal of British policy: A degree of self-government was restored to Burma, and Aung San in September became the country's acting Prime Minister.

Among his first acts was the announcement of a firm timetable for completion of the independence process; the schedule established a deadline of January 1948 for the transfer of power. The British, realizing that they lacked the means to force continued British rule on the unwilling Burmese, accepted this timetable, and Aung San was invited to London for talks with Prime Minister Clement Attlee. The negotiations went smoothly and led to elections in April of 1947 for members of a constituent assembly, which convened in June. The principal action taken by the assembly was a decision to adopt full independence—outside the British Commonwealth.

Just as Aung San began to see his great hopes for Burma fulfilled, he was struck down. Former Prime Minister U Saw, attempting a desperate coup, organized a mass assassination attempt in Rangoon. Aung San and eight of his colleagues went down in a hail of machine-gun fire. In the shock and grief that followed, one Burmese journal compared Aung San's killing to the assassination of Abraham Lincoln; on the front page, the editors published the full text of Walt Whitman's "O Captain! My Captain!"—the classic anthem of mourning for Lincoln. (It begins: "Exult O shores, and ring O bells! / But I with mournful tread, / Walk the deck my Captain lies, / Fallen cold and dead.")

Aung San's death at 32 failed to bring U Saw to power, or to slow the momentum of Burma's climb toward freedom. The British asked Thakin Nu, speaker of the constituent assembly and longtime associate of Aung San, to form a new Cabinet. At 4:20 a.m. on January 4, 1948—right on Aung San's schedule, and at an hour chosen as auspicious by Burmese astrologers—independence was declared. In a broadcast that day Prime Minister Thakin Nu—later known as U Nu—paid tribute to Aung San as the man whose efforts had brought his countrymen "the coveted crown of complete freedom." Thakin Nu went on to sum up the emotions of the Burmese after years of colonial subjugation. "We lost our independence without losing our self-respect," he said. "We clung to our culture and our traditions and these we now hold to cherish and to develop in accordance with the genius of our people.

"This Day of Independence dawns on a people not only free but united," Thakin Nu continued. "This is also a day for solemn thought, for in a sense, our work has just begun."

A FRIENDLY CONFRONTATION

As the umpire signals the count, an American GI prepares to pitch to a Japanese batter in a Tokyo softball game in October 1945, just two months after V-J Day.

CAPTIVATING THE CONQUERORS

A GI ponders the sign of a makeshift Tokyo laundry. For many Japanese, doing laundry for the Occupation forces was a vital source of income.

After almost four years of bitter warfare, the 450,000 American troops who landed in Japan expected the worst. "Don't forget," cautioned one of the American officers, "the Jap is still the slimy, sneaky treacherous animal who was doing his best a few weeks ago to kill and torture you." What the GIs found, however, was not smoldering hatred, but a people who almost without exception were docile, courteous and respectful.

The Japanese seemed fascinated by their American conquerors. Children called out greetings in broken English—"herro, GI, herro, good-by"—and their parents bowed to passing American jeeps. "The people are most friendly," wrote Navy Captain Benton W. Decker, who took command of the Yokosuka Naval base near Tokyo. "I walk through the town and up the crowded alleys with no fear."

Communication was a serious problem at first: There were many Japanese who spoke some English, but fewer than 1,000 American soldiers knew enough Japanese to serve as interpreters. Very quickly, however, victors and vanquished found that they shared a common addiction: baseball. The game was the national sport of the Japanese—they had been playing it since the 1870s, almost as long as the Americans had. Soon teams of GIs were engaged in friendly competition with local clubs throughout Japan.

The Occupation authorities encouraged such encounters as part of a larger program for the reconciliation of East and West. At the same time, individual Americans began plumbing the mysteries of Japan's culture. They found Japanese styles and tastes decidedly exotic: Both men and women had shed their drab wartime clothes and often walked the rubble-strewn streets of their cities wearing brightly colored kimonos; their shoes were odd-looking wooden clogs "with heels at both ends," as one correspondent put it. And a favorite Japanese dish consisted of finely sliced raw fish.

Occupation duty left most of the American soldiers with a surplus of free time. Armed only with cameras, they toured the length and breadth of the conquered islands—and were themselves captivated.

Visiting an American Army rest center located near Nagoya on the east coast of Japan, a pair of GIs contemplate a Buddhist statue and take its picture.

A U.S. Army sergeant carries ashore his baby daughter, who with his wife has arrived at Yokohama in 1947 on a U.S. transport ship.

STATESIDE •GRILL•

WILL OPEN AS AN

American Style

RESTAURANT

WHEN WE CAN OBTAIN FOOD

Please be as patient as Possible

Two American couples await a steak dinner in 1946 at a newly opened enlisted men's club whose sign requests the guests' forebearance.

INSTANT HOMES AWAY FROM HOME

No one knew how long the Occupation forces would be in Japan, but by most estimates it was to be years. Accordingly, the Americans moved in to stay—which for most of them meant trying to make their new homes as much as possible like the ones they had left behind.

Thousands of wives were transported from the United States at government expense to join their soldier-husbands. Many brought children as well. The dependents were afraid of what they would find. One soldier whose wife was reluctant to come complained that "she still thinks we're living in foxholes."

Instead of foxholes, GIs and their families settled into former Japanese military bases as well as the new Quonset-hut villages, with such names as Washington Heights and Jefferson Acres, that abutted every large U.S. base in Japan. In these instant subdivisions, they went about creating a hometown life style—replete with hamburgers, soap flakes, cigarettes, cameras and radios that had been shipped from the States and were available at low cost in the nearby Post Exchange.

Most American bases were furnished with gymnasiums, athletic fields and reasonably well-stocked clubs for both officers and enlisted men. In fact, amenities at some bases rivaled anything to be found at home, including pleasant Japanese waitresses and live music with dinner.

A soldier and his family walk through the gateway to an Army-built housing compound; hardly palatial, it at least offered terraced lawns and palm trees.

PLUNGING INTO AN EXOTIC CULTURE

The strange new world outside the gates of their compounds was a source of constant fascination for the American Occupation troops and their families. Military wives joined clubs dedicated to learning Japanese culture, and they devoted hours to mastering such crafts as miniature-tree growing *(bonsai),* paper folding *(origami)* and flower arranging *(ikebana).* Many of the soldiers, during their liberal off-duty time, took up such ancient martial pursuits as longbow archery, judo and karate.

Soldiers touring the countryside while on leave partook of one of Japan's long-established pleasures—a stay in a *ryokan,* or traditional inn. There they might soak in a communal hot bath, or *ofuro,* and then retire to their rooms to enjoy warm sake and a feast that started with *ushio jiru*— or fish-head soup—before they bedded down between cotton comforters on the straw-matted floor.

Occupation wives attending a class at an American Red Cross club in Tokyo learn the subtleties of Japanese flower arranging.

At a resort hotel on the island of Kyushu, in southern Japan, two Americans share a hot bath with a pair of Japanese businessmen. Buckets on the floor contain water for cleansing oneself before entering the tub.

Dressed in skirtlike hakamas and peaked caps, a group of American GIs are instructed in the art of kyudo, or ancient Japanese archery.

A receiver on a Japanese college football team awaits a pass in a game against a team of artillerymen from the U.S. 24th Division. The contest, played on Thanksgiving Day, 1949, before 2,000 spectators to raise money for the Japanese Community Chest, was won by the Americans, who outweighed their opponents by 42 pounds per man.

INTRODUCING SANTA, FASHIONS AND FOOTBALL

Even as the Americans explored Japanese culture, they set out with the zeal of missionaries to convert the Japanese to American ways. The campaign began with instruction in Western political democracy, and it soon broadened to include American sports, American fashion styles and even the techniques of Madison Avenue merchandising. The newcomers also promoted such familiar American institutions as volunteer charity drives, chambers of commerce and athletic associations.

One charitable service Japan needed badly was aid for the thousands of youngsters who had been orphaned during the War. American soldiers joined forces with existing Japanese organizations to help the children. Often one or more GIs would ''adopt'' a Japanese orphan, contributing money to the child's upkeep, paying regular visits and sending gifts. In at least one instance, a U.S. Army regiment helped to subsidize an entire orphanage.

A new American look in bathing suits is shown off by live models in the window of a department store in Tokyo. Such eye-catching displays would have been unlikely in Japan before the War.

Children assembled from five orphanages in the Osaka area are greeted by Santa Claus, as portrayed by Sergeant H. W. Wittmis of the U.S. 25th Division.

On a rainy night in Tokyo, a lone American soldier strikes up a conversation with a Japanese woman.

A sign on a home near Tokyo's red-light district pointedly warns away any roving GI who might mistakenly seek entry. All large Japanese cities had brothel areas—off limits to military personnel, but patronized anyway.

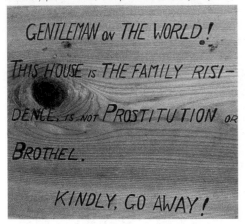

GENTLEMAN ON THE WORLD!

THIS HOUSE IS THE FAMILY RISI-DENCE, IS NOT PROSTITUTION OR BROTHEL.

KINDLY, GO AWAY!

SOME DO'S AND DON'TS OF FRATERNIZATION

For thousands of GIs, the most urgent aspect of their stay in Japan was the search for female companionship. Unlike American authorities in Germany, General MacArthur did not try to stop fraternization. But his headquarters did lay down some rules of conduct: no visits to brothels, no joy rides for dates in government jeeps, no kissing in public. At the same time, it was officially acceptable to hold hands, or to have dinner at a girl friend's house—if the GI brought his own food.

It was easy enough for an American to pick up a streetwalker or a bar girl in a nightclub. And if he could afford it, he could enjoy the company of geishas —trained professional entertainers whose services as a rule did not include sex.

On duty and off, the GIs also met many ordinary young Japanese women and were fascinated by their petite beauty and modest ways. Getting to know them better could be a challenge: Japanese frowned on informal American-style dating, and some refused to let their daughters have anything to do with the Americans. But many GIs found ways around the barriers of custom and language—and fully 6,000 of them brought home Japanese brides.

Kimono-clad geishas, or "artistic persons," lead stocking-footed visitors through a traditional folk dance. Graceful and intelligent, the geishas were also trained to sing and to make lighthearted conversation.

At a nightclub in Osaka, American soldiers dance with hostesses provided, for a stiff fee, by the management.

A FAIR TO SHOWCASE AMERICA

After five years of occupation, the effort to Americanize the Japanese had not abated. In 1950, when the Tokyo newspaper *Asahi Shimbun* organized the America Fair near Osaka, the Occupation authorities strongly supported the project.

On 75 acres in and around Nishinomiya Stadium, the fair's sponsors erected models of an ambitious sampling of American landmarks: the White House, the Capitol, Abe Lincoln's log-cabin birthplace, an Arizona ranch and a Pittsburgh steel mill, panoramas of the New York and Chicago skylines—even a realistic Niagara Falls.

The fair attracted Japanese and Americans alike by the trainload. Nearly two million people came to admire the exhibits, which, as one visitor reflected, left the "Occupation GIs homesick and the Japanese bug-eyed."

A GI visitor to the America Fair shows off a meticulously detailed papier-mâché reproduction of the façade of the United States Capitol to Japanese friends.

Fairgoers throng around an intricate scale model of downtown Washington, D.C., displayed inside a replica of the White House.

A large-scale model of the Golden Gate Bridge in San Francisco is complete with cityscape and ships. In the background can be seen the tail fin of a mock-up B-377 Stratocruiser that was also on display.

Fashioned by Japanese artists, reproductions of Mount Rushmore's quartet of great American Presidents gaze out somberly at visitors to the 1950 Osaka fair.

2

A BENIGN INVASION

Under the hot afternoon sun of August 30, 1945, a U.S. transport plane put down at Atsugi airfield near Yokohama, Japan. From the aircraft, his corncob pipe clenched at a jaunty angle, stepped General of the Army Douglas MacArthur, newly designated Supreme Commander, Allied Powers—the military governor of vanquished Japan. The acronym SCAP, which referred both to MacArthur and to his headquarters organization, would soon become the symbol of ultimate power as the famed American general guided the defeated nation into a lengthy occupation that did not end until April 1952. During this crucial period of rebirth the United States through MacArthur would play two roles, as conqueror and reformer, that were unique in history.

By the time MacArthur flew into Atsugi, the hostilities had ceased. It had been two weeks since Emperor Hirohito, in the wake of the atomic bombing of Hiroshima and Nagasaki, had instructed his countrymen to surrender. At first, Allied leaders questioned whether the Japanese military would obey fully. Though devastated from the air, Japan was far from prostrate. More than 250,000 heavily armed Japanese troops guarded the Kwanto plain near Yokohama and Tokyo. Troops stationed elsewhere in Japan brought the total in the home islands to more than two million.

The first contingents of American troops to arrive in Japan did not know what to expect and disembarked from their planes with some apprehension. But these forces, only a few thousand strong, were not molested in any way. Man, woman and child, the Japanese honored their venerated Emperor's order to cease fighting.

Hirohito and Prime Minister Kantaro Suzuki's Cabinet had accepted the tough Potsdam Declaration issued jointly on July 26 by President Harry S. Truman, Prime Minister Winston Churchill and Generalissimo Chiang Kai-shek, President of the Nationalist government of the Republic of China. In return for a surrender, the Allies offered Japan a number of concessions that softened somewhat the terms imposed on Germany a few months earlier.

Members of the Japanese armed forces were to be disarmed and allowed to return home, instead of being held prisoner—as had been the case with the Germans, who were held for periods up to three years after the Wehrmacht surrendered. More important, the Japanese nation would be permitted to continue functioning as such, a privilege not extended to Germany. Japanese industry and trade, stripped of its warmaking potential, would function at a level sufficient to keep the population employed and prevent the nation's economy from collapsing. And in the proclamation, an end to the Occupation itself was foreshadowed. Once the Japanese people had established a "peacefully inclined and responsible government," the Allies would depart.

Such an eventuality seemed remote indeed to those familiar with Japan's warlike history. The island nation's relationship with the United States and the Western world had begun nearly a century earlier, under the guns of a flotilla commanded by Commodore Matthew Calbraith Perry. Perry had forced Japan's rulers, the military government of the Tokugawa shogunate, to agree to open ports to American trade; the precedent led to similar arrangements with other Western nations. But opposition to these concessions helped bring down the shogunate and generated a profound change in the nature of the imperial throne.

Since the 12th Century, the Emperors of Japan had in effect been hostage to a succession of feudal warlords. In 1603, the rule of Japan was concentrated under the Tokugawa, who continued to exclude the Emperor from any real power. The forces that brought the shogunate down, however, moved in 1868 to prevent future dictatorships by restoring the Emperor (then a boy of 15 named Mutsuhito) to a position of visible authority. As was later confirmed in a written constitution, the Emperor personified Japanese sovereignty; his powers included the right to declare war, to make peace and to conclude treaties.

From this fundamental realignment came an era that came to be known as the Meiji Restoration: *Meiji* means "Enlightened Rule," and restoration referred to the renewed status of the Emperor. Energetic and able, the leaders of the Meiji Restoration turned Japan from a feudal backwater into a world military power capable of defeating China in 1895 and Russia in 1905. They generated an industrial base that essentially was presided over by a small number of entrepreneurial families called *zaibatsu*. In the 1880s these Meiji activists modernized the government by introducing a parliamentary system adapted from the West with a bicameral legislature, the Diet. Political parties nominated candidates to an elected lower chamber, the House of Representatives.

Membership in the upper chamber, the House of Peers, was based largely on inherited titles of nobility.

The rise of prosperity during and after World War I—in which Japan was a belligerent on the side of the Allies—favored a liberal domestic and foreign policy. But there remained in Japan a powerful faction of ultranationalist politicians and military officers. These extremists gained strength during the worldwide Depression in the early 1930s, and through strong-arm measures that included assassination they came to dominate Japanese political life. International aggression soon followed. A Japanese army took over the Chinese territory of Manchuria in 1931; a puppet regime was set up and the region was renamed Manchukuo. China itself was invaded in 1937. Following the fall of France in 1940, Japan sent troops to occupy French Indochina and signed a military agreement with Germany and Italy; at home, the government maintained control through censorship, intimidation and raw police power.

Throughout World War II, with the more or less willing support of the great industrial families and the implicit consent of Mutsuhito's grandson, Emperor Hirohito, Japan was ruled as a totalitarian machine by such dedicated militarists as Hideki Tojo, Prime Minister from 1941 to 1944. This was the all-powerful faction whose members made the fateful decision to attack Pearl Harbor; they were the leaders who bore responsibility for defeat—and the humiliating presence of foreign conquerors on Japanese territory.

It was against this background of fierce nationalism and mistrust of foreigners, of oligarchy and military adventurism that Douglas MacArthur set out to achieve nothing less than a political and social revolution in Japan. It might be expected that the Japanese would work to balk him at every turn. But MacArthur was invested by the Allies with supreme power and was backed by overwhelming force of arms. Moreover, he was careful to introduce democratic reforms in a manner calculated to make them as palatable as possible to the majority of Japanese—by firm suggestion and persuasion rather than by fiat and raw power. This approach was enhanced by two circumstances not clearly foreseen in the immediate aftermath of surrender: the instinctive belief among the Japanese people in the liberating reforms that were imposed on them, and a dramatic shift in the United States' view of Japan in an emerging atmosphere of Cold

War tension with the Soviet Union. Initially regarded by Americans as a beaten enemy, Japan was increasingly embraced as a potentially strong and influential ally.

Shortly after his arrival at Atsugi airfield, MacArthur and his entourage drove to Yokohama, where they were to establish headquarters for the first few days of the Occupation. Japanese soldiers, rifles in hand, lined the road. There were two divisions of them—approximately 30,000 men. Curiously, the troops faced away from the highway, offering their backs to the motorcade. Only later did the wary Americans learn that the apparently disdainful attitude of the soldiers was a gesture of respect, and that in facing outward they were guarding MacArthur just as they would the person of their own Emperor. It was as if the soldiers were offering their allegiance to the man who, they realized, was to be the paramount power in their land for the foreseeable future.

MacArthur's supremacy was the result of decisions made at Potsdam and at earlier conferences, where the Allies had agreed that the United States would play the central role in the Occupation of Japan, acknowledging the fact that victory in the Pacific war had been almost exclusively an Ameri-

can enterprise. China, the Soviet Union and Britain expected and received a voice in directing the Occupation, but U.S. policy, embodied in a joint Pentagon-State Department directive, left MacArthur more or less free to ignore the Allies for whom he was acting.

All the Allies were represented in a body called the Far Eastern Commission. But the commission was based in faraway Washington, and it was paralyzed from the outset by the fact that each of its principal members (the United States, the Soviet Union, Great Britain and China) had veto power. Americans dominated the deliberations of another group—the Tokyo-based Allied Council. MacArthur reduced this body to ineffectuality by holding it strictly to its advisory role, though it became a forum for Soviet propaganda and displays of intransigence over policy, and for occasional British complaints about SCAP's high-handedness.

The British Commonwealth's military share in the Occupation was fulfilled primarily by Australian and New Zealand units, and even these troops ultimately came under MacArthur's direct control. The Soviets were frustrated nonparticipants in the military occupation. At the end of the War they had urgently wanted an occupation zone on the

island of Hokkaido, close to the U.S.S.R. MacArthur, who observed how the Soviets were creating a new set of problems in divided Europe, helped blunt their ambitions in Asia. Soviet troops, he said, could take up positions in a zone on Honshu, the main island, wedged between two U.S. combat divisions. The Russians declined and quietly dropped their bid for a direct role in the Occupation.

In early September, MacArthur moved his headquarters from Yokohama to Tokyo, settling in a building near the Imperial Palace that had been the central office of the Dai Ichi Insurance Company. The general valued the impression he would make on the rank-conscious Japanese by choosing this address. He knew that the building overlooked a square in which he was to have been publicly hanged after the War; such, at any rate, had been the prediction of Tokyo Rose, the radio siren who had spun records of American popular songs and tried to seduce GIs into surrendering.

In this headquarters building—Dai Ichi, the former corporate name, was loosely and aptly translated as "Number One"—MacArthur was a remote and mysterious figure. One man who worked for three years no more than 30 paces from MacArthur's office was never introduced to him. The Supreme Commander closeted himself in an interior office, furnished with a desk, two inelegant but comfortable leather sofas and some chairs. He lived in the vacant U.S. Embassy—joined late in September by his wife, Jean, and his seven-year-old son, Arthur—and commuted daily by Cadillac to the Dai Ichi, about two miles away.

The Supreme Commander's routine was simple and exceedingly regular. He and his staff worked seven days a week. After beginning his day at the Embassy with a look at newspapers and mail, MacArthur arrived at his office at 10:40 a.m.; he returned to the Embassy between 2 and 2:30 for lunch and sometimes a nap; he was back at the Dai Ichi by 4 or 4:30 for a stint that lasted until he had cleared his desk—usually between 8 and 9 p.m. For MacArthur's staff, the working day began at 8 a.m. and ended when the general called a halt. One aide protested that the pace was killing the staff; MacArthur, serious, asked: "What better fate for a man than to die in performance of his duty?"

The regularity of the schedule—and the fact that the trips to and from the office drew crowds of curious Japanese—concerned members of MacArthur's entourage, who feared

an assassination attempt. "He's a target slower than a duck at an amusement park," warned a staff colonel. MacArthur himself, at least outwardly, was utterly indifferent. "In the Orient," he pointed out, "the man who shows no fear is master. I count on the Japanese people to protect me."

MacArthur genuinely respected the people of Japan and wished them well. In his speech accepting the formal surrender of Japan aboard the U.S.S. *Missouri* on September 2, he had promised to carry out his responsibilities as Supreme Commander "with justice and tolerance, while taking all necessary dispositions to ensure that the terms of surrender are fully, promptly and faithfully complied with."

In sharp contrast to the rules established for Allied soldiers occupying Germany, GIs in Japan from the outset were allowed to fraternize with the Japanese. They had this dispensation despite criticism from those within and without the Allied governments who objected to personal relationships on the grounds that they cosseted a beaten enemy.

MacArthur felt that orders against soldiers mingling with local civilians were unenforceable. Remembering the Puccini opera about a love affair between a 19th Century American Naval officer and a Japanese woman, and citing his own soldier-father as authority, MacArthur rationalized his position this way: "They keep trying to get me to stop all this Madam Butterflying around. I won't do it. My father told me never to give an order unless I was certain it would be carried out. I wouldn't issue a no-fraternization order for all the tea in China."

MacArthur's personal style appealed to the Japanese. They liked the Supreme Commander's flair for the dramatic, as demonstrated by his appearance as unarmed conqueror among his fully armed enemies. MacArthur's habit of demanding loyalty and absolute obedience from his own men also was in tune with Japanese ways, and his aura of decisiveness and authority struck a responsive chord. The general's presence in Japan therefore appeared to many as a sign, in itself, of hope for the future. In the autumn of 1945, the Japanese people could see very few such signs.

The Japanese were in desperate need of such strong but humane leadership. According to Edwin O. Reischauer, a postwar American Ambassador to Japan, the men who in 1941 had set off to conquer Southeast Asia "returned after

Arriving at Atsugi airfield near Yokohama on the 30th of August, 1945, General Douglas MacArthur pauses before stepping down from his C-54 transport, nicknamed Bataan. An advance contingent of the U.S. 11th Airborne Division had secured the field only two days earlier, and MacArthur's early appearance in the enemy's midst was considered a bold act, a foretaste of his style as Supreme Commander in Japan.

the War to a Japan changed physically and spiritually almost beyond recognition." Sheer physical destruction had wrought the most palpable change. Out of a 1940 population of 73 million, roughly 1,850,000 Japanese had died—668,000 of them killed by the relentless American bombing campaign against the home islands. More than two million buildings had been destroyed and 40 per cent of Japan's urban areas had been damaged or lay in ruins.

Other statistics were equally dismaying. Industrial production had dropped to one seventh the level of 1941. If not smashed or standing idle, factories were occupied in such activities as converting soldiers' discarded steel helmets into kitchen utensils—to replace those melted in the heat of the American fire bombings. Other factories were fabricating crude shoes out of wood scraps, or using wood pulp to mill a kind of cheap cloth that rain, according to one observer, could turn into a substance resembling soggy newspaper.

Food in Japan would be desperately short for years. In 1945, outright starvation threatened. There were dire predictions that 10 million Japanese, one person in seven, would perish for lack of food. Housewives foraged for edible weeds. People in small boats competed for garbage thrown off the U.S. Navy ships anchored in Tokyo Bay; fearful of saboteurs, the Navy drove the boats away until a Japanese noblewoman appealed to the Occupation authorities: If she could collect the Navy's garbage, she said, she could feed hundreds of people who might otherwise starve. After that the Navy cooperated by turning over discarded food from the fleet to the Japanese.

Ship commanders afloat could not see the faces of deprivation. Captain Benton W. Decker, who took over command of the Japanese Navy base at Yokosuka near Yokohama, was closer to the suffering. He brought members of the city's women's club into the mess hall to gather leftovers. The women were given bits of meat, bread, salad, butter and half-glasses of milk, which they distributed throughout Yokosuka along with chocolate and K rations donated by Becker. Years later, Yokosukans erected a statue of the American captain in a park near the city hall.

Food shortages benefited some Japanese farmers as the first winter of Occupation came on. After feeding his family, a farmer could sell his surplus on a black market where prices were uncontrolled—and rose with the increasing

scarcity of produce. But food was so scarce generally that the black market did little to mitigate the hunger among city dwellers. Though an average of 60 per cent of an urban family's income went for food, it was seldom that anyone ate 2,000 calories a day, or 50 per cent of the normal U.S. Army ration. Consumption often fell below 1,500 calories, and people spent their weekends traveling to the country to trade whatever they had—even heirloom furniture and family jewels—for a few sweet potatoes.

To ease the hunger that he feared might lead to riots and insurrection, MacArthur set up U.S. Army soup kitchens throughout Japan early in the Occupation and requested that Allied military sources supply what food had accumulated in warehouses throughout the Pacific theater. Some critics in Washington complained about what they regarded as the "unauthorized" use of this food to sustain the erstwhile enemy. MacArthur's response was to ask for more food to be shipped directly from the United States. He cabled grimly: GIVE ME BREAD OR GIVE ME BULLETS.

As though hunger and the prospect of an unheated winter—coal production in November 1945 was one eighth of the prewar rate—were not affliction enough, many Japa-

A young Japanese railway worker scoops up a precious windfall, rice that was dumped from a train by black marketeers when they were apprehended by police. Because of food shortages after the War, the distribution of rice was controlled by the government, but large amounts of it were smuggled from farm to city for sale at exorbitant prices.

nese lived in fear that they would be savaged by the Occupation troops. Brutal treatment at the hands of a victorious enemy was a matter of course in the Orient; the vanquished Japanese were resigned to the prospect of rape and pillage.

MacArthur would stand for none of that. SCAP issued an order mandating a five-year jail sentence for any GI caught molesting a Japanese. Petty theft committed against civilians could bring a sentence of 10 years at hard labor and a dishonorable discharge. Such penalties applied to every soldier in the Occupation force, which at its peak in October of 1945 numbered more than 450,000 men. The force consisted of the U.S. Sixth Army under General Walter Krueger and the Eighth Army commanded by Lieut. General Robert L. Eichelberger, augmented later by a substantial contingent of British Commonwealth troops. These units were composed of combat veterans who retained vivid memories of Japanese ferocity in the Pacific island war. A few of them took a measure of vengeance, and paid the price. But the vast majority quickly put bitterness behind them, and their courteous behavior won the gratitude of the Japanese.

The paramount military objective of the Allied Occupation was contained in SCAP's General Order No. 1, issued on September 2, 1945, which directed that Japan's extensive military forces be disarmed. Even this urgent goal was achieved in a manner harmonious with MacArthur's long-term objective of fostering Japanese independence. Instead of directing the Occupation troops to disarm Japan's legions, MacArthur instructed that the Japanese commanders carry out the order. To the relief of many, this was done without incident. Men demobilized from units based in Japan dispersed to their homes—grateful for the early timing and the uneventful manner of their discharge.

In need of repatriation from overseas at the War's end were three million Japanese troops and about the same number of civilians. In one of the greatest and most orderly mass movements of all time, 4.5 million of these people were returned to their homeland within 10 months after the surrender, and an additional 500,000 came home in the ensuing six months. At the peak of this process, 167 Japanese ships and 200 Japanese-manned American vessels—half of them landing craft—were disembarking 185,000 persons a week at reception centers in Japanese ports. The repatriation program, otherwise so successful, suffered one major setback, which was traceable to the Soviets. The Russians, after declaring war against Japan on August 8, 1945, had sliced eastward across Manchuria, capturing more than 600,000 Japanese. By late 1947, almost all of these prisoners were deemed to be still in Soviet hands, despite pressure from SCAP through the Allied Council.

It was not until 16 months after V-J Day that the Russians would even agree to the principle of repatriation. In subsequent years, they shipped home Japanese prisoners in small groups, usually heavily indoctrinated with Communist ideology in the hope that they would have an impact on Japanese politics. This effort backfired; the Soviet treatment of the prisoners had been too harsh. By early 1949, an estimated 460,000 of them were still unaccounted for, the majority probably dead of starvation or disease.

With this one grim exception, repatriation and demobilization were among the easier aspects of MacArthur's neutralizing process. Another fairly uncomplicated matter was the dismantling, under Eighth Army supervision, of arsenals, arms factories and military bases. Arms were broken up or dumped into the sea; the machinery for manufacturing warplanes and artillery was taken apart and scrapped. Anything that could be converted to peacetime use—food, uniforms, boots, medical supplies—was salvaged; about seven million blankets and more than 21 million pairs of socks were handed over to the Japanese for distribution to civilians.

Far more difficult was the task of purging Japan's institutions and leadership of all militaristic taint. Among the purge's major aims were the trial and punishment of war criminals and the ferreting out of those leaders identified with Japan's era of aggression. Also important was the suppression of any organization devoted to militarism—notably the state-supported Shinto religion.

The dragnet for war criminals began with the roundup of well-known figures. Armed with a copy of *Who's Who in Japan* and a sheaf of dossiers compiled during the War, SCAP intelligence officers worked feverishly to create preliminary lists of prominent Japanese to be arrested and held for trial. Among those hunted down were two former Prime Ministers—Hideki Tojo and Koki Hirota, who had allowed militarists to gain power in the mid-1930s—and the American-born Tokyo Rose. Soon the Sugamo Prison in

Tokyo was crowded with 1,128 suspects. Among them were some surprises, including a German Gestapo colonel named Joseph Meisinger, known as the "Butcher of Warsaw," who was wanted by Allied authorities in Europe.

The Allies brought 28 persons accused of major war crimes to trial in May of 1946. The joint trial lasted for 30 months and produced a transcript 48,412 pages long that included 4,336 exhibits and the testimony of 1,198 witnesses. Ultimately the long process resulted in sentences of death for seven defendants, including Tojo and Hirota. MacArthur, vested with the power to overturn the sentences, refrained from exercising it; a plea for a stay of execution filed with the U.S. Supreme Court also was turned down. On December 23, 1948, the condemned seven men, shouting a last defiant *"Banzai!"* before they mounted the scaffold, were hanged at Sugamo Prison.

The purge of militarists led to the expulsion and exclusion of 200,000 functionaries from Japanese government jobs. It also brought a sweeping overhaul of the national police, an organization once feared as much in Japan as the Gestapo was in Germany. The police force was decentralized and its top officers dismissed. Every city or town of more than 5,000 people was made responsible for running its own force, which was to answer only to local civilian authorities.

A second purge focused on the *zaibatsu,* the family-owned financial, commercial and industrial combines that were formed in the 19th Century. By the 1940s, the *zaibatsu* controlled 80 per cent of Japan's major business activity through a dozen conglomerates. Some were dominant in specific fields, such as Kawasaki in shipbuilding and steel, and Furukawa in copper and electric power. But the largest combines, such as Mitsui and Mitsubishi, ruled vast banking and trade networks affecting dozens of enterprises and hundreds of thousands of employees. Through a series of SCAP-

inspired laws enacted by the Diet, these corporate bodies were broken up, their executives were let go and their stocks and other assets auctioned off.

Of 1,200 smaller companies slated for comparable "deconcentration," only nine were eventually dissolved, because the law proved to be too sweeping. Japanese industrial activity, already crippled, approached a state of paralysis. The confiscation of corporate assets resulted in financial stagnation, since sufficient capital to purchase such assets at auction was scarce—and most of what did exist was underground money in the hands of known criminals, who had continued to profit during the War. The Japanese government, stuck with the confiscated assets, watched their value decline. The decentralization program was gradually curtailed. At the same time, however, a ban against the manufacture of war matériel of any kind, from airplanes to ball bearings, was strictly enforced—although banning the latter would have a damaging effect on peacetime industry.

The attempt to break Japan's corporate oligarchy demonstrated that the purges were a mixed blessing. No mechanism of appeal existed, and thus there was no official way to judge wartime culpability. Many potentially useful and well-intentioned people needlessly lost their jobs—and their talents were lost to their country at a critical time.

In contrast to this rigidity, a lack of thoroughness caused the authorities to miss some who deserved to be ousted; others, banned but still secretly in touch with those in power, continued to wield their influence indirectly. Yet for all their shortcomings and occasional injustices, the purges broke the hold of Japan's militant establishment and opened the way for a new generation of national leaders.

The political organs that these new leaders were to use in governing Japan became the target of the most comprehensive reforms introduced by the Occupation. The process began forcefully in October 1945, when MacArthur gave the Japanese government a list of changes to be implemented immediately, including the granting of voting rights to women for the first time in Japanese history. MacArthur had already decreed that Japanese newspapers were to be free to print anything they pleased—except "destructive" criticism of the Occupation. In practice, Japanese newspapers were not allowed to discuss the extent of SCAP's involvement with the Japanese government; American censors also suppressed news and editorial material from abroad, furnished by the Associated Press and other agencies, that they feared might undermine Japanese confidence in the Allies.

Even Hirohito, sensing the need for reform, began nudging Japan's ancient imperial throne in a new direction. The debate over how to handle the Emperor had begun well before the War ended. Many on the Allied side wanted to depose Hirohito and try him as a war criminal; according to this argument, the Emperor deserved punishment because he had allowed Japan's aggression in the Far East, even if he had not actually set it in motion. But there were many who proposed a milder solution. They felt that prosecuting the Emperor would generate such lasting bitterness that Japan would be decades in rejoining the society of peaceful nations, and that the costs of occupying and governing the country in the meantime would be prohibitive.

Emperor Hirohito visits the residents of a new housing project near Tokyo. By tradition a distant, godlike figure—few Japanese had caught even a glimpse of him before 1945—Hirohito paid a great service to Japan's democratization by such well-publicized mingling with his people.

Flanked by American MPs, former Prime Minister Hideki Tojo (upper center) testifies in his own defense in December of 1947 before the International Military Tribunal, which tried him for conspiring to conduct aggressive war and for violating the laws of war. Before the trial, Tojo had bungled an attempt at suicide; the tribunal sentenced him to death.

It was President Truman who decided to leave the question of the Emperor's future to the Japanese. Truman's decision was never stated in so many words; but its import, agreed to by the other Allies, appeared in a clause of the Potsdam Proclamation that allowed the Japanese to choose their own peaceable form of government. Because his people wanted him, the Emperor remained on his throne.

The imperial office did not remain unchanged, however. Hirohito "humanized" it—in the word used by Kazuo Kawai, then the editor of the *Nippon Times*. The humanizing process began with the monarch's initial meeting with General MacArthur, an occasion on which Hirohito deliberately shed his traditional aura of inviolate supremacy. One morning in late September 1945, Hirohito sent word to the Dai Ichi that he wished to see the Supreme Commander. MacArthur felt that his position as representative of the victorious Allies prevented his going to the palace to visit the vanquished Emperor; on the other hand, he felt that forcing Hirohito to attend him at the Dai Ichi would have been needlessly degrading for the Emperor. Instead, it was arranged for the two men to meet at the U.S. Embassy.

Alone except for an interpreter, the Emperor was greeted by MacArthur inside the Embassy and conducted into a reception room. There MacArthur, who was unaccompanied by any aide, showed Hirohito to a seat by the fireplace and offered him an American cigarette. "I noticed how his hand shook as I lighted it for him," MacArthur later recalled. "I tried to make it as easy for him as I could, but I knew how deep and dreadful must be his agony of humiliation."

In agreeing to the meeting, MacArthur had been apprehensive that the Emperor would plead for clemency in case he should be charged as a war criminal. (Unbeknownst to Hirohito, MacArthur already had removed his name from the list of accused.) Instead of self-justification, however, what MacArthur heard was an assumption of ultimate guilt:

"I come to you, General MacArthur," the Emperor said, "to offer myself to the judgment of the powers you represent as the one to bear sole responsibility for every political and military decision made and action taken by my people in the conduct of the War."

As MacArthur remembered it later, the statement stirred him "to the very marrow of my bones. He was an Emperor by inherent birth, but in that instant I knew I faced the First Gentleman of Japan in his own right." Thereafter, the Emperor called on the Supreme Commander several times, developing a cordial relationship that could not have been dreamed of at any earlier time.

For Hirohito, shedding his aura of supremacy also meant stepping out of his role as a demigod. Ever since the mythical beginnings of the imperial institution in 660 B.C., Emperors had been deemed divine descendants of a primal sun goddess. According to traditional belief, the Emperor shared this inheritance with his people, who were thought of as members of a large family with the monarch at its head, all sharing his divinity.

SCAP had abolished government support for the Shinto religion—of which the Emperor was, in effect, the high priest—because of its use by the extreme nationalists to support Japan's expansive militarism. "The Japanese people were told," MacArthur later wrote, "that the Emperor was divine himself and that the highest purpose of every subject's life was death in his service."

Although the Japanese did not actually regard the Emperor as a god in the Western sense, MacArthur's headquarters was worried about the persistence of a divine aura. The

Americans feared that it would undermine the transformation of the imperial throne from a seat of potential power to a symbol, that it would therefore feed Western apprehensions of future Japanese militarism. The Emperor was urged to renounce his divinity. Protesting that it would embarrass him to give up what he did not possess, the Emperor nevertheless agreed, conceding that doing as he was asked might allay Western suspicion of Japan's future intentions.

On January 1, 1946, Hirohito issued a statement renouncing his divine status. The Emperor said that the ties between him and his people had "always stood upon mutual trust and affection. They do not depend on mere legends and myths. They are not predicated on the false conception that the Emperor is divine and that the Japanese people are superior to other races and fated to rule the world."

In response, MacArthur said, "The Emperor's New Year's message pleases me very much. By it he undertakes a leading part in the democratization of his people." The Supreme Commander also stated that Shinto priests would be permitted to continue preaching their faith, "so long as church and state were separated."

A major effect of Hirohito's renunciation of divinity was

to liberate him from a confining pedestal; his entourage and the American Occupation authorities now prevailed on him to move among the people, attending art galleries, concerts and sports events. On these expeditions, Hirohito was sometimes bumped and pushed by news photographers, and the imperial dignity suffered in other ways. On a visit by Hirohito to a coal mine, a miner touched off a national controversy over how the Emperor should now be greeted. The traditional form of greeting for the miner would have been a bow, to which the Emperor would have bowed in response. When the miner tried to shake hands, the flustered Emperor insisted on mutual bows. Irked, the miner complained to reporters, and Japan's newspapers initiated a debate over the new etiquette. Both the incident and the controversy surrounding it would have been unthinkable before the War.

The Emperor's shifting status had obvious implications for Japan's political future: A monarch breaking precedent to mingle with his people was a clear harbinger of democracy.

From the autumn of 1945 on, MacArthur proceeded on a carefully planned sequence of steps aimed at making Japan a democracy: The Japanese were to get the chance to draft a new constitution, using as a starting point the structure of the 1889 Meiji charter. If the Japanese dragged their feet in this endeavor, SCAP would offer its own cogent suggestions for Constitutional change; as a last resort, the Occupation would hand down a directive specifying reforms that must be carried out. An election for Diet members to be held in April of 1946, it was felt, would be in effect a popular referendum on the Constitution.

First, there had to be a constitution. A Japanese government committee assigned to draft one in October 1945 brooded for months without producing anything useful. Liberal members of the committee urged substantial changes in the old Constitution, conservatives wanted none. In February, MacArthur told Brigadier General Courtney Whitney, one of his closest wartime aides and now the head of SCAP's section on government, to design a model constitution for presentation to the Japanese.

Working around the clock for a week, Whitney's team wrote a charter that in a number of ways resembled Western models. The new draft called for a tripartite government: an independent judiciary, an executive branch consisting of a

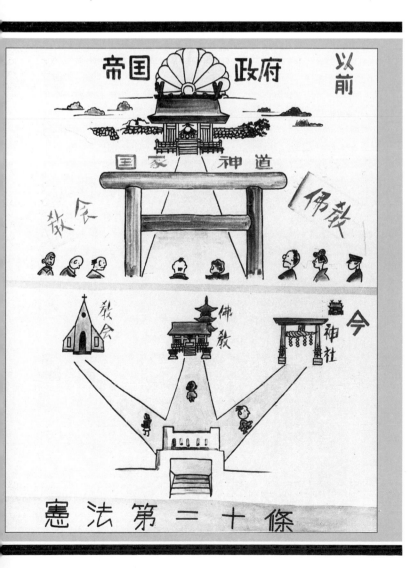

Graphic posters issued by MacArthur's headquarters in 1947 illustrate for the Japanese the many virtues of their new Constitution. The poster at far left provides a before-and-after look at government spending: In the old days (top), a citizen's taxes funneled into a cash box, to be squandered by irresponsible bureaucrats; now, tax receipts were to be allocated by law, to pay for schools, roads and public-health services. In the poster at left, a shrine with the imperial chrysanthemum symbolizes the state-supported Shinto rite of Emperor-veneration that had been obligatory for all Japanese, apart from whatever religion they practiced. The new Constitution abolished compulsory rites: Shintoism existed on an equal basis with other religions, none of which received government aid.

prime minister and a cabinet, and a one-chamber legislature. The old House of Peers was to be abolished, along with titles of nobility; the House of Representatives was retained. The people, backed by a bill of rights that included an article establishing equality of the sexes, were to be sovereign. In the new constitution, a final phase in the democratization of the imperial throne was reached: The Emperor, once the focus of sovereign power, was reduced to "a symbol of the state," a status comparable to that of constitutional monarchs in Great Britain, Norway and the Netherlands. He retained no political power and his political activities were limited to ceremonial functions.

In the most radical departure from its predecessor—and from every other national charter—the new Constitution's Article 9 foreswore war:

> Aspiring sincerely to an international peace based on justice and order, the Japanese people forever renounce war as a sovereign right of the nation and the threat or use of force as means of settling international disputes.
>
> In order to accomplish the aim of the preceding paragraph, land, sea and air forces, as well as other war potential, will never be maintained. The right of belligerency of the state will not be recognized.

Later, under pressure of rising tension between the United States and the Soviet Union, legal opinion in Japan and the United States developed formulas citing the initial phrases of both paragraphs of Article 9 as justification for the so-called self-defense forces that Japan was to form in the wake of the Occupation. MacArthur, for one, viewed Article 9 as prohibiting only aggressive moves by Japan, not any action taken in defense of the country against outside attack.

The initial Japanese reaction to the American-designed constitution was a bit sour. On February 13, General Whitney handed the document to Foreign Minister Shigeru Yoshida, Dr. Joji Matsumoto, chairman of the Constitutional Revision Committee, and Jiro Shirasu, head of the so-called Central Liaison Office, the primary link between SCAP and the Japanese government. The three reacted to the model charter, according to a SCAP aide who accompanied Whitney, "with a distinct sense of shock." As Whitney remembered it, "Mr. Shirasu straightened up as if he had sat on something. Dr. Matsumoto sucked in his breath. Mr. Yoshida's face was a black cloud."

As time passed, however, the shock wore off. With some revision, made in consultation with SCAP over the next three weeks, the Constitution won official Japanese acceptance. MacArthur's personal authority undoubtedly played a part in this acquiescence. In addition, the men who voted on the measure inside the government may have been aware—though nothing was ever said—that the Supreme Commander was prepared if necessary to go over their heads and present the Constitution directly to the people.

In the meantime, Japanese newspapers were full of voluble comment on the charter. From this press discussion, three reactions seemed to foretell the favorable reception of the Constitution by ordinary Japanese. One was relief, because the clause abandoning war conveyed a sense of Japan's restoration to the world of peace-loving countries. Another was a growing perception of self-worth, because power had shifted away from the minority that had ruled throughout Japanese history, therefore raising the masses from *shimmin* (subjects) to *jimmin* (the people). Finally, as one newspaper commentator pointed out, the new charter was "markedly thorough in establishing the basic human rights of the people as eternal and not to be violated."

Insistent as always that the Japanese take the lead in working out their postwar destiny, MacArthur waited while the government's lawyers and the two Houses of the Diet had a chance to study and digest the draft. The Japanese leaders proposed a number of changes at this stage—the most important of those accepted by SCAP being the addition of a second Diet chamber, called the House of Councilors; acceptance was granted on condition that all members of the new House be elected rather than hereditary, and that the House of Councilors be the lower chamber of the Diet instead of the upper, as the old House of Peers had been.

Submitted to the Diet—which was still operating under the Meiji Constitution—the final draft charter passed by a vote of 421 to 8 in the House of Representatives. Not surprisingly, since the new Constitution abolished the House of Peers, its reception there was not enthusiastic. But only a minority openly attacked it. At a ceremony on May 3, 1947, the Emperor—waving his hat to the crowd as he stood in the rain—proclaimed the Constitution the law of the land,

LAND OF THEIR OWN AT LONG LAST

Until 1945, almost half of Japan's farmland was worked by sharecroppers, who had to hand over roughly 50 per cent of each harvest to their landlords. Burdened with oppressive poverty, the tenant farmers had little stake in the process of democracy that the Americans were trying to install in Japan. MacArthur's solution was a sweeping redistribution of land. In 1946, with firm guidance from MacArthur's staff, the Japanese Diet passed the Farm Land Reform Act, which in effect turned over the land to those who farmed it.

Over the next three years, landlords had to sell five million acres of agricultural land to the government; the government in turn sold it to the former tenants at modest prices, with payment spread over 30 years.

Individual plots were small; 7.5 acres was the largest holding allowed by the new law in the more productive areas, and the average parcel was a scant 2.5 acres. Yet many farmers were able to double their previous incomes. And the social benefits were enormous. More than two million hitherto landless tenants and their families were now property owners, with an entrepreneur's vested interest in the future of the new Japan.

In the first transaction under Japan's 1946 land reform law, a government official (left) hands a former tenant the deed to his rice field near Yokohama.

and exhorted his people to exercise their sovereign rights.

The right of the ballot had already been exercised by 27 million Japanese in the 1946 elections—3 out of 4 among those eligible voted, including more than 13 million women. Among the 466 new members of the House of Representatives, 38 were women—one of them a prostitute who polled more than 250,000 votes.

Such equality for women was totally new in Japan. Among the 700 largely reformist laws passed by the Diet during the Occupation were a number aimed at putting an end to sex discrimination. Women, long barred from divorcing their husbands (who could shed their wives with relative ease), were accorded that right. For the first time, women were allowed to own property independent of their husbands, and they could share equally with their brothers the family inheritance. By the third year of the Occupation, nearly 2,000 policewomen were serving throughout the country. And as MacArthur rode to and from the Dai Ichi every day, he was gratified to see another manifestation of the feminist surge: girls in shorts batting and fielding along with boys in sand-lot games of baseball, which the Japanese had learned from Americans in the 19th Century.

Discrimination based on sex still prevailed in the Japanese educational system, however. Founded on a prewar European model and rigidly controlled by the Ministry of Education in Tokyo, the school system required six years of compulsory education for all children, and during these years classes were mixed. Children who continued their education attended separate schools. In practice few girls reached high school or university. In fact, barely 3.5 per cent of all students advanced as far as the 11th year; one half of 1 per cent made it to the university level.

Reforms passed in the Diet, and overseen by SCAP, transformed the entire system. An American model lengthened the compulsory stages, revised the curriculum and abolished traditional rote-learning methods; new textbooks discarded notions of emperor-veneration and militaristic patriotism. Coeducation was broadened at the college level, and many new schools were founded throughout Japan.

A basic element of the educational reform program was new construction—needed, for example, to house such innovations as three-year junior-high schools. Unfortunately, SCAP directives to build these schools conflicted with other SCAP orders restricting the ability of local Japanese communities to finance them; to foster fiscal responsibility under a democracy, SCAP insisted that money to pay for the buildings had to come out of current revenue, and many localities simply did not have the funds. On asking SCAP how they were to reconcile these conflicting demands, officials were abruptly told that the Americans were not running the Japanese government, only recommending policies; it was up to the Japanese to implement them any way they could. In the face of this impasse, several officials resigned, the building program stalled, and classes continued to be held in temporary quarters such as abandoned barracks. The building program was eventually completed, financed in many instances by expedients that included "voluntary" contributions by parents that were actually obligatory—forced by social and governmental pressures in communities avid to take advantage of the new educational program.

In a later critique of the Occupation, journalist Kawai pointed to the school construction program as an illustrative summary of the Occupation's workings: SCAP introduced policies that were legislated and enforced by the Japanese government, which took the brunt of criticism when things went wrong. The final result, however, was good: By shaking up old methods, Kawai concluded, SCAP caused a general soul-searching throughout the system, and young people benefited by a better education.

Two other instances, agonizing for all concerned, reveal how SCAP policy, exercised through Diet and Cabinet channels, developed as it was filtered through Japanese realities both early and late in the Occupation. One case, resulting in a rare military crackdown, involved the labor movement, for which SCAP had nurtured high hopes as an instrument for liberalizing the economy; the other, culminating in a proof of Japanese democracy, evolved from MacArthur's urge to decentralize the government.

Guided by Washington policy directives, and by MacArthur's belief that a liberated working class was the bulwark of a democratic society, SCAP pushed hard from the beginning to strengthen Japanese labor. Before the War, frustrated by hostile employers and by a government that was indifferent when not downright antagonistic, Japanese unions had barely clung to existence. A law enacted by the Diet in late 1945—even before the passage of Constitutional reforms—freed labor to organize and engage in collective bargaining. It also guaranteed most workers the right to strike. Other laws passed subsequently matched American legislation in their liberal provisions on such key issues as hours, vacations, sick leave and child labor.

Thus encouraged, the Japanese labor movement grew rapidly, accompanied by a wave of strikes and such unprecedented demands as the use of company facilities for union activities conducted on company time. There was an ominous increase in political activity by unions, and such radical actions as take-overs of company property by the workers, acts that SCAP suspected were Communist inspired.

SCAP's tolerance for the apparently runaway labor movement snapped in late January 1947, when unions mobilized for a general strike. A threat to call out U.S. troops headed off that strike, and in later demonstrations by strikers and other labor activists, American soldiers in jeeps—and even formations of tanks—backed up Japanese police. The early liberality of SCAP's labor policy increasingly yielded to a sterner attitude; by 1948, for example, the right to strike was withdrawn from all government employees.

One of the Occupation's last reforms was a drive to raise local taxes to pay for the operation of municipal and regional governments. A bill based on SCAP recommendations and introduced in the Diet in March 1950 was opposed by many legislators, both because they felt its provisions were too rigid and because they faced a June election. When the Japanese Prime Minister warned SCAP that the bill was in trouble and offered a compromise draft that would satisfy the lawmakers, Occupation bureaucrats rejected it. The original bill failed to pass.

Furious, the Supreme Commander called in his top aides and asked for an explanation. Justin Williams Sr., a civilian legislative expert attached to the government section, reminded his chief that in democratizing the Japanese government, he had encouraged it to come up with just such a negative vote. Acknowledging the point, MacArthur authorized a press release indicating that the Diet had been "entirely within its right to reject the local tax bill, that in a democracy it sometimes takes a little longer to conduct the nation's business." An amended local tax bill passed easily in the next session of the Diet.

By the time of the tax bill controversy, SCAP had met its basic objective: to replace Japan's authoritarian wartime regime with one committed to peace and democracy.

At the outset of the Occupation, American food shipments were intended mainly to prevent starvation and social unrest, but the urge to strengthen Japan as an Asian bulwark against the Soviet Union led to an increase in aid, since even a fully recovered agriculture could not alone have fed the Japanese people. Between direct shipments from the United States and American-financed purchases from elsewhere in the world, Japanese food imports increased from just over one million tons in 1947 to nearly 1.8 million tons the following year. By 1949, the Japanese were beginning to wean themselves from American aid—able, at any rate, to pay for 40 per cent of their own food imports. During that year, potatoes and sweet potatoes were removed from the list of rationed foods—although rice, the national staple, continued to be rationed for several years.

Inflation, a problem that had threatened MacArthur's efforts to rebuild the Japanese economy, also was being brought under control. After watching prices rise by 135 per cent in 1947 and an additional 65 per cent the following year, SCAP in 1949 imposed an austerity program on the country to hold down the spiral, and pressured the Diet into passing—and abiding by—a balanced budget. The resulting fall in prices helped produce the first postwar surge in Japanese exports, primarily of cotton textiles. To serve the new overseas markets and to supply domestic needs, Japanese industrial potential was bolstered by a steady flow of American dollars—$1.7 billion by mid-1950, funneled directly into the economy. And by the early 1950s, per capita productivity had regained prewar levels.

In June of 1950, events overtook both Japan and its Supreme Commander. The armies of Communist North Korea crossed the 38th parallel into South Korea, and a new war broke out—almost two years before a formal peace treaty was signed by Japan and all the Allies except the U.S.S.R. The Korean emergency transformed General MacArthur into a warrior once again. He was named to command the United Nations forces resisting the Communists. Japan became an essential forward base for the American troops and matériel needed for the struggle on mainland Asia. Just nine years after Pearl Harbor, it ceased being an enemy—and increasingly became an American ally and friend.

JAPAN REBORN

As Japan rebuilds, a Shinto priest invokes good fortune during the dedication ceremony for a new sawmill under construction in Tokyo in late 1946.

FIRST STEPS IN A MIRACLE OF RECOVERY

Prewar Japan had been Asia's most industrialized nation by far, and as a trader it had ranked fifth in the world. But in 1945, Japan's economy lay shattered: The months of relentless U.S. bombing had leveled its cities, wrecked much of its coastal transport system and destroyed its manufacturing capacity. Even those factories that survived were geared largely to turning out the machines of war—such as fighter aircraft—that were forbidden to a vanquished nation.

Of necessity, simple sustenance became the first goal of the Japanese—as well as their American occupiers, who began pouring relief aid into Japan at a rate that reached $400 million per year. But it became clear that if Japan was once again to support itself, its industrial base must be rebuilt—and with American help. Late in 1948, the same year the Marshall Plan was initiated in Europe, a group of American planners, including executives recruited from private business, charted an ambitious new economic course for Japan. It called for self-sufficiency within five years.

Triggering such a recovery required additional American outlays beyond the cost of basic relief: $74 million in fiscal 1949 and $165 million in 1950, used mainly to import raw materials. This pump priming was the stimulus the Japanese needed to launch what was to become a miraculous economic revival. The comeback was accelerated in 1950 by the onset of the Korean War, during which Japan became an essential supply and staging base, repair facility and rest area for American combat forces.

By 1954, no further aid was required from the United States. Japan's gross national product and the personal income of its people had matched prewar peak figures and would continue to rise. In the rebuilt cities, shops bulged with consumer goods, new cars jammed the streets and, in the words of a contemporary newspaper editor, "smartly dressed people were working and playing in an almost carnival atmosphere of buoyancy and vitality."

A bilingual notice posted in a machine-tool factory at Chiba in eastern Honshu exhorts Japanese workers to help revive their country's shattered economy.

Housebuilders trailing ropes erect a scaffold in Hiroshima in 1947. Two years earlier the first atomic bomb had leveled nearly three quarters of the city.

REBUILDING THE BASICS WITH SAND AND WOOD

Two urgent postwar goals for the Japanese were the replacement of housing—25 per cent of which had been destroyed—and repair of the railroads. The rail system was vital to a country that even before the War had poor highways and only one motor vehicle per 600 people. The wartime manpower shortage had slowed the replacement of rails on Japan's 25,000 miles of track to barely 3 per cent of what was needed. Rolling stock too had been destroyed or was in disrepair.

Trains were so scarce during the first months of peace that passengers had to wait as long as three days just to get standing room out of Tokyo. But that would not be true for long. Construction gangs, made up in part by women, were already laying track and restoring roadbeds. Renovated factories began turning out steam locomotives and the electrically powered passenger trains that would make Japan's rail system one of the fastest and most efficient in the world.

The simplicity of Japanese domestic architecture helped facilitate the housing renewal; a typical house—small, made of wood and paper—could be put up quickly and cost about one tenth as much as a European-style masonry dwelling.

But the style had its drawbacks. Houses rarely lasted more than 30 years even in normal times. Thus, although the Japanese replaced the 2.7 million houses damaged or destroyed during the War, housing lost to other causes (ranging from natural decay to fires resulting from earthquakes) combined with a growing demand to sustain the shortage: Ten years after the surrender, Japan still had nearly three million fewer houses than it needed.

Women members of a railroad construction crew heft wooden ties that will be used to repair war-damaged roadbed on the hard-hit southern Japanese island of Kyushu.

In late 1945, Japanese children led by former soldiers tote bags of sand up a riverbank near Tokyo, as another group at right fills more bags. In the immediate postwar period, sandbags were used, with wire, charred wood and scrap metal, to build makeshift shanties.

At an electric power plant near Tokyo in 1946, workers take tango lessons in a twice-weekly dancing class sponsored by their union, in a room furnished by the company.

SECURITY AND BENEFITS FOR LOYAL EMPLOYEES

American Occupation policy encouraged Japanese labor to organize, and unions grew enormously, from fewer than one half million members before the War to seven million in 1949. The strike became a legitimate tactic. But for many workers the right to bargain collectively was over-shadowed by the traditional, almost fa-milial relationship between the Japanese worker and his employer.

Although the unions agitated for higher wages—and for equal pay for women— the companies held the workers' loyalty by giving special allowances based on such standards as the employee's age and the size of his family. When it came to job security, the unions did not have to fight: Most companies felt an obligation to keep their employees on the payroll even when there was almost no work to be done.

Editorial workers in the city room of the Asahi Shimbun, Tokyo's leading newspaper, prepare a two-page daily edition in 1949. In spite of a paper shortage that kept issues thin, the newspaper maintained a full staff of 2,500 people working in three shifts.

Visiting Americans and their hosts inspect a
quality-control process for sorting light bulbs at
Tokyo's Shibaura Electric Company in
1951. The highest-quality bulbs were exported.

YANKEE KNOW-HOW TO BOOST EXPORTS

A high priority in the American plan for putting Japan back on its feet was to restore its capacity to manufacture goods that it could sell abroad. Washington's projection called for a five-fold increase in Japanese exports, from $259 million in 1948 to $1.3 billion in 1953.

It was a tall order. But the Japanese fulfilled it, working with American production experts and under financial guidelines set by a tough Detroit banker, Joseph Dodge, whom President Truman named in 1949 to oversee Japan's economy. To keep the recovery from creating as many problems as it solved, Dodge insisted on a balanced government budget and higher taxes to curb runaway inflation.

The textile industry had accounted for almost half of Japan's prewar export income, and with U.S. aid, particularly in the import of raw cotton, it became one of the first to revive. By 1951, Japan was exporting one billion square yards of cotton cloth—more than any other nation.

Flanked by Japanese colleagues, an American textile expert checks yarn on a spindle at a rehabilitated rayon mill near Osaka. Before the War, Japan led the world in rayon production.

The 1948 Datsun two-door deluxe sedan, a prototype designed for eventual export, had a top speed of 35 miles per hour.

THE FIRST TRICKLE OF CARS, CAMERAS AND TVs

The heavy industries in Japan needed time to rebound, but by 1951 the production of coal, iron and steel had reached almost 80 per cent of wartime peaks. The nation's battered shipyards were restored and modernized, and Japan—which had to import almost every barrel of petroleum it used—soon developed into one of the major builders of oil tankers.

It was in some relatively new areas, however, that Japan's recovery was about to take wing. In July of 1950 the four-year-old Tokyo Telecommunications Engineering Corporation, later renamed Sony, marketed Japan's first magnetic-tape recorder. In 1952, Japan's automotive factories exported their first 1,000 cars—small vehicles sent mostly to South America and the Middle East. The next year, with technical help from such American firms as RCA, the fledgling Japanese television industry produced and sold its first 14,000 TV sets.

A lens cleaner at the Nippon Kogaku Company removes dust particles from Nikon camera components before their assembly. In 1952, Japan exported 72,000 cameras to Venezuela, Singapore and the United States.

Visitors to the Japan Broadcasting Company in 1948 watch a demonstration of television on a cumbersome experimental console. The screen itself measured only 8 by 10 inches.

Shoppers stroll the main commercial street of Hiroshima in 1952, shortly after the end of the American Occupation. In the seven years since the Bomb, 65 per

cent of Hiroshima had been rebuilt and the city was reviving as an industrial and commercial center for foodstuffs, textiles, machinery and rubber products.

3

An electric silence settled over the Parliament in New Delhi as Jawaharlal Nehru rose to speak. It was a few minutes before midnight on August 14, 1947. Nehru, who was about to become the first Prime Minister of India, would now formally declare his nation's independence as a dominion within the British Commonwealth. In so doing, he was bidding a peaceful farewell to the British, who had come to India three centuries earlier as merchants and stayed as conquerors to build an empire.

Nehru, wearing as always a fresh rose in his buttonhole, gazed around at the packed benches of Parliament Hall, where members of the Indian Constituent Assembly had convened to assume full power over their new nation.

"Long years ago," Nehru began, "we made a tryst with destiny, and now the time comes when we shall redeem our pledge, not wholly or in full measure, but very substantially. At the stroke of the midnight hour, while the world sleeps, India will awake to life and freedom.

"We end today a period of ill fortune," Nehru continued, "and India discovers herself again. This is no time for petty and destructive criticism, no time for ill will or blaming others. We have to build the noble mansion of free India where all her children may dwell."

As Nehru finished speaking a herald stepped forward and raised a conch-shell horn, reserved since ancient times for occasions of great ceremony. The spine-tingling call of the conch filled the hall, as the clock over the speaker's stand tolled midnight. Indian independence was a reality. Exactly two years after the Japanese surrender ended a war that had accelerated the processes of political change already under way, the people of India had reclaimed their land from European intruders and brought the colonial era decisively to an end. Britain's fabled Indian Empire was no more.

Outside in the streets of New Delhi, crowds cheered and sang. In the neighboring old city of Delhi, light flickered from tiny oil lamps in the alleys, blazed from the strings of bulbs festooning mosques and temples. At Cawnpore, on the Ganges River in north-central India, scene of grisly atrocities during the mutiny of 1857 when Indian troops rose against their British officers, Indians and Englishmen now embraced each other. In Simla, the elegant resort in the foothills of the Himalayas used by the British as a summer capital, Indian men clad in the traditional loincloths called

INDIA'S VIOLENT DESTINY

dhotis, and women in the flowing dresses known as saris, frolicked merrily down the Mall, an avenue once off limits to any Indian wearing traditional dress. In Calcutta, street signs in English were torn down along the main thoroughfare, Clive Street, and replaced with new ones bearing the name Subhas Road, commemorating Subhas Chandra Bose, an Indian revolutionary hero. In towns, villages and cities from Madras in the east to Bombay in the west, from Trivandrum in the south to Patna in the north, a free people celebrated by turning midnight into a festival of light, or by gathering at temples to scatter rose petals at the feet of their multifarious goddesses and gods.

Yet not everyone in India celebrated. Vapal P. Menon, a high-ranking Indian lawyer-bureaucrat who had worked closely with the last British Viceroy, Lord Louis Mountbatten, to help bring about this moment, sat at home and listened to the swelling sounds of festivity. Menon did not cheer. Instead he said, "Now our nightmares really start."

The nightmares in fact had already begun, born of ancient quarrels damped or diverted by the British but never resolved. On independence night, murderous mobs roamed the northern city of Lahore, in the heart of the Punjab, a Muslim stronghold; the disorders were harbingers of an onslaught of violence, mostly between India's two predominant religious groups, Hindus and Muslims. Their mutual hatred reflected a kind of madness suffered by peoples whose religious and cultural differences were too great to be resolved through one mighty, sweeping change.

Hinduism, with hundreds of millions of followers, was the overwhelmingly dominant religion in India, a fact both feared and resented by tens of millions of Muslims who despised every Hindu belief. Less numerous than either Hindus or Muslims were the Sikhs, a militant sect antagonistic to both Muslims and Hindus. The Muslims drew the special wrath of the Sikhs, who refused to forget that they had been persecuted at Muslim hands two centuries earlier during the Mogul empire.

In the weeks leading up to independence, armed bands of Sikhs and Hindus had rampaged through the Amritsar area 30 miles to the east of Lahore, setting fire to Muslim villages, slaughtering the residents, splashing acid into Muslim faces. Now vengeful Muslim mobs assaulted the Hindu and Sikh neighborhoods in Lahore's ancient quarter, called the Old City, cutting off the occupants' water supply and trapping them inside a circle of fire. Hindu homes were broken into and plundered. A Sikh temple, crowded with refugees who had been promised protection there by Muslim authorities, was set afire by killer gangs, whose members roared with glee at the agonized screams of their immolated victims. Muslim police made no attempt to quell the terror. They too wanted revenge.

Such horror stunned the world. Virtually no one, Indian, British or otherwise, had fully anticipated the bloodshed that independence would unleash. With hindsight, however, it was clear that violent death and disunity were familiar legacies for India. There had been no Indian nation since the last days of the Mogul emperors, and even their rule had never encompassed the whole of the subcontinent. India had no discernible national identity when British traders arrived in the 17th Century. After many struggles British troops and colonial administrators succeeded, by the middle of the 19th Century, in bringing order to India for the first time, pacifying a diversity of warring provinces and pulling them together under a succession of viceroys responsible to the British government in London.

Even at its peak, however, the British union was compromised by a gross anomaly: More than 560 states, which were scattered throughout the subcontinent and occupied two fifths of its area, were ruled by Indian princes known variously as nizams, nawabs, rajas and maharajas. These isolated states remained virtually independent of British India, although their rulers came to acknowledge the supremacy of the British crown and accept the guidance of British officials in their respective domains.

Aside from its political diversity, India under the administration known as the British raj (an Indian word meaning rule or dominion) was anything but culturally homogeneous. Perhaps 1,500 languages and dialects splintered the country. Religious differences extended beyond the large populations of Hindus, Muslims and Sikhs to such small minorities as Christians and Buddhists. There also were Jains, members of a Hindu sect founded in the Sixth Century, and Parsis, followers of an ancient faith called Zoroastrianism, which had originated in Persia.

Small wonder that India's surge of nationalism, when it

came, was an upheaval; originally representing the yearning of oppressed people to be free of colonial rule, nationalism became a convulsively divisive movement that almost defeated itself.

Of all India's problems the most severe by far was the unrelenting antagonism between its 250 million Hindus and 90 million Muslims. The chasm between the two communities was virtually unbridgeable. Their religious differences were so numerous as to color every thought and act of life. The Hindus, whose forebears had been in India for centuries before the birth of Christ, worshipped a deity that was manifest in every form and concept in the universe, from commonplace animals to the outermost stars. Paintings and statues of more than three million gods and goddesses representing crops, weather, water, fire, and even such physical ailments as smallpox, were objects of worship. And of all the animals revered by the Hindus, the cow inspired the deepest veneration.

By contrast, the Muslim faith was relatively new to the subcontinent, having been introduced by seafaring traders from Arabia in the Eighth Century and spread by the Mogul conquerors. For Muslims, there was but one God—Allah—and one Prophet, Muhammad. They considered the idols of the Hindus an abomination. Particularly abhorrent and incomprehensible was the cult of the cow. In the Muslim view, the worship by man of a dumb animal was both degrading and senseless, especially when millions of Indians starved while 200 million sacred cattle fed relatively well.

As great an obstacle to Hindu-Muslim cooperation was the Hindu caste system, a social structure ranging from elite Brahmans to despised untouchables. To the Muslims, Hinduism perpetuated social inequities that were an affront to Allah. Islam became a sort of brotherhood that welcomed refugee untouchables from the harsh caste system.

Those Hindus whose status placed them above the untouchable level regarded Muslims themselves as untouchables, and treated them accordingly. A Brahman recoiled in horror at the slightest accidental touch of a follower of Islam. Eating or even touching food within sight of a Muslim was an anathema to upper-caste Hindus.

As though their differences were not enough, India's well-to-do Hindus, possibly because they embraced with ease a variety of idols—and ideas—had quickly seized the educational opportunities offered by the British. Under the paternalistic eye of their mentors, they became India's financiers, bankers, insurance brokers, lawyers, industrialists and administrators. Upper-class Muslims, because they were intent on preserving their Islamic traditions, made little effort to educate themselves in Western culture; most were landlords or career military men. The Muslim creed forbade usury, a stricture that, as Muslims saw the matter, excluded them from effective participation in the business community. The Hindus thus were able to assert a disproportionate economic domination over Muslims.

The first visible stirrings of an Indian political identity had come in 1885, when Allan Octavian Hume, a retired British official of the Indian Civil Service urged Indian graduates of Calcutta University to found an organization for the expression of their political grievances and objectives. Both Hume and his fellow founders intended the Indian National Congress, as they called the organization, to function strictly within the framework of the British regime. They could not imagine the passions they would unleash.

The core of the Indian National Congress was Hindu. Many Muslims, who constituted less than 25 per cent of India's population, were disturbed by the new movement. They worried about undue Hindu dominance if the Congress Party should ever gain greater political power. In 1906, the Islamic community formed its own organization to safeguard the political rights of the Muslims in India: the All-India Muslim League, which eventually would be dominated by a zealot named Muhammad Ali Jinnah. India's two constituencies were thus sharply defined.

World War I brought with it the first real surge of Indian nationalism. The European conflict was not India's war—though in the beginning all the disparate elements in India, from factory hands to princes, united behind Britain's war effort. But the ostensibly loyal subjects of the King-Emperor, George V, soon became restless and disillusioned. As the War dragged on, Britain appeared less awesome, only one among a number of powerful nations. And it seemed increasingly odd to Indians that so superior a British culture—indeed, Western civilization in general—should have allowed such a bloody war. Yearning for more responsibility in the conduct of its own national affairs, India repeatedly

Indian soldiers enforce a round-the-clock curfew in July 1946 on a riot-torn street in Ahmadabad, near India's west coast; clashes between rival religious communities had killed 19 people and injured 130. The decorated enclosure beside the soldiers is a small Hindu temple.

was told: "After the War." Yet it seemed that the War would never end. As British prestige waned, Hindus and Muslims put aside their differences—for the moment—and joined in a demand for self-rule.

When peace finally came in 1918, Britain continued to hold back. The British raj extended promised reforms with one hand and then took them away with the other. The Indians gained a measure of self-rule with the establishment of national and provincial legislatures, but summary justice was meted out to agitators with the suspension of jury trials for political offenses. Indian protests against such repression led to riots; the riots in turn brought savage reprisals by British troops. Mohandas Karamchand Gandhi—soon to become active in the nationalist movement and revered as Mahatma, or Great Soul—was a longtime friend of Britain's, and a dedicated apostle of nonviolence; yet even Gandhi now lost faith in British intentions. The supposedly "beneficent institutions of the British government," he declared, "are like the fabled snake with a brilliant jewel on its head, but which has fangs full of poison."

In the 1920s, young Jawaharlal Nehru joined Gandhi as a leader of Indian nationalism, and the Congress Party became a political force to be reckoned with by the British. The personalities and methods of the two men were quite different. Gandhi was a charismatic spiritual leader who used civil disobedience and passive resistance as tools to achieve Indian self-expression. Nehru, scion of an aristocratic family, was a sophisticated, articulate politician with a more international point of view than Gandhi. Gandhi brought Nehru forward as his lieutenant in order to capture the young intellectuals in the nationalist movement for the Congress Party. Under the umbrella of a party formerly dedicated to winning piecemeal reforms from the British, the aims of Gandhi and Nehru fused into one goal: democratic self-government for India.

In 1935, Britain broadened Indian self-government. By 1937, entirely Indian legislatures functioned in each province (and were optional in the princely states), and Indians were granted greater representation in the federal legislature in New Delhi. The Congress Party and the Muslim League

elected members in 1937 to speak in these forums and even to make policy in matters concerning local and regional administration. Yet decisions involving defense, foreign affairs and finance remained in the hands of the British Viceroy, who in extreme circumstances could suspend representative government altogether.

It took another war to precipitate the ultimate break. More than any nationalist movement, the global catastrophe of World War II brought about the end of the British raj—and the agonizing mutilation of the Indian subcontinent that followed. In September of 1938, when the shadow of coming conflict was unmistakable, Nehru sent a letter of warning to the *Manchester Guardian,* a leading British newspaper:

"The people of India have no intention of submitting to any foreign decision on war. They alone can decide and certainly they will not accept the dictation of the British government," wrote Nehru. "If Britain is on the side of democracy, then its first task is to eliminate empire from India. That is the sequence of events in Indian eyes, and to that sequence the people of India will adhere."

On September 3, 1939, the current Viceroy, the Marquess of Linlithgow, without consulting any Indian leader proclaimed India at war with Germany in a fight for democracy and freedom.

The Indian reaction was predictable. "Whose freedom?" demanded Nehru. Only a few weeks earlier, in a Congress Party resolution challenging the British government, he had declared: "India cannot associate itself with such a government or be asked to give her resources for democratic freedom, which is denied to her and which is likely to be betrayed." Only a free India, Nehru asserted, could support Britain in the war against Nazism.

The British government, committed to the defense of liberty almost everywhere, still was not ready to extend democracy's blessings to India. Britain held back in spite of the threat by Nehru and his Congress Party colleagues to withhold support for the war effort. London's priorities once more urged delay in granting Indian self-rule: Wartime, Britain argued, was no time to launch an independent India. Nevertheless, most British leaders realized that no matter how much they disliked the idea, the transfer of power must eventually take place.

London had no intention, however, of granting true self-government to an India riven with internal strife. As the British saw it, they had pasted and patched the bits and pieces of India into one structure; they did not intend to let their edifice crumble when it came time for them to leave. Yet the British ignored an inconvenient fact: Most Indians did not necessarily equate independence with unity. The great mass of the people of India were barely aware of politics; they knew little more than a continuing daily struggle for subsistence. Spiritual leader Gandhi suggested that British notions linking democracy and unity were stumbling blocks to independence. His solution: "Let them withdraw from India and I promise that the Congress and the League will find it to their interest to come together and devise a homemade solution for the government of India. It may not be scientific; it may not be after any Western pattern, but it will be durable."

Muhammad Ali Jinnah, speaking for his people, crystallized the Muslim distrust of democracy: Rule by majority vote meant Muslim subjugation. "Democracy," he declared, "can only mean Hindu raj all over India." When, in January 1940, Gandhi tried to obtain Jinnah's cooperation in what he called "building up the Indian nation," Jinnah sneered. "You start," he said, "with the theory of an Indian nation that does not exist."

Presiding over a meeting of the Muslim League in March of 1940, Jinnah developed the theme that Hindus and Muslims were distinct and separate peoples. He persuaded the league to resolve that India should be divided into two homelands. The idea of an independent Muslim nation, to be called Pakistan, was thus declared as a goal. The name Pakistan combined two words in Urdu, meaning "spiritually pure" and "land," and had been coined in the 1930s by a group of Muslim students at Oxford. The students based their thinking on the ideas of Muhammad Iqbal, a poet and philosopher who was an early leader of the Muslim League; Iqbal is given credit for conceiving the idea of a Muslim homeland consisting of the Punjab, Kashmir, Sind and the Pathan tribal area known as the North-West Frontier Province.

The British could not support this separatist aim. They envisioned a united, democratic government as a legacy of

British rule. But democracy implied the ascendancy of the Hindus and a government controlled by their Congress Party. The British feared that transferring power to the Hindus without safeguards for the Muslim minority would inevitably ignite a civil war between Hindus and Muslims. Delay, for the British, remained the best answer.

In the spring of 1940, Hitler's troops stormed through Western Europe to the shores of the English Channel and challenged the very existence of Great Britain. More than two million Indian subjects became soldiers and were trained in new skills; many reached officer rank. A small Indian Air Force and Navy came into being. Indian units fought superbly in North Africa, the Middle East, Europe and Southeast Asia. But despite such participation, support for the British cause was less than wholehearted. Nehru and Gandhi would spend much of the War in prison for their vociferous—though always peaceful—noncooperation.

Anti-British feeling would take more extreme form in the so-called Indian National Army, formed in 1943 by onetime Congress Party President Subhas Chandra Bose from among Indian troops captured by the Japanese in Burma and Malaya. The INA's mission was to invade India along with Japanese troops—whose war cry was "Asia for the Asians"—and liberate their country from the British. (As a military force, the 14,000-man INA proved to be of little help to the Japanese. Many Indians volunteered simply to escape Japanese prison camps; others were said to have been forced to join by Bose's officers. Ultimately, the INA forces disintegrated during the 1944-1945 Allied offensive into Burma.)

By the middle of 1942, India was in turmoil in anticipation of a possible Japanese invasion. Gandhi was reluctant to accept a "post-dated check" for home rule after the War, and he hoped to neutralize the Japanese threat by first ousting the British. He called upon the British to pull out voluntarily and "leave India in God's hands." Swayed by Gandhi, the Congress Party formally adopted the cry "Quit India!" and on the 8th of August, 1942, urged a "mass struggle" that would take the form of civil disobedience on a mighty scale. Most Congress Party leaders immediately and enthusiastically backed the plan.

Gandhi, Nehru and a number of other activists were arrested within hours of the "Quit India" resolution, and the Congress Party was declared illegal. What had been a non-violent freedom campaign suddenly turned violent. Armed with dynamite, brickbats and knives, nationalist extremists cut telephone and telegraph wires in 2,500 locations, blew up bridges and burned government buildings. They derailed trains and murdered fellow Indians who refused to join them. Saboteurs tore up railroad tracks and smashed signaling devices. By mid-September, 150 railway stations had been damaged or destroyed and 550 post offices—symbols of the British raj—had been attacked. Communications between Bengal and Assam in the northeast and the rest of India became virtually nonexistent; the flow of war supplies to the Allied forces preparing to defend the India-Burma border against the Japanese dwindled to a trickle.

But by the end of September the viceregal government had struck back with British and loyal Indian troops; on a number of occasions RAF planes roared down to strafe mobs. One after another, the wildfires of protest were stamped out. As Indian journalist Durga Das noted, "The raj, employing all the instruments of suppression at its command, had imposed on the country a sullen, frustrated quiet." This festering calm continued for almost three years, until two atomic blasts in August 1945 brought a sudden end to the war with Japan.

Peace inspired little jubilation in India. Britons cheered and staged celebrations in all the major cities. But the great mass of Indians, who were not deeply involved, could only shrug at its outcome. Yet the War had wrought great changes for India as well as for Britain. Events had overtaken the British Empire. A new pattern had been slowly forming; now it rapidly took shape and the pieces of the puzzle tumbled into place.

In India, a major change lay in the perceived self-image of middle-class Indians who had served as military officers or had undertaken new wartime responsibilities in government, business and industry. Circumstances had confronted them—and the British—with proof of their skills as administrators, technicians and industrialists. These people no longer were content to be second-class citizens in their own land. Nor did they consider captured members of the Indian National Army guilty of treason, as the British charged. Subhas Bose had died from injuries suffered in an airplane crash and could not be tried; instead, three other INA officers were selected for public trial at Delhi in November of 1945.

The British asserted that the officers were traitors because they had broken their soldiers' oath to the crown. The defense countered that the men owed nothing either to their colonial masters or to Japanese militarism; they simply had been fighting for national freedom.

In proceeding to trial, the British made a profound tactical error: They undermined their case by choosing to prosecute, as a group, a Hindu, a Muslim and a Sikh. Putting the three on trial together unified antagonists who were ordinarily far apart; it gave the trial a symbolic significance that struck a chord throughout India and aroused public opinion as never before. The chief defense lawyer, Bhulabhai Desai, making much of the national solidarity represented by the accused trio, attacked the prosecution claim that Indians owed allegiance to Britain. "Unless you sell your soul," Desai declared, "how can you ever say, when you are fighting to liberate your own country, that there is some other allegiance which prevents you from doing so? If that were so, there would be nothing but permanent slavery."

The three defendants, now popularly regarded as martyrs

to the cause of freedom, became national heroes. And when the court convicted them, an angry outcry arose in every major city. To preserve public order, the British military commander in India, General Sir Claude Auchinleck, hastily ordered their release.

The unfortunate trial and its outcome dealt a sharp blow to British prestige and gave the nationalist movement a great surge. The issue, Nehru said, had been "a trial of strength between the will of the Indian people and the will of those who held power in India, and it was the will of the people that triumphed in the end."

At the same time, the right arm of British imperialism—its military structure—was undermined. The INA trials had raised a serious problem for Indians serving in the armed forces. If opposing the crown had been in any way justifiable, then the reasons for their own loyalty were put into question; if Indian nationalism could come before duty to Britain, what Indian would choose the foreign master?

Such a dilemma was bound to breed trouble, and on February 19, 1946, about 3,000 enlisted men of the Royal Indian Navy mutinied in Bombay. Protesting against a system of discrimination that provided them poorer food and living conditions than British seamen, rioting Indian sailors attacked British officers and men. They hoisted an orange, green and white flag in the name of the Congress Party on several vessels in the harbor, and paraded through Bombay streets on foot and in commandeered trucks.

Sparks leaped from Bombay to Navy establishments in Karachi, Calcutta, New Delhi and Madras. Slogans such as Quit India and *Jai Hind* (Hail India) were scrawled on city walls. British military police fired on the Bombay demonstrators, who retaliated with gunfire and hand grenades; one person was killed and nine injured. Industrial workers in Bombay went on sympathy strikes, as did more than 1,000 men in Royal Indian Air Force camps in the area.

The outbreaks were spontaneous, and were not approved by Indian leaders, either Hindu or Muslim. Nevertheless, the troubles continued. By February 22 the mutinous sailors, having seized nearly 20 Navy vessels in Bombay's harbor, were turning their guns on the city. Just one day later, however, they abruptly surrendered in response to joint Muslim-Hindu pleas by Muhammad Ali Jinnah and Vallabhbhai Patel, a prominent Congress Party leader. On

Photographed in 1948, the year after he became India's first Prime Minister, Jawaharlal Nehru wears the traditional Indian hat that he was seldom without. Although Nehru did not share Mohandas Gandhi's religious zeal or his austere life style, he found in Gandhi a personal model for integrity and courage, "a symbol of uncompromising truth." Gandhi, in turn, chose Nehru as his political heir.

shore, however, the mob violence continued. Bombay was subjected to an orgy of arson, vandalism and looting. For several days, trying to make themselves heard above the din of street warfare, Jinnah and Patel appealed in vain to sailors to lay down their arms and to civilians to avoid the conflict. By February 24 the official casualty count totaled 187 killed and 1,000 injured.

When the frenzy finally subsided at the end of the month, Nehru suggested that the time had come for his countrymen to direct their energies into constructive channels. Nehru was concerned that such anarchy would backfire and endanger the larger cause of independence. Yet members of both parties attributed the violence to genuine Indian resentment of foreign domination. A Congress Party spokesman, Minoo Masani, declared on the floor of the New Delhi legislature that "the real cause of this mutiny is the existence of British rule in the country."

For once, the Muslim League was in full agreement with the Congress Party. Addressing remarks to the viceregal government representatives in the legislature, a prominent Muslim from Bengal, Abdur Rahman Siddiqi, issued a warning: "Your age is finished and a new age has dawned. Unless you go with the spirit of the age there will be trouble and misery for my own countrymen as well as for those who would like to crush them."

In Britain, these warnings did not sit well with such champions of empire as Winston Churchill, who had declared early in the War: "I have not become the King's First Minister in order to preside over the liquidation of the British Empire." Churchill, however, was no longer in office. He, along with the Conservative Party, had lost power to Clement Attlee's Labor Party in the election of 1945, and Labor was resigned to divesting itself of empire.

The British people, exhausted by war, had neither the desire nor strength to resist independence movements. Victory had almost defeated them. Britain was bankrupt; there was no money in the exchequer to pay off the nation's crippling war debt. Factories were closing, coal production diminishing, electric power failing. Millions of Britons were unemployed. Sales taxes on some items were as high as 100 per cent, but there was little to buy. As the famed British economist Lord John Maynard Keynes put it: "We are a poor nation and we must learn to live accordingly."

For a country adjusting to hard times, India had become a costly burden. Britain had been drawing upon India as if it were a bank account, using India's manpower, capital, goods, food supplies, services, manufacturing capabilities and other resources until it was deeply in debt to its own colony. By the end of the War, Britain owed India the equivalent of four billion dollars. At the same time Britain had incurred the enmity of the Indians by answering their pleas for independence with promises of "tomorrow." Now tomorrow had dawned, and for most Britons the only remaining questions were when to transfer power and, most important, who should receive it?

In February 1946, Prime Minister Attlee announced that a three-man Cabinet Mission would visit India and attempt to establish a practical framework for independence. The emissaries chosen were Sir Richard Stafford Cripps, President of the Board of Trade (the British equivalent of the U.S. Department of Commerce); Lord Frederick Pethick-Lawrence, the Cabinet Secretary of State for India; and Albert V. Alexander, First Lord of the Admiralty.

Vallabhbhai Patel, Nehru's political ally and sometime rival, was a masterful organizer and power broker who was able to mold the Congress Party into a formidable political force. Patel might have become Prime Minister when India was granted its independence in 1947, but Gandhi favored Nehru for that job and persuaded Patel to accept the administrative post of Deputy Prime Minister in the new government.

73

Charged with the task of promoting a Hindu-Muslim coalition that could set the stage for self-rule, the team—ironically dubbed the "Magi," or "three wise men," by the Viceroy, Lord Archibald Wavell—had two primary objectives. One was to organize a body of Indian leaders who would devise a constitution for a free India. The other was to form an interim Indian government, an executive council representing the major political parties that would run India until the constitution had been drawn up. At the same time, the commission had to resolve the profound complication represented by Jinnah's dream of a separate Pakistan.

The "three wise men" had varying qualifications for the job. Cripps, a brilliant lawyer, had long advocated Indian independence. In 1942 he had formulated a plan for self-government to be implemented after the War; Gandhi had aborted it with his Quit India campaign. Pethick-Lawrence, described by Wavell as a "charming old gentleman"—he was 75 years old—deeply respected the Indians and believed himself to be on a divine mission. "We are but the instruments of powers far greater than ourselves, whose will," he said, "will in the end be done." The commission's third member, Alexander, was described by a contemporary as a plain, no-nonsense fellow, a sort of John Bull "who wants Cheddar cheese and English food and is so proud of the Navy." Alexander had had no prior experience with the complexities of Indian politics.

Lord Wavell, the viceroy the commission would have to work with, was more warrior than diplomat. An associate described him as "suspicious of new-fangled ideas, straightforward, blunt." But Wavell knew India, as commander in chief of British forces beginning in 1942, and as Viceroy since 1943; he had also served there as a junior officer before World War I.

These men understood that the problem they confronted was enormous and complex, rooted in the age-old animosity between India's Hindu and Muslim communities. Now the underlying friction between the two populations increased as independence, with its promise of power, became imminent; far from acting as a unifying factor—as the INA trials had—the proximity of freedom became the catalyst for an ever-deepening split.

The Cabinet Mission arrived on March 24. Just meeting with the enormous cast of characters involved in the independence movement and sorting out their points of view was a monumental task. Heading the list, of course, were Gandhi, Nehru and Jinnah. Next came a mixed lot of scarcely less important figures: Vallabhbhai Patel, powerful head of the Congress Central Parliamentary Board and a dedicated political creature contemptuous of half measures; Tara Singh, a third-grade schoolteacher who represented the five million Sikhs of the Punjab and harbored a fanatical hatred for Muslims; H. Shaheed Suhrawardy, Chief Minister of the important Muslim-majority province of Bengal, described by Wavell as "inefficient, conceited and crooked," a flamboyant politician with a private army of thugs and a taste for high life.

It soon became clear to the British team that they were dealing with individuals who were simultaneously inflexible and volatile in asserting their goals. Jinnah demanded a Pakistan consisting of six of the British Indian provinces: four located in the northwestern part of the country, the Punjab, Sind and Baluchistan and the North-West Frontier Province; and two in the northeast, Assam and Bengal. In addition, Jinnah had designs on Kashmir. But, as the mission pointed out, such a state would include large areas where the population comprised substantial numbers of non-Muslims. The non-Muslim population, 38 per cent in the northwestern group of provinces and 48 per cent in the northeastern group, would not necessarily agree to incorporation in a separate Muslim state.

To India's Hindu majority, mutilation of their homeland still represented sacrilege. With an old man's passion, Gandhi declared repeatedly: "You shall have to divide my body before you divide India." And Nehru insisted, "Nothing on earth, not even the United Nations, is going to bring about the Pakistan that Jinnah wants."

"No power on earth," Jinnah raged in his turn, "can prevent Pakistan." And Jinnah's colleague, Firoz Khan Noon, warned that if India were to remain united under a Hindu substitute for the British raj, the ferocity of Muslim uprisings would outdo even the terrible 13th Century depredations of Genghis Khan.

Faced with the threat of civil war, the three British Commissioners attempted to compromise. The plan they developed called for a united India: a Hindu-Muslim coalition

Muslim leader Muhammad Ali Jinnah (center) confers in May 1946 with two members of the British Cabinet Mission sent to negotiate Indian independence: Lord Pethick-Lawrence (left) and Albert V. Alexander. Jinnah was a luxury-loving, aristocratic man who held himself aloof from India's masses and even was disdainful of much about his own religion, but he had won the support of millions of Muslims for his uncompromising insistence on a separate Pakistan.

within a three-tiered government, functioning under a new charter to be drawn up by a constituent assembly. The first tier, a federation of all the provinces, would deal with defense, communications and foreign affairs. The second tier, unions of provinces grouped according to Muslim or Hindu interests, would control all other federal government functions. The third tier, the individual provincial governments, would take care of affairs on the local level. The states ruled by princes would have representatives in the constituent assembly and would negotiate alliances within the Hindu or Muslim groups. The plan was a complex but sincere attempt to combine the Congress Party's desire for union and the Muslim League's strident calls for a separate state, and it was approved by both organizations—with reservations.

The British Cabinet Mission flew back to London at the end of June, hoping that a process of compromise had been set in motion. But within a month, all was in shambles. Nehru said in a press conference that the Congress Party was bound to nothing more than entering the Constituent Assembly to help draft a new constitution. He implied that

the grouping plan, designed by the British to mollify the minority Muslims, might not be adhered to by his majority faction. And when the Congress Party refused to send delegates, Viceroy Wavell shelved the plans for an interim Hindu-Muslim coalition government.

Jinnah felt trapped and betrayed. On July 29, 1946, at a Muslim League meeting in Bombay, he declared: "This day we bid good-by to constitutional methods." Jinnah's alternative was what he called "direct action," an implicit signal for Muslims to demonstrate their support for partition and Pakistan. August 16 was to be Direct Action Day.

Jinnah did not specify what he had in mind for the day. But the phrase "direct action" and Jinnah's attitude were suggestive. H. Shaheed Suhrawardy, the corrupt Chief Minister of Bengal, chose to interpret the suggestion as a personal opportunity. Suhrawardy had private dreams of making Bengal an independent state, and a vague idea that he could serve his own interests by turning Direct Action Day into a jihad—a Muslim holy war—against the Hindus. Declaring

August 16 a public holiday for the Muslims of Calcutta, Suhrawardy used the occasion to make an inflammatory speech to a large gathering in the city, thus setting off a series of bloody events.

Masses of Muslims marched in holiday demonstrations of solidarity for Suhrawardy and—incidentally—for Pakistan. Professional troublemakers moved among the already-aroused crowds, suggesting that the Hindus were preparing to massacre all the Muslims in Bengal. "Arm yourselves!" cried the agitators. "Kill them before they kill you!" The Muslim poor of Calcutta, who were living in the world's foulest slums, hurled themselves into an orgy of hatred. Streaming into the business center, they sacked Hindu shops and slaughtered the owners. Panic-stricken Hindus began pouring out of the center city, but the mobs caught up with them on the streets and in alleyways, prolonging the awful day into a night of murder, rape and pillage. Gutters literally flowed with blood. Many Hindus who had not fled rallied and rampaged through Calcutta in quest of revenge. Sikhs, loathing Muslims, vigorously joined in.

The next day, Michael Edwardes, a British writer who entered Calcutta by bus from the airfield, described the aftermath: "Fires glowed on either side and the bodies of men, women and children, hideously mutilated, squelched under the wheels of the bus. The hot air smelt of fire and blood, and the mad yelling of the mob echoed in the alleys."

The killing in Calcutta went on for three more days. Watching from a boat on the Hooghly River, a Briton named Radclyffe Sidebottom saw people with their hands tied brought to the river's edge and then pushed down the bank into the water, where men in dinghies prodded them under with poles. Others were dispatched in a different manner. "You could see them being laid on their faces," Sidebottom reported, "with their heads poking out over the Howrah Bridge and being beheaded into the river, their bodies thrown in afterward. After the riot the river was literally choked with dead bodies."

At the end of the four-day-long massacre—described by a British-owned newspaper, *The Statesman,* as the "Great Killing"—more than 4,000 people had lost their lives and 10,000 had been injured. An estimated 100,000 people were homeless. It was civil war. As Michael Edwardes noted, however, "No British were assaulted; on the contrary,

the few who were out in the streets received only politeness from men whose fingers were still wet with blood."

Wavell, horrified by the mass violence, appealed again to Muslim League and Congress Party leaders to reconcile their differences. Jinnah was not interested. To him, the Great Killing was proof that there must be either a Pakistan or all-out war. He accused the Congress Party of fomenting the riots, but he could not disguise his satisfaction with the results of Direct Action Day: It must now be obvious that Muslim and Hindu could not live together.

"We shall have India divided," he thundered, "or we shall have India destroyed."

Reaction in London to the Great Killing was somber. Wavell's attempts to cobble together an effective interim coalition government during the autumn of 1946 proved useless. Thwarted by Jinnah's noncooperation, the doughty soldier began to feel the strain. He had trouble sleeping and suffered migraine headaches and nosebleeds.

In December, Wavell and the coalition leaders were summoned to London to review progress on the Cabinet Mission's plan. After two days of talks without making headway, they lunched with King George VI. The King, sitting between Nehru and Jinnah, decided that "the leaders of the two parties will never agree."

On February 20, 1947, the final phase of the British raj began. Prime Minister Attlee announced to the House of Commons that His Majesty's government wished to make it clear that "it is their definite intention to take the necessary steps to effect the transference of power into Indian hands by a date not later than June 1948."

Attlee added that there would be a change of Viceroy. Lord Wavell was to be replaced by Lord Louis Mountbatten, Viscount of Burma. Mountbatten, 46, was a great-grandson of Queen Victoria and a cousin of King George VI; during the War's climactic years he had been Supreme Allied Commander, Southeast Asia. Presiding over the British retreat from India was not a task he relished, but he was an enormously capable man and was widely considered an excellent choice.

Nevertheless, the coldly stated fact of quitting India was not easily swallowed. Winston Churchill rose to denounce the move in one last passionate attempt to halt history in its

The victims of four days of religious rioting, their corpses picked clean
by vultures before a burial party could reach them, fill a narrow street in
Calcutta in late August of 1946. The butchery was triggered when
Muhammad Ali Jinnah, leader of the Muslim League, called on his people
to demonstrate against the Hindu-dominated Congress Party.

tracks. "It is with deep grief," he rumbled, "that I watch the clattering down of the British Empire with all its glories and all the services it has rendered mankind. Many have defended Britain against her foes. None can defend her against herself. . . . Let us not add by shameful flight, by a premature, hurried scuttle—at least let us not add to the pangs of sorrow so many of us feel, the taint and sneer of shame."

Churchill spoke in vain. Well convinced that it was time to shift British responsibilities onto Indian shoulders, the House of Commons voted overwhelmingly to end British rule by June 1948.

Lord and Lady Mountbatten arrived in New Delhi on March 22, 1947. The new Viceroy found India in what he described as "a most unsettled state." Ceaseless rioting had ripped the country apart. Nehru, touring disaster areas in the Punjab in November, had been sickened by the ghastly scenes. "Murder stalks the streets," he wrote to a friend, "and the most amazing cruelties are indulged in by both the individual and the mob. It is extraordinary how our peaceful population has become militant and bloodthirsty. Riot is not the word for it—it is just a sadistic desire to kill."

Lord Hastings Ismay, once Winston Churchill's chief of staff and now Mountbatten's, had had experience in India. He surveyed the breakdown of the nation and voiced his opinion that "India was a ship on fire in midocean with ammunition in her hold." Mountbatten's task was to put out the fire before it reached the ammunition, and he knew he must act quickly. He sent urgent messages to Nehru, Gandhi and Jinnah, requesting private meetings in New Delhi.

Louis Mountbatten was no stranger to Jawaharlal Nehru. The two men had met in Singapore after the War and had liked each other at once. Meeting again in the Viceroy's study, they quickly renewed the friendship. Mountbatten combined toughness with charm; Nehru, subtle grace with pragmatism. Like-minded in many ways, they agreed that the partition of India would be a tragedy and that an early resolution of the Indian problem was essential if open warfare was to be avoided.

It was important that Mountbatten persuade all of India's leaders to trust him, and he was a man who very seldom failed. Even Gandhi, presenting himself to the Viceroy in loincloth and sandals, felt at ease with the elegant English-

man. Mountbatten, in turn, saw Gandhi as a saintly pacifist who looked rather like a "sweet, sad sparrow."

When Jinnah's turn came, however, neither Mountbatten's warmth nor his powers of persuasion made any impression on the remote and chilly Muslim leader. Pencil-thin from a wasting chest ailment, single-minded in his aim of carving a Muslim state out of the body of India, Jinnah was frigidly courteous but unbending in his first meeting with the Viceroy. For almost two hours, Mountbatten tried all the social and diplomatic tricks at his command to make Jinnah's acquaintance as a human being.

When at last the Muslim leader left Mountbatten's study, it was on a formal but somewhat defrosted note. "My God, he was cold!" Mountbatten told a member of his staff. "It took most of the interview to unfreeze him."

In the days that followed it became apparent that even the slight thaw had been temporary. Jinnah refused to consider an Indian union. He insisted that a "surgical operation" was the only cure for India's illness, and that all of Bengal and the Punjab would have to be included in his new state, not just their Muslim areas.

Meanwhile, rioting and bloodshed continued in both those provinces, as well as in the North-West Frontier Province. The need for action was becoming increasingly urgent. Mountbatten tried to gain a point by reminding Jinnah that if India were to be partitioned on the basis of its Muslim population, only half of Bengal and half of the Punjab belonged with Pakistan.

Jinnah could not see why, just for the sake of 40 million Hindus and Sikhs, he should have to accept a shrunken, "moth-eaten" Pakistan. He refused—at first. Then, on reflection, he changed his mind. No one knows precisely why; perhaps Jinnah feared that further rigidity might cost him what he had already gained. "Better a moth-eaten Pakistan," he said to Ismay, "than no Pakistan at all."

A move toward a settlement also came from the Hindu side. With great reluctance, Nehru and his colleague Vallabhbhai Patel were coming to the conclusion that partition was preferable to unending chaos, though Gandhi was still deeply opposed to a dismembered India. Anticipating a workable basis for unified self-government, Nehru and Patel started pushing Mountbatten to draw up a blueprint for British withdrawal.

Under the pressure, Mountbatten produced a plan. Attlee, in offering self-government to India by June 1948, had warned that if the Indian parties did not cooperate, the transfer of power would have to be made on the basis of what seemed best to all parties when the deadline came; power might even be turned over to individual provinces. Accordingly, Mountbatten formulated a plan for partition based on decisions made by the provinces themselves. Those with substantial Muslim majorities could simply affirm that they indeed wanted to be a part of the new state of Pakistan. Provinces in which Muslims barely outnumbered Hindus—for example, Bengal and the Punjab—would be divided between India and Pakistan, if either faction favored a division. Precise boundaries were to be determined later by a special commission. For the moment, the hope that partition would put an end to strife was great enough to produce an agreement, in principle, between the Congress Party and the Muslim League to abide by Mountbatten's plan.

Taking his cue, Mountbatten on June 3 dramatically accelerated the pace of events: He moved up the deadline of June 1948 to August 15, 1947, leaving Britain and India little more than two months to work out all the details of transfer against the background of a worsening blood bath.

Mountbatten's plan split British India into two independent states, one Muslim and one Hindu. Areas with a Hindu majority, including substantial slices of Bengal and the Punjab, would form the new India; areas with a Muslim majority would form the state of Pakistan, consisting of the North-West Frontier Province, Baluchistan, Sind, part of Assam, the western half of the Punjab—and East Bengal. A complicating factor in the package was that East Bengal and Assam lay 1,000 miles away from the rest of Pakistan, with no land corridor to link the two. There would be two Pakistans: East and West.

Immediately after Mountbatten's plan was accepted, Sir Cyril Radcliffe—a lawyer who had never served in or even visited India—was handed a most unenviable job and given less than six weeks in which to accomplish it. As chairman of the newly established Boundary Commission, he was to preside over the dismemberment of Bengal, Assam and the Punjab. Known for his brilliance as a trial lawyer, Radcliffe had been chosen largely because he knew so little about India and would presumably harbor few prejudices about the place.

The territory to be divided encompassed 175,000 square miles and was inhabited by about 90 million people. One official cheerfully told Radcliffe that, apart from drawing a couple of arbitrary lines, "you will have nothing to worry about." But Radcliffe took the assignment more seriously than that, fearing that haste could result in terrible mistakes. Ostensibly he was to have the help of Indian high court judges as legal experts, but in fact he would have to make all the boundary decisions himself. Patiently, yet painfully aware of how little time and knowledge he had, Radcliffe worked on his maps and drew his boundary line through factory complexes, irrigation systems and railroads—a reluctant hand performing the surgical operation forced upon British India by its inhabitants.

The issue of the princely states was not Radcliffe's problem but Mountbatten's. As representative of the crown it was the Viceroy's duty to deal with the termination of the treaties they enjoyed under British rule. The princes were independent rulers of their respective domains—free, except in cases of glaringly conspicuous misrule, to do exactly as they pleased throughout their realms. Collectively, their territories contained approximately 80 million people, nearly one quarter of India's total population. They ranged in size from tiny Bilbari—a titular estate two square miles in area, with a population of fewer than 30 people—to Hyderabad, 82,000 square miles in area, with a population of 16 million. The rulers, variously, were fabulously rich or almost poor, self-indulgent or spartan, wildly eccentric or extremely enlightened.

As Mountbatten explained to this mixed lot, the forthcoming partition of British India meant that each must make a choice: to join Congress Party-ruled India or the unformed nation of Pakistan—or to remain independent. Essentially, the Viceroy pointed out, each ruler was to make his own decision; but Mountbatten strongly advised them to accede to one or another of the new nations, taking into account the geographical location of their states and the religious preferences of their peoples.

For some wealthy, powerful maharajas, the prospect of being swallowed up by an avowedly egalitarian state had little to recommend it. The principality of Junagadh, north

A GILDED WORLD SOON TO END

As the day of independence approached and their British protectors prepared to depart, India's several hundred hereditary nobles became an endangered breed. In a time of sweeping change, these feudal lords were regarded as anachronisms with no place in India's democratic future.

A majority of the local rulers were little more than tribal chieftains. But many of the khans, nawabs, rajas, jagirdars and maharajas were men of enormous wealth whose lavish life styles were all the more incongruous in a nation burdened with frightful poverty. A study done by *Life* correspondent Richard Neville in 1947 of 85 of the richest and most important nobles revealed a statistical profile of stunning opulence: On the average, each owned five palaces; rode on 9.2 elephants, in 3.4 Rolls-Royce automobiles and 2.8 private railroad cars; and had 5.8 wives or concubines and 12.6 children. Fond of sports, the typical noble had bagged 22.5 tigers in his lifetime.

For these aristocrats and their entourages, life could be a never-ending holiday. A certain Nawab of Rampur, who was fond of jazz bands and theatricals, kept a troupe of 500 actors and musicians to amuse him. And the Maharaja of Gwalior played with an elaborate set of electric trains that transported his meals from the kitchen to the royal banquet hall along 250 feet of solid silver track.

In his uniform as a lieutenant general in the imperial service, the Maharaja of Bikaner stands in his palace courtyard. The honeycomb of upper-story rooms housed his concubines, but the Maharaja's truest loves were his crack camel corps and hunting for grouse.

Escorted by lancers and swordsmen and protected from the sun by an umbrella, the Maharaja of Gwalior reclines in a golden howdah atop his elephant during a procession in celebration of a Hindu holiday.

Lesser nobles pay court to the Maharaja of Baroda on his birthday in 1948, as the days of such pomp and privilege draw to a close.

Portraits of Britain's George V and Queen Mary in a palace chamber reflect the Maharaja of Mysore's debt to his imperial protectors.

of Bombay, was only 3,300 square miles in extent but its Nawab was wealthy and self-willed. Uninterested in the needs and wishes of his subjects, the Nawab was devoted only to his dogs, which lived in kennel-apartments, each equipped with bed, bath, valet, electricity and telephone. A Muslim himself, he ruled a population that was overwhelmingly Hindu.

The even wealthier Maharaja of Kashmir, Sir Hari Singh, had been known to buy hundreds of dancing girls valued at $80,000 apiece. Because he was a Hindu, Singh held live cattle in high regard, and although 75 per cent of his four million subjects were Muslims for whom there was nothing sacred about a cow, he punished hungry subjects who butchered cows with seven years in prison.

Possibly the most powerful—certainly the richest—of the princes was the Nizam of Hyderabad, whose vast state in south-central India was populated primarily by Hindus. The Nizam, a Muslim, was an aging miser reputed to be the wealthiest man in the world. Strewn around the basement and attic of his palace, loosely wrapped in crumbling newspaper, were about $10 million in bank notes, vulnerable to the nibbling of the palace rats. No matter: The Nizam had more durable property so valuable that no one had a precise idea of its worth; estimates ran well above $50 million for his hoard of gold bars and coins, and close to $100 million for his jewelry collection, which included two diamonds the size of limes.

Other princes were a striking contrast. The Maharaja of Baroda, in the western part of India, supported a system of free and universal education that his grandfather had introduced before the turn of the century. In the far south, under Maharaja Bala Rama Varma, the untouchables of Travancore were allowed to worship in Hindu temples—a privilege unheard of elsewhere. Farther north, Mysore's prince had assembled the finest science faculty in Asia at a private university in his capital. In Jaipur, southwest of Delhi, the Maharaja, a descendant of a renowned 18th Century astronomer, sponsored one of the best-equipped observatories in the world.

Early in July 1947, a special team headed by Vallabhbhai Patel and Vapal P. Menon began appealing to the princes to make their choice. On behalf of the forthcoming nation of India they offered to ease the pain of surrendering authority to the Indian union with offers of tax-free state pensions and guarantees that the princes would retain their personal wealth, along with their much-valued right to British titles and decorations. Patel and Menon enlisted the help of Mountbatten, who badgered and bantered with the princes to persuade them to join one side or the other. Warning of "anarchy and chaos which will overwhelm great and small in a common ruin" if the princes did not come to a decision by August 15, Patel and Menon used all their skill and tact to persuade the rulers to throw in their lot with India.

One prince after another signed the Act of Accession. By August almost every princely state contained within the geographical limits of Hindu India had declared itself part of the new state. Five others with Muslim populations, Muslim leaders and borders contiguous with those of Pakistan opted to join Jinnah's government. There were three holdouts, states in which the ruler and the majority of the people were not of the same religion: Junagadh, Hyderabad and Kashmir. For the moment, nothing much could be done about their recalcitrance. The stage for independence was set.

In London on July 18, the Clerk of Parliament read out the titles of the 18 bills requiring royal assent that day: Among them were the South Metropolitan Gas Bill (authorizing maintenance funds for gasworks), the Felixstowe Pier Bill (concerning dock regulations at a harbor in Suffolk), and the Indian Independence Bill. To each the Parliamentary Clerk of the Crown, representing King George VI, gave a brief, formal assent. In such workaday legislative company did the British Indian Empire formally come to an end.

In Bengal and the Punjab, the two major territories that were to be divided between Pakistan and India, the minorities in each area realized that they must flee to avoid the risk of being slaughtered. They began a mass migration to new homes in areas dominated by their respective coreligionists. In New Delhi, and in government offices all over India, representatives of India and the future state of Pakistan earnestly and sometimes furiously haggled like divorcing couples over the division of property, from gold ingots to cash, trucks to typewriters, aircraft to encyclopedias.

Some 60,000 Englishmen who had served as administrators, clerks, soldiers, policemen, inspectors and technicians, packed their souvenirs, held farewell parties, said

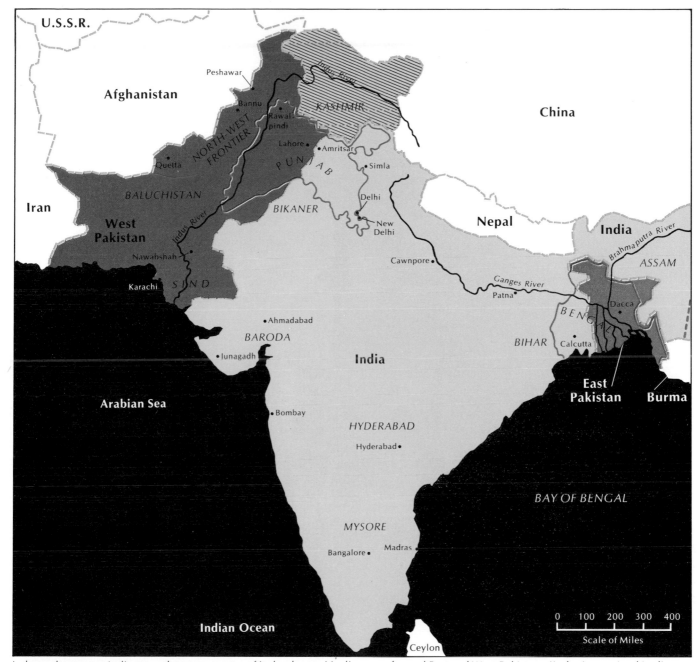

U.S.S.R.

Afghanistan

Peshawar

Bannu

Rawal-
pindi

NORTH-WEST FRONTIER

Quetta

BALUCHISTAN

Iran

West
Pakistan

Indus River

Nawabshah

Karachi

SIND

Arabian Sea

KASHMIR

Lahore

Amritsar

PUNJAB

Simla

BIKANER

Delhi

New
Delhi

China

Nepal

India

Brahmaputra River

ASSAM

Cawnpore

Ganges River

Patna

BENGAL

BIHAR

Dacca

Calcutta

East
Pakistan

Burma

Ahmadabad

BARODA

Junagadh

India

Bombay

HYDERABAD

Hyderabad

BAY OF BENGAL

MYSORE

Bangalore

Madras

Indian Ocean

Ceylon

0 100 200 300 400

Scale of Miles

Independence cost India more than one quarter of its land area: Muslim areas formed East and West Pakistan; Kashmir remained in dispute.

PARTITION: AN UNHAPPY COMPROMISE

When Parliament ratified a bill granting independence to the separate nations of India and Pakistan in July of 1947, a British peer hailed the compromise as a "peace treaty without a war." He was only partially right. A rebellion against British rule had been prevented, but the arbitrary borders that were imposed almost guaranteed bloodshed.

Predominantly Muslim regions in the east and west *(shown in red)* became Pakistan. The borders with Hindu India *(gray)* were primarily the existing provincial boundaries. Major new borders had to be drawn only through Bengal and the Punjab, provinces of mixed populations. But these lines were often impractical. Bengal's jute plantations, for example, ended up on one side of the border and the jute mills on the oth- er. In the Punjab, the line divided an irrigation system and the rivers supplying it. Inevitably, everyone felt cheated.

No map could account for the minority Hindu or Muslim communities left isolated on what turned out to be the wrong side of the border. Nor could it solve the problem of Kashmir, a princely state in the north *(diagonal lines)* whose ruler delayed joining either nation; Kashmir thus was doomed to be fought over by both.

good-by to their Indian friends and departed. Others, owners of plantations or private businesses—many of whom knew no other homeland—remained behind, and became witnesses to a blood bath.

Even before Sir Cyril Radcliffe's hastily drawn boundary lines were released, the chaos had begun. The Sikhs, whose traditional Punjab homeland was being sliced in half, had been whipped into a frenzy by the rabble-rousing Tara Singh, and were on a rampage. On the eve of independence, thousands of people—Muslims, Hindus and Sikhs—were attacked in their homes and slaughtered in the streets of Amritsar and Lahore as each faction rose in turn against another. While their villages burned, the number of Indians on the roads seeking sanctuary swelled enormously. Moving slowly and carrying all the possessions they could, the migrants offered easy targets for roving bands of killers.

A special Punjab Boundary Force of 55,000 Indian Army troops, including many Gurkhas from Nepal and led in part by British officers, took up positions in the boundary area to assist Indian and Pakistani civil forces in controlling the violence. But the civil forces broke down entirely and the Boundary Force, too small for the task, was overwhelmed as if by an erupting volcano.

Violence also threatened in Bengal, where one million people would soon be on the move, and where the dreadful precedent of the Great Calcutta Killing one year earlier was still fresh in the minds of almost everyone. Viceroy Mountbatten, desperate to maintain order and calm in Calcutta, beseeched Gandhi to go to the city to become his "one-man boundary force."

An even more compelling plea to Gandhi came from the former Muslim minister of Bengal under the British, H. Shaheed Suhrawardy—the same man who had incited the Muslims to riot on Jinnah's Direct Action Day in 1946. Suhrawardy recognized that his own political future would be threatened by further trouble in Bengal; Jinnah had already named another person to serve as the administrator for the new East Pakistan.

Gandhi accepted both pleas on the condition that Suhrawardy reside with him—in a house in a poor neighborhood—to present a picture of Hindu-Muslim solidarity. "Suhrawardy and I are going to stay together in a Muslim

A crowd gathers at quayside in Bombay as an honor guard of Indian soldiers and sailors forms up to salute a detachment of the Somerset Light Infantry, the last British troops to leave India, on February 28, 1948. After a symbolic parade through the Gateway of India, a massive stone arch built to honor the 1911 visit of King George V and Queen Mary, the British proceeded by launch to a troopship waiting to take them home.

quarter," he informed an astonished Patel, naming the area, a cesspool slum called Beliaghata. It was, Patel noted, "a veritable shambles and a notorious den of gangsters and hooligans"—a repulsive place for a frail old man like his leader to stay.

Passions were already high in Calcutta when Gandhi, together with Suhrawardy, moved into a filthy derelict house in Beliaghata on the 13th of August. Young Hindu extremists taunted Gandhi for protecting Muslims and greeted Suhrawardy with a barrage of flying bottles and insulting screams—"Muslim pig!"

But Gandhi was prepared to fast to the death if the people of Calcutta refused to heed his pleas for peace. He was there, he said, to serve Hindus and Muslims alike. "I have nearly reached the end of my life's journey," he observed. "If you again go mad I will not be a living witness to it." And he reasoned with the demonstrators for many hours, until their anger cooled. Suhrawardy, standing beside Gandhi, joined in the old man's pleas. Together the two peacemakers addressed huge crowds of Muslims and Hindus, preaching brotherhood.

At midnight the next day, the British Indian Empire ended. Mixed groups of Hindus and Muslims paraded by the thousands through the streets of Calcutta, welcoming independence and shouting: *"Hindu Muslim bhai bhai"*—"Hindus and Muslims are brothers." Bengal, at least, was spared a massacre.

Far to the west in the city of Karachi, very early on the morning of August 14, 1947, Muhammad Ali Jinnah was installed as Governor General—his own choice of title—over the newly created Dominion of Pakistan. Aging and ill, he was savoring a wondrous triumph. "I never expected to see Pakistan in my lifetime," he told an aide. Yet it was a strange sort of nation: a widely separated East and West, with little in common besides a majority religion.

The following morning in New Delhi, to a 21-gun salute and the raising of a new national flag, Lord Mountbatten officially became Britain's ex-Viceroy and—at the request of Nehru and the Congress Party—the first Governor General of the Dominion of India. The city, bulging with an excess population of almost 100,000 refugees, was free of violence and a scene of joy. Even Prime Minister Nehru, his heart sore for the burning Punjab, felt a moment of jubilation as New Delhi laughed and cheered.

But New Delhi's happiness was fleeting and illusory. The victims of partition continued to pour into the capital, bringing their sick, their maimed and dead, and orphaned children and widows, along with the pitiful remnants of their possessions and tales of brutality encountered on the long migration. The city smoldered and burst into flames of retaliatory hatred. Ten days of bloody disorder ended only when Gandhi the peacemaker arrived from Calcutta and a military force of 5,000 men finally regained control. More than 1,000 people had died.

Elsewhere, atrocity reigned. In Lahore, West Pakistan, Muslims were roasting Sikhs and Hindus alive wherever they could trap them. In Amritsar, the Sikhs continued their rampage, descending on Muslim neighborhoods to murder the men and then rape and slaughter the women. At the Amritsar railroad station, a train chugged in with carloads of wounded and dead Hindus and Sikhs from Lahore—hundreds of them, many chopped to pieces, their blood coagulating on the floors.

Trailing across the Punjab in opposite directions were more than 10 million people, with their bullock-drawn carts, backpacks, cooking utensils, straw pallets, farm tools and gaunt animals. Human vultures stalked the two-way columns robbing and butchering the stragglers. Most of those who finally reached their destinations were gathered into camps where they stayed for weeks with no provision for food or shelter, drenched by monsoon rains, and prey to cholera and other diseases.

The Britons who chose to remain could do little to help. Rupert Mayne, whose family had been in India since 1761, was traveling in the Punjab at the time of the great exodus.

Between Amritsar and Lahore, Mayne saw "mile upon mile of people going east and going west carrying their belongings. The Hindus and the Sikhs from Pakistan moving on one side of the road, the Muhammadans on the other. Every now and again some goat or something would run across the road and then there would be a beat-up trying to get it back again." Starvation deepened the misery. "Even the bark of the trees had been eaten up to a height of 10 feet," Mayne wrote, "as high as a person could stand upon another person's shoulders."

As Mayne stood watching the humanity stream by, a small thing happened that epitomized what he considered a tragic moment in history. "A figure came out from the huge line of refugees, stood to attention and asked me to help him." The man said that he was a veteran of the War, that he had been "with the 4th Indian Division through the desert and in Italy. What could I do to save him? All I could do was look at him and say, 'Your politicians asked for *swaraj*,'" referring to the Indians' term for self-rule, "'and this is *swaraj*.'"

For the next nine months a tidal wave of anarchy surged across the two newly independent countries. All through this grim period the three holdout princely states remained in a turmoil of indecision about their future. The Muslim Nawab of Junagadh finally decided to join Pakistan; he made his decision in spite of his state's contiguity to India, and without consulting his predominantly Hindu subjects. The decision aroused the fury both of his people and of India, which within a year seized the state by force. The Nizam of Hyderabad refused to join India, although surrounded by it, and declared his intention to remain independent. This arrangement suited nobody but the Nizam, and India could not permit it to continue; Hyderabad was forcibly absorbed in its turn.

The most explosive situation existed in Kashmir, contiguous to both Pakistan and India. Kashmir's Muslim majority propelled it toward a connection with Pakistan. Its Hindu Maharaja, Hari Singh, refused to join the Muslim state and yet—with delusions of independence like those of Hyderabad's Nizam—dithered about joining India. While he hesitated, warriors from a seminomadic Muslim tribe living in what was now northern Pakistan invaded Kashmir, with the connivance of the Jinnah government. They indulged in an indiscriminate orgy of murder and pillage on their way toward the capital. Suddenly desperate, Hari Singh appealed to India for military help. He got it—after hastily agreeing to join India.

Order was restored in the capital, but Pakistan felt cheated: To the Karachi government, a state that was 70 per cent Muslim did not belong in Hindu India. An undeclared war over Kashmir continued to simmer. Although a cease-fire arranged by the United Nations would put a temporary stop to the fighting in 1949, disagreement over a permanent settlement would lead to sporadic hostilities during the decades that followed.

Only gradually did an emergency committee organized by Nehru, Patel and Mountbatten devise an effective plan for policing the caravans of migrants and bring civil order to India. One modestly encouraging sign was a cryptic report received by the emergency committee late in 1947. "The practice of throwing Muslims from train windows," it said, "is on the decline."

By the time the cross-migration ended in the spring of 1948, between 10 and 16 million people had been transplanted. As for the number who perished, estimates ranged from 200,000 to one million. Even then, peace came hard. The unresolved issue of Kashmir was poisoning relations between India and Pakistan. Mohandas Gandhi was assassinated on January 30, 1948, by a Hindu fanatic named Nathuram V. Godse, who had taken it into his head that Gandhi had sold out to the Muslim cause. Muhammad Ali Jinnah, the stubborn creator of Pakistan, succumbed to his long-term disease on September 11, 1948. The palaces of the Maharajas, symbols of another time, became museums, schools and hotels—or fell into ruins.

THE APOSTLE OF FREEDOM

Mohandas Gandhi sits cross-legged by one of the spinning wheels that he worked daily. The wheel symbolized his hope of reviving India's pride in its custom

A LIFE DEDICATED TO NONVIOLENT CHANGE

As a stiff-collared young barrister in the early 1900s, Mohandas Gandhi achieved prominence as a spokesman for Indian residents of South Africa.

Mohandas Karamchand Gandhi was a complex, paradoxical man who in his lifetime of nearly fourscore years achieved almost godlike stature. "I never knew a more deeply religious man," wrote the American correspondent William L. Shirer, "nor a subtler politician." Trained as an attorney, Gandhi dedicated himself to the cause of freeing his people from British rule. The Mahatma, or Great Soul, accomplished his aims in divergent ways: Celibate and a vegetarian, he wore a loincloth to indicate his rejection of material possessions, and his life style of voluntary poverty earned the reverence of millions who were poor without choice; with the British authorities he asserted his belief through the brilliant use of nonviolent resistance.

Born near Bombay in 1869, Gandhi overrode the objections of his Hindu family in 1888 and ventured to London, where he studied law. Lonely, a misfit in his Bombay-tailored clothes, he tried at first to cut an elegant English figure, affecting a top hat and silver-headed cane. But he found such foppery too costly, and contrary to his nature.

After being admitted to the bar, Gandhi was glad to return to India; once at home, however, he found it difficult to establish a legal practice, and he gratefully accepted a commission that took him to another part of the Empire, South Africa. The case was settled in six months, but Gandhi stayed on for 21 years—succeeding as a lawyer and becoming the leader of a campaign to end British discrimination against Indians living in South Africa. He developed a form of protest, based on nonviolent resistance, called *Satyagraha,* or "holding to the truth"; it became the core of his political philosophy.

In 1915, back in India, Gandhi began a long drive, punctuated by stints in jail, to expel the British through nonviolent strikes and boycotts. He had detractors—among them his great rival, the Muslim leader Muhammad Ali Jinnah, who once called him a "cunning Hindu fox." Yet by the end of World War II, Gandhi's determined but peaceful tactics had made him admired around the world as an apostle

Conspicuous in a robe of homespun cotton, Gandhi attends a London conference on India in 1931. His goal of independence was called a ''vain dream.''

A HISTORIC MARCH OF PROTEST

By 1930, Gandhi's struggle against the British raj had earned him many months in jail. Yet he persistently sought new ways to rally his countrymen in peaceful confrontation with their British rulers.

To inspire a bold new drive for *swaraj*—self-rule—Gandhi seized on an issue that had the broadest possible appeal. The processing and the sale of salt were government monopolies; when Indians purchased salt they had to pay a sales tax that amounted to half the retail price. Gandhi launched a campaign to turn the salt tax into a symbol of colonial oppression.

On March 12, 1930, the Mahatma and about 80 of his disciples set out on foot from their home base near Ahmadabad on the Sabarmati River, heading for the coastal village of Dandi, about 200 miles to the south. Gandhi, carrying a pilgrim's staff, led his followers along a route lined by thousands of peasants, who strewed his path with flower petals.

The marchers' ranks swelled as the days went by. At every halt the Mahatma addressed vast audiences—standing in rows at roadsides or perched on walls, roofs and trees—exhorting them to join his movement of noncooperation. Even the English-language newspaper *Bombay Chronicle* described such occasions as ''magnificent and soul-stirring.''

On April 6, Gandhi bathed in the sea near Dandi; as thousands watched, he scooped up crystals of salt—formed by evaporation on the tidal flats—in open defiance of the law. Overnight, tens of thousands of his supporters rushed to India's coastlines to demonstrate against the salt tax. British authorities responded by arresting thousands of Indians. Gandhi, on his way back to prison, was triumphant. ''The honor of India,'' he said, ''has been symbolized by a fistful of salt in the hand of a man of nonviolence.''

The melodramatic episode imparted tremendous strength to Gandhi's popularity with the masses. Against a background of angry protest, the British convened in London a series of so-called Round Table Conferences on India. In 1931, Gandhi, free once more, used the conferences as a platform for his unswerving demand for national independence.

In 1930, a bare-chested Mohandas Gandhi and his followers march to the Arabian Sea in a symbolic challenge to the British salt tax.

In March 1931 a throng of more than 100,000 hears Gandhi speak from a stand near Ahmadabad, where he had begun the Salt March one year earlier.

Gandhi arrives at Buckingham Palace in 1931 to have tea with King George V. Asked about his scanty garb, Gandhi quipped: "The King was wearing enough for us both."

Amid comfortable surroundings that he d___ himself, Gandhi confers amiably with Lord Louis M___batten in the British Viceroy's study in 1947

BESEECHING THE BRITISH TO "QUIT INDIA"

Gandhi's demands for independence at the 1931 London conference were unavailing. During the next decade he left the front line of politics to such key associates as Jawaharlal Nehru and concentrated instead on social reforms—among them improving the lot of women and the untouchables in Hindu society.

During the Second World War, Gandhi rejoined the political fray as a leader of the "Quit India" campaign, a vast civil-disobedience movement. Once more the Mahatma was arrested and violence broke out. When the British blamed it on Gandhi, he responded with a 21-day fast that seriously impaired his health. The British refused to submit to his "political black-mail," releasing him only because, at the age of 74, he had contracted malaria.

Once the War ended, the British were willing at last to grant India's freedom. But the centuries-old enmity between Hindus and Muslims blighted any hope for a peaceful, unified independence: The alternative—partition—was a solution that Gandhi abhorred.

During the religious warfare that bloodied his country in 1947, Gandhi spent his waning energy trying, through sheer will, to relieve the hostility between Muslim and Hindu. By facing down angry mobs he brought a measure of peace, but only where he could appear in person, and then only for brief periods of time. When offered congratulations for bringing independence to India, the old man lamented, "Would it not be more appropriate to send condolences?"

Jawaharlal Ne___ Gandhi's protégé and a future Prime Minister of Ind___ istens intently to his mentor at a meeting of the Congress Party in 1946

9

A DEATH FAST TO END THE BLOODSHED

On January 13, 1948, Gandhi began a fast to the death at a friend's New Delhi home. Formerly he had used the fast as a weapon against the British; now he hoped it would bring his own people to their senses in this awful first year of independence.

Once more the magic worked. At first, hate-filled refugees, displaced by the independence accord, screamed, "Let Gandhi die!" But as he grew weaker, public concern for him rose like a tide. Gandhi was almost comatose on his sixth day of fasting when Hindu and Muslim leaders gathered anxiously by his bed with a signed peace charter. In it, they vowed to seek harmony not only in New Delhi, but throughout the subcontinent. Gandhi broke his fast; that night he was carried outside the house, where he waved to a crowd that greeted him with thunderous cheers.

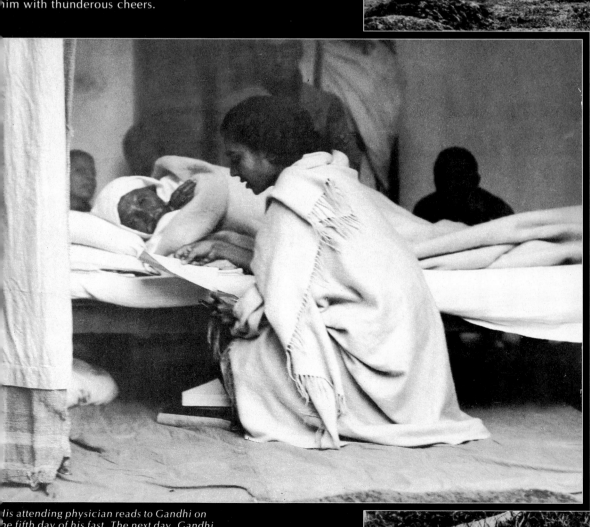

His attending physician reads to Gandhi on the fifth day of his fast. The next day, Gandhi drank fruit juice laced with glucose, and he told his followers: "If we remember that all life is one, there is no reason why we should eat one another as enemies."

"THE LIGHT HAS GONE OUT OF OUR LIVES"

The surge of relief that Gandhi had broken his fast was felt far beyond India. "The mystery and power of a frail 78-year-old man," said the London *News Chronicle*, "shakes the world and inspires it with new hope." As for India itself, it seemed that peace and sanity might now triumph.

Physically drained by his ordeal, the Mahatma had to be carried to his daily prayer meetings in the garden of his host's house. But his mind was keen and his spirits were high. In less than a week he was on his feet and making plans to march again—this time across the ravaged cente

Enfeebled by his fast, Gandhi is carried to a prayer meeting in late January of 1948.

of India to lead minority Muslims who had fled to Pakistan back to their homes in India, and Hindus back to Pakistan.

On January 30, 1948, as Gandhi walked into the garden, a man pushed through the crowd, bowed gravely to Gandhi and shot him three times. Delhi was near the flash point. Word spread that the Mahatma had been murdered by a Muslim—which, if true, would have sparked a vengeful massacre. But the killer, Nathuram V. Godse, turned out to be a Hindu, who hated Gandhi for treating Muslims as brothers and blamed him for India's partition.

The world mourned. Nehru spoke for hundreds of millions when he said: "The light has gone out of our lives and there is darkness everywhere."

The face of Nehru reflects his grief, hours after he learned of Gandhi's death

Hindu women keep vigil through the night beside Gandhi's petal-strewn bier; the Mahatma's neck is a garland of his own homespun cloth

With an honor guard of policemen, airmen,
soldiers and sailors, Gandhi's body is drawn
through the streets of New Delhi on a gun
carriage wreathed in flowers. He was cremated
that day by the Jumna River, a stream flowing
into the Ganges that the Hindus hold sacred.
Nehru in a eulogy predicted that Gandhi's light
"will shine 1,000 years from now."

4

As the sun burned through the steamy humidity of a Javanese morning on August 17, 1945, an excited crowd assembled in front of a house on Pengangasaan Timur, a street in Djakarta, the capital of the Japanese-occupied Netherlands East Indies. Some of the younger men in the crowd carried spears of sharpened bamboo; others bore shovels, sticks and cleavers. A few carried contraband Japanese firearms.

Japan had capitulated to the Allies two days earlier, but the Japanese Army still held power in Djakarta, and the crowd gathered on Pengangasaan Timur did not want the occupying forces to interfere with the dramatic ceremony that was about to unfold. They knew that the Japanese had received orders from the Allies to maintain the status quo. In the front room of the house, a young militiaman stationed himself by a window with a telephone in his hand, holding a line open to his headquarters. The militia had been trained by the Japanese to help repel an Allied invasion, but now members of the Djakarta unit were standing by to battle the Japanese if they tried to halt the morning's program.

In spite of the tension, the crowd was orderly. After a while, however, a few people began calling out: "Now, *Bung,* now. Speak the words of freedom now. The sun is getting hot." They used the Indonesian word *Bung,* which means "brother," to invoke their leader, who was still inside the house.

Shortly before 10 a.m., the man they were waiting for stepped out onto the veranda. He was weary, having been up most of the night preparing for this moment. He had, in fact, been preparing for it most of his life. He was 44 years old, an engineer by training, a dedicated nationalist by calling—and a spellbinding orator in several languages. The Allies considered him a collaborator and a traitor, because he had worked with the Japanese after their 1942 conquest of the Netherlands East Indies and because of the virulent anti-Western speeches he had made during the War. But most of the 70 million people of the tropical archipelago regarded him as a hero.

Sukarno—like many of his compatriots he had only one name—stepped to a microphone that his supporters had stolen from the Japanese. Taking from his pocket a piece of lined paper that had been torn out of a student's notebook the night before, he delivered one of the shortest, yet most consequential political statements of the postwar era.

DEFEAT FOR THE DUTCH

"We the people of Indonesia," he said, "hereby declare Indonesia's independence. Matters concerning the transfer of power and other matters will be executed in an orderly manner and in the shortest possible time." The brief document bore two signatures, which Sukarno solemnly read aloud, his own and that of Mohammad Hatta, a fellow independence leader.

A militia officer walked to a makeshift flagpole in front of the house and raised a red and white flag that Sukarno's wife had sewn a few hours earlier. The crowd sang "Indonesia Raya" ("Great Indonesia")—a revolutionary song that earlier had been designated as the national anthem—and dispersed to spread the news of the independence declaration. "Okay, all clear," the militiaman in the window told his headquarters, and hung up the phone.

The brevity and informality of the ceremony, held outside Sukarno's own house, had been dictated by the suddenness of Japan's surrender. But the proclamation marked neither the beginning nor the end of Indonesia's struggle for independence. For decades, Sukarno and other educated Indonesians had been speaking out against colonial rule and as a result had spent years in prison or in exile. For centuries, in fact, the Indonesian population had been too timid and disunited to present an effective challenge to their Dutch masters. Then the Japanese arrived. By overrunning the bulk of the Netherlands East Indian empire in barely two months, they proved that the white man was not invincible. When Japan was defeated in its turn, Indonesian nationalist leaders, urged on by their followers, seized the moment to throw off their country's chains. Or so they intended; a time of severe testing still lay ahead.

The Indonesians, like other peoples of Southeast Asia, had suffered under the Japanese. But they had been spared the wholesale ravages of combat: Allied counteroffensives had concentrated on the eastern islands of the archipelago—chiefly New Guinea and the oil facilities on the island of Borneo. It was not until the world rearranged itself following the War that Indonesians faced death in battle. Almost five years of bloodshed, internal strife and complex international diplomacy would intervene before Sukarno could make good the promise of independence contained in the speech from his veranda.

More than 300 years had passed since the Dutch became the dominant power in the East Indies, commencing with the conquest of the Spice Islands, the Moluccas, which had been Christopher Columbus' goal. During that period the Netherlands had extended its control to most of the archipelago, whose thousands of islands stretch for more than 3,000 miles along the equator, astride some of the world's most important shipping lanes. The colony was governed at first by a private concern, the Dutch East India Company, and later by the Netherlands government. Dutch rule was often oppressive, though generally indirect. Most Indonesians continued to live as subjects of the more or less despotic petty kings and nobles of the islands. The Dutch enlisted these notables as colonial partners, called regents, and allowed them to skim lucrative revenues from the products of their subjects' labor.

Beginning in the 1830s, Indonesian peasants worked under a government-controlled cultivation system that concentrated on commercial crops such as coffee, sugar and indigo. Labor on these crops was compulsory, and the farmer was subject to a tax payable to the government out of his harvest. Theoretically, he was liable for only a portion of the crop, but the nobles and the managers who ran the system for the Dutch were permitted to squeeze the farmer for much more than the amount of official tax. Often the farmer had little or nothing left over to sell so that he could feed himself and his family.

Starvation was inevitable. A succession of famines between 1843 and 1848 reduced the population of one region from 336,000 to 120,000; in another area the population fell from 89,500 to a mere 9,000. For the Dutch, however, the system was tremendously profitable. Between 1840 and 1880, the Indies each year contributed nearly one third of the Netherlands' national budget.

Eventually a series of reforms improved the lot of the peasants. Forced labor and the cultivation system gave way to a system in which farmers contracted with private entrepreneurs for their labor and were paid wages. Much of the farming was concentrated on properties leased by Dutch companies from Indonesians, who were established by law as the only legal owners of land they had traditionally cultivated or of jungle areas they were able to clear. The law was intended to stop the Dutch and immigrant Chinese practice of buying up land from Indonesian farmers and chieftains whenever the Indonesians fell into debt, as they often did. Other reforms encouraged the growth of commerce in the islands and attracted a burgeoning population of Dutch entrepreneurs and Chinese merchants.

Stimulated by private enterprise and by the opening of the Suez Canal in 1869, the Indies trade prospered. Few Indonesians grew wealthy, however. In addition to the Dutch, it was the Chinese who had the know-how and the aggressiveness to invest in land leasing and other enterprises. As late as 1935, Indonesian proprietors owned only 865 of the more than 5,000 businesses employing six or more people in the Indies.

For the Dutch, profits from the Indies had become more important than ever. By the beginning of World War II, the $1.4 billion invested in the colony was yielding an annual profit of $100 million, and Dutch imperialists boasted that "Indonesia is the cork on which Netherlands prosperity floats." Unfortunately for the Dutch, the sheer weight of their investment made them more dependent on their colony than any other European power.

The vulnerability of their position was not apparent to the Dutch who administered the Indies. Their blindness was caused in part by a gratifying sense of social dominance. They were the undisputed masters of a society that was stratified along racial and ethnic lines. Beneath the Dutch were Eurasians of mixed Dutch and Asian blood; below the Eurasians came the Chinese; and at the bottom were the native Indonesians—"inlanders," as the Dutch called them. Signs on swimming pools announced, "No dogs or inlanders allowed," and inlander streetcar conductors were expected to bow to their Dutch passengers.

Such abasement extended to education. In 1899, only 13 Indonesian students were attending Dutch secondary schools in the Indies. In time, the Dutch ever-so-slowly opened to Indonesians the European-style schools they had established to educate their own children. They also began to sponsor schools where subjects were taught in the local language, though these institutions covered only the first three grades. By the beginning of the War, more than two million Indonesians were attending these three-year elementary schools, and another 80,000 were enrolled in the Dutch-language primary schools.

Yet only 230 Indonesians had graduated from the islands' three university-level schools, and fewer still had traveled to the Netherlands for advanced training. Thus, educated Indonesians made up only a tiny handful in a population of 70 million. But they were a significant few—exposed to Western ideas and yet frustrated by a colonial society that refused to give them the jobs or status that their education had earned them. They were the cutting edge of the anticolonial movement.

Until 1926, the most outspoken faction in the fledgling movement was the Communist Party of Indonesia. The

Communists identified their enemy as the Dutch commercial and plantation interests. From the educated Indonesians' point of view, to be a Marxist at a time when anticolonial sentiment was taking shape was to be a patriot; thus, although they rejected organized Communism's bid for power, most of the later leaders of the Indonesian independence movement regarded Communists as fellow revolutionaries. Marxism, according to one observer, became the "major ideological training for Indonesian politicians."

The bulk of the population, however, was apathetic toward Communism. Its appeal was directed toward a relatively small urban proletariat, rather than the agrarian majority. Moreover, the Islamic leaders, who wielded great influence on Indonesia's Muslim masses, opposed Communism on religious grounds. When the Communists attempted a revolution in 1926, the peasants ignored it. Without their support, the uprising collapsed. Dutch police put down the revolt in a few days and arrested 13,000 people, sending nearly 5,000 of them to jail or into exile. The result was an end to overt Communist activity in the Indies for two decades. Though a vestige of the party continued to exist underground, non-Communists dominated the leadership of the nationalist movement until the late 1940s, when the Communists mounted a belated bid for power.

For many years, the most important anticolonial organization in Indonesia was a group called Sarekat Islam, or the Islamic Union. The common bond of Islam, shared by 85 per cent of all Indonesians, was a powerful symbol of their national identity in the face of economic oppression by the Dutch—and by the Chinese. Sarekat Islam got its start in 1904 as the Islamic Trading Association; its founders were Javanese merchants who sought to protect themselves from competition by Chinese entrepreneurs. The movement later turned political. The head of Sarekat Islam was a friend of Sukarno's father.

Sukarno was born at dawn on June 6, 1901, on Java, the most populous of the islands. According to Javanese legend the hour of his birth, a propitious moment, endowed him with mystical powers. In a sense, the legend was borne out: Sukarno's ability to sway a crowd with his voice and to mold the emotions of millions with his brilliant sense of drama often seemed magical indeed. A British observer wrote that, for Sukarno, the Indonesians "will sit in silence for hours, listening as if to the Almighty; with him they will laugh as easily as children at Charlie Chaplin; at his orders they will fight, kill, work, change their previous ideas, follow dumbly—almost anything. He can *conduct* a large crowd as if he were in control of an orchestra of tens of thousands. It will shout the answers he wants to the questions he puts; it will cheer, howl, sob, roar, bellow, laugh—all in unison."

Sukarno's father was a schoolteacher who insisted that the boy study hard. His mother claimed that her family had fought the Dutch in the 19th Century when they took over her native island of Bali (the last major island of the Indies to be brought under Dutch control). The mother imbued her son with hatred of the colonial oppressors. Through his father's politically connected friends, young Sukarno was exposed to the seething currents of the anticolonial movement, including Marxism. He became a local chairman of Young Java, an organization for youthful nationalists.

In 1923, addressing a huge outdoor rally, Sukarno predicted a "volcanic explosion" of nationalism and challenged the Dutch to prevent it. In response, the Dutch police halted the rally and sent everyone home. The dean at the engineering school Sukarno was attending—the Bandung Technical College—warned him that politics would interfere with his studies, and made him promise to address no more rallies.

Once his engineering degree was safely in his pocket, Sukarno plunged back into politics. In 1927 he helped to found the Nationalist Indonesian Association, an organization dedicated to gaining independence. Soon he succeeded in bringing several rival elements into a single federation under the association's banner. In the Javanese tradition of striving to accommodate competing philosophies, Sukarno tried to combine the conflicting political currents of his time into one deep and surging stream. "I am a convinced nationalist, a convinced Muslim, a convinced Marxist," he once said—insisting that he saw no problem in reconciling the three.

While Sukarno was becoming the emotional voice of Indonesian aspirations, Mohammad Hatta was emerging as the pragmatic intellectual of the independence movement. Born in Sumatra in 1902, Hatta spent 10 years studying eco-

Wary of Japanese troops still patrolling the city, nationalist leader Sukarno declares Indonesian independence on August 17, 1945, in a modest ceremony at his home in Djakarta. At right is his associate, Mohammad Hatta; at left, Latief Hendraningrat, deputy chief of the local militia.

nomics in the Netherlands, where he became chairman of the Indonesian students' association and edited a newspaper espousing independence. He was arrested by the Dutch in 1927 for his political activities.

Hatta was released following his trial, at which he made an impassioned speech defending Indonesian nationalism. He returned to Indonesia, where he soon became a rival to Sukarno. In 1929 the Dutch arrested Sukarno and his top lieutenants on charges of disturbing public order. Sukarno was convicted and spent the next two years in prison. Some of his followers, trying to carry on without their spellbinding leader, founded a more moderate political organization called Partindo, the Indonesian Party. But Hatta and a young, hard-headed Sumatran named Sutan Sjahrir—who had also been educated in the Netherlands—split away. They thought it was futile to rely on a single leader such as Sukarno, whose arrest could decapitate the movement. Their view of the future emphasized education—the development of an ever-widening circle of trained adherents who could keep the momentum of the revolution going whether or not their leaders were in jail.

When he was released in December of 1931, Sukarno embraced Partindo, became its chairman, resumed his rousing speechmaking and continued his pamphleteering for another 13 months before the Dutch cracked down again. This time the authorities did not even bother to try Sukarno. He was exiled, with his family, to the island of Flores near the eastern tip of Java—and moved later to Benkulen, a remote town in southern Sumatra. He remained isolated from his adoring crowds for more than eight years. The Netherlands authorities also sent Hatta and Sjahrir into exile in February of 1934. The Dutch breathed easier. The lid, they thought, was on.

Keeping it on once the Japanese came streaming into Sumatra from Malaya in early 1942 proved an insuperable challenge. The Dutch made a desperate attempt to whisk Sukarno off to Australia, fearing that he would collaborate with the invaders. Sukarno and his family were escorted on a rugged day-and-night trek on foot and by truck over jungle paths from Benkulen to Padang, in western Sumatra, where a ship bound for Australia was to evacuate them. But the Japanese Navy sank the ship before the party arrived at the port, and the Dutch escort scattered, abandoning Sukarno to the Japanese.

Aware of Sukarno's immense popularity, the Japanese handled him with caution. Like other Indonesian leaders, he was offered a chance to cooperate with the conquerors. Sukarno accepted; he regarded the Japanese occupation as a "magnificent opportunity to educate and ready our people." He later insisted that he made it clear to the Japanese colonel commanding in Sumatra that he would collaborate only in order to advance the cause of eventual independence. He sought and received assurances that the Japanese intended to establish a free Indonesia.

War and occupation brought about a coalition among Sukarno and his fellow nationalists. Allowed by the Japanese to return to Djakarta, Sukarno was reunited with Hatta and Sjahrir, who had also returned from exile. The three men buried their differences and pledged to help one another. They agreed that Sukarno and Hatta, being so well known, would work aboveground, visibly collaborating, while Sjahrir went underground and fought against the Japanese.

Another underground force was directed by a nationalist politician named Amir Sjarifuddin, whose abhorrence of Nazi- and Japanese-style totalitarianism had led him to organize an anti-Axis front in the late 1930s. The Dutch helped to finance Sjarifuddin's resistance activities, which proved to be limited. Sjarifuddin was captured by the Japanese in 1943. They were preparing to execute him when Sukarno and Hatta intervened, warning that his execution would hamper the mobilization of the Indonesian people behind the Japanese war effort. Sjarifuddin's sentence was commuted to life in prison.

The wrath of the Japanese reached far beyond the resistance. The Japanese imprisoned all civilians who were Dutch or Eurasian, and conditions in the camps were abominable. Treatment of the Indonesians themselves was usually rude and sometimes harsh. The Japanese looted the islands of food and supplies and drafted an estimated 270,000 laborers for construction and maintenance projects in Indonesia and elsewhere in their Empire. Tens of thousands of these workers perished.

The Japanese issued an order that at all public meetings Indonesians must bow in the direction of the Emperor in Tokyo. This decree infuriated devout Muslims, who normally made such obeisance only in their prayers—bowing five times each day in the direction of Mecca. Muslim leaders opposed the order, and the Japanese, who hoped to control the Islamic majority through their religious leaders, quietly withdrew it.

Late in 1943, as the tide of the Pacific war turned against the Empire, the Japanese began to enlist large numbers of Indonesians to defend their country in case of invasion by the Allies. The occupation authorities raised and trained an Indonesian militia called the Defenders of the Fatherland (known as PETA, from its Indonesian name, Pembala Tanah Air). By the end of the War, PETA had become a well-disciplined military force that numbered 40,000 men in Java and another 30,000 in Sumatra. They were commanded by Japanese but had their own junior officers. Sukarno and Hatta, under the pretext of making the soldiers eager to fight, were able to imbue them with nationalist fervor. Although the Japanese ordered PETA disbanded after their surrender, its troops were to become the nucleus of the Republic of Indonesia's first army.

In September 1944, as the perimeter of their Empire receded, the Japanese formally promised independence to the East Indies as part of a community of Asian nations that Japan expected to dominate. Indonesians were permitted to fly their national flag and sing their national anthem.

The Japanese had already granted their limited version of independence to Burma and the Philippines. They had delayed giving the same privilege to Indonesia, however, believing that the archipelago's abundant resources had to be more closely controlled in order to feed Japan's wartime needs. But ultimately the Supreme Council in Tokyo decided that the Indonesians might make stronger allies if they were given independence, with the understanding that they would maintain "close and inseparable relations with the Empire."

In the spring of 1945, after the neighboring Philippines had been retaken by American forces, Japan set up a committee of Indonesians, including Sukarno, to discuss a constitution. The committee hammered out a draft calling for a centralized republic headed by a strong president. Before the conference ended, the Japanese authorized a declaration of independence for early September.

On August 9, without warning, Sukarno and Hatta were flown to Saigon, headquarters for all the Japanese forces in Southeast Asia. There, Field Marshal Hisaichi Terauchi telescoped the timetable, setting independence for August 24. He told Sukarno and Hatta: "It is up to you now. The Imperial Government puts the process of independence totally in your hands." The Japanese, he explained, would henceforth maintain only an advisory role. A few hours later, the Indonesian leaders learned that an atomic bomb had been dropped on Hiroshima, but they could not guess how close Japan was to capitulation.

Sukarno and Hatta returned to a restless Djakarta on August 14. The city was bursting with rumors that Japan was surrendering. The talk upset Sukarno and his colleagues, who expected that in a few more weeks the Japanese would hand power over to them in a relatively painless transfer. If the rumors turned out to be true, the Indonesian leaders asked themselves, What happens now?

The next 72 hours were a crucial time. Many younger Indonesian nationalists were spoiling for a fight. Their hatred for the Japanese occupation was so strong that they could not accept the idea of independence as a gift from Japan. The leaders of the young nationalists were called *pemudas*, an Indonesian term that means "youth" but carries overtones of fervid revolutionary zeal. Many were educated, and therefore an elite. Nevertheless, the pemudas perceived themselves as the true spokesmen for the people, separate from most of the older leaders, who they felt had been compromised by their cooperation with the Japanese.

Of the older leaders, the pemudas had turned primarily to Sutan Sjahrir, who had not collaborated. Sjahrir was convinced that the Japanese were indeed on the verge of surrender, and he was afraid that the victorious Allies would not accept any independence that could be construed as Japanese inspired. He urged Sukarno and Hatta to proclaim independence on their own, rather than through the Japanese-sponsored committee. As Sukarno and Hatta saw it, however, their first priority was to obtain official confirmation of the surrender from the Japanese, and make sure Japanese troops would not oppose an early independence proclamation.

Such a peaceful outcome was not what Sjahrir and the pemudas wanted. They laid plans to take over the Djakarta radio station on August 15, hoping that Sukarno could be persuaded to broadcast a call for the people to seize their independence. Sukarno and Hatta refused to go along, and Sjahrir abandoned the plan. But the militant pemudas were not so easily discouraged.

On the night of the 15th, a delegation of angry youths armed with guns and knives confronted Sukarno and Hatta at Sukarno's house. Insisting that all was in readiness for an armed uprising, they demanded that Sukarno immediately give the word for the revolution to begin. Sukarno told them that the Japanese would crush any such move, but the young men threatened to act without him if he did not declare independence immediately.

Sukarno retorted, "Don't threaten me." He bowed his head toward them and said, "Here is my neck. Kill me now. Go on, cut off my head. You can kill me but I will never risk unnecessary bloodshed because you want to do things your way." The youths departed, with mixed feelings of anger and dejection.

To mollify the pemudas, Sukarno and Hatta agreed to sign the independence proclamation alone on August 17, 1945, instead of including members of the constitutional committee organized by the Japanese. But the committee continued to function as a legislative body; following the proclamation, it elected Sukarno and Hatta President and Vice President of the Republic of Indonesia.

News of the independence declaration was broadcast throughout Java, though most Indonesians outside the capital thought it was a Japanese trick—and regarded the Japanese surrender itself as much more important. To rally the masses behind the new Republic, Sukarno decreed a powerful new symbol: "Merdeka" ("Freedom"), spoken as a greeting with the hand raised, fingers spread. It was soon heard everywhere.

The fledgling state went about establishing itself and extending its writ from Java to the other islands in the archipelago. But it was operating in a strange limbo. August ended, and September was half over, yet the Japanese remained as armed occupiers, waiting for Allied troops to arrive and receive their surrender—and hoping in the meantime to avoid trouble.

As the weeks passed, the Japanese, striving to maintain a disintegrating status quo, were facing problems within their own ranks. Most of their troops were demoralized, and they were fearful of the growing pemuda unrest. They saw little point in risking their lives to help the Allies; they just wanted to go home.

Confusion among the Allies hampered their liberation of Indonesia. One major problem was a massive last-minute change of assignments and responsibilities. Originally it had been assumed that American troops would liberate the Indies. But when General Douglas MacArthur received orders to prepare an invasion of Japan, responsibility for Indonesia was transferred from his Southwest Pacific Command to Lord Louis Mountbatten's basically British Southeast Asia Command, with headquarters in Ceylon.

The Dutch, lacking the military power to reoccupy the Indies on their own, drew up an agreement with the British on August 24. British troops would occupy the Indies, wielding transitional authority until the Dutch could bring in their own forces. Until then, units of the Netherlands Indies Civil Administration (NICA) would accompany the British to exercise civil authority and enforce prewar laws.

The agreement rested on a sweeping assumption: that the Indonesian people would accept the return of the Dutch. The Dutch were well aware of the republican movement, but they dismissed it as a puppet regime established by the

Acting on behalf of the Dutch, British officers (above) interrogate nationalists who had taken over one of Djakarta's leading banks. At right, Dutch troops, who started to replace the British occupation force early in 1946, frisk Indonesian civilians at a street checkpoint in Djakarta.

Japanese, and credited it with little popular support. The British, at least for a time, accepted this interpretation.

Mountbatten, struggling to assemble an Allied occupation force to cover all of Southeast Asia, had available only three divisions—mostly Indians and Gurkhas commanded by British officers—to deal with the 735,000 square miles of the Indies. This contingent of about 30,000 men was obviously inadequate. Mountbatten asked for help from Australia. He requested that its forces, which already held parts of Borneo and New Guinea, occupy the eastern half of the archipelago, leaving only Sumatra, Java, Bali and Lombok for the British themselves to worry about.

Time was slipping by. An Allied mission made up of about 50 military and civilian personnel landed in Djakarta on September 16. But it was September 29 before the first sizable units were ready to come ashore—more than six weeks after the War had ended.

The Indonesian Republic had made good use of the time. Sukarno had appointed a Cabinet. Many of its members had headed bureaucratic departments under the Japanese, who took less and less responsibility for overseeing the new government. By late September, Indonesian officials in Java were reporting directly to the Republic. To encourage Japanese acquiescence, Sukarno made it his policy to assume power slowly—working through the existing bureaucratic mechanism and taking over from within, rather than seizing control by force.

This methodical approach suited the pemudas no better than before. They had lost none of their yearning for dramatic demonstrations. On September 19, against the advice of many older leaders and without Japanese permission, they staged a rally in Djakarta and invited Sukarno to speak. Japanese troops and tanks ringed the plaza where the rally was held, their guns trained on the crowd of 200,000 people. Sukarno, though fearful of bloodshed, had agreed to appear. He spoke for about two minutes, stating merely that his government would defend the independence proclamation; then he asked the crowd to trust him and go home quietly. The people dispersed—once again demonstrating Sukarno's hold on them.

Sukarno could postpone violence, but he could not completely prevent it. The Republic was forming a military and police force. However, there were difficulties; though the PETA militia was available as a nucleus, the Japanese had disarmed and disbanded most of its units, and regrouping was a slow business. Meanwhile, pemudas and other nationalists managed to obtain firearms from the increasingly demoralized Japanese. Some weapons they received simply

109

for the asking; the Japanese were anxious to avoid any confrontation. In one case, a Japanese commander even suggested to pemuda leaders that they stage a mock attack so that the commander could later claim he had been forced to surrender his unit's arms. In other instances, the Japanese fought hard, not only to hold on to their weapons, but also to block the assertion of military authority by the Republic, which was clearly a threat to the status quo. Still other Japanese troops simply sealed themselves inside their garrisons and waited for Allied troops to arrive.

When the British finally landed they were totally unprepared to deal with the situation that confronted them: a hodgepodge of freshly instituted Republican government authorities, nervous Japanese troops and armed pemudas aching to fight someone. Compounding the confusion was the fact that the Allies had no detailed plan to deal with the future of recaptured colonial lands.

The fundamentals of Allied policy had been engraved in the Atlantic Charter of 1941. It established a general Allied objective to secure the right of self-determination for all peoples. As for the East Indies in particular, the Netherlands' exiled Queen Wilhelmina had made a promise in 1942 to improve the lot of Indonesians after the War. The extent of the royal promise, however, was vague. The Dutch badly wanted the Indies back as a primary element in rebuilding their war-shattered economy.

A few Dutch troops came ashore with the British during the first weeks of October 1945. Dutch POWs, released from their camps by the Japanese, began to congregate in Djakarta. But additional landings of Dutch troops were halted when the nationalists complained that their presence would touch off riots. The modest troop strength of the British, deployed mostly in western Java, left them with a huge problem in carrying out their basic mandates: to disarm and repatriate the Japanese, evacuate Allied prisoners of war and internees, and keep the peace.

Outside Java and Sumatra, the occupation went smoothly enough. Australian troops moved during September and October to take control of the less densely populated eastern islands, bringing Dutch units along with them. Transfer of control in these areas presented few problems, because in most places the nationalists were not yet organized.

By December, most of the Australian units had been replaced by the Dutch, and nationalist sympathizers had gone underground.

But in Java and Sumatra—strongholds of the Indonesian Republic—the difficulties mounted. The British did what they could. Mountbatten ordered Japanese troops to continue to maintain law and order temporarily. He also ordered his own forces to cooperate with the Republic, which seemed to be running what government there was. Mountbatten urged Hubertus J. van Mook, the prewar Lieutenant Governor who had returned from wartime exile in Australia and was presently the senior Dutch official in the Indies, to recognize this reality and negotiate with Sukarno. Lieut. General Sir Philip Christison, the Allied military commander, insisted that British troops were in Indonesia only to accept the Japanese surrender, take care of the prisoners, and keep order in the areas where they needed to operate. He had no intention, Christison asserted, of meddling in the country's internal politics.

As the Indonesians read it, Christison's statement implied recognition of the Republic. They broadcast their own message, declaring that the British had come as guests of the Indonesians. The broadcast infuriated the Netherlands government in The Hague. The Dutch charged that the British were violating their August agreement to hold the territory for the Netherlands, and forbade van Mook to negotiate with Sukarno, whom they regarded as a traitor.

Sukarno and his colleagues realized that to survive as a government they had to prove to the world that they indeed governed. That meant maintaining order and creating an aura of responsibility calculated to earn international respect. Sukarno and Hatta sent out instructions not to interfere with British troops.

But once again the pemudas had different ideas. In the hinterlands, pemudas and other dissidents used weapons seized from the Japanese to attack Dutch civilians, who were emerging from their internment camps. The pemudas also terrorized local officials, many now employed by the Republic, who were judged to have worked too closely with the Japanese, or were regarded as pro-Dutch. Such officials often were aristocrats who had been regents under the Dutch, and numerous old scores were settled in blood.

For their part, the Dutch were only exacerbating the situa-

Soldiers of the 5th Indian Infantry Division, part of the Allied occupation force in Indonesia, sprint across a street in Surabaya during a fire fight in November of 1945. The pitched battle in Surabaya was the first major uprising by the Indonesians, and it was the last engagement in which Indians served in combat under British command.

tion. An American military observer reported that the Dutch troops were inclined to shoot at anything they thought was suspicious and "were not above forcing an Indonesian's house and dragging off, without charges or warrant, some or all of the inhabitants." The observer concluded that the Dutch were trying to buy time—stirring up trouble to keep the British involved until the Netherlands was strong enough to take over again. The British, however, were not pleased. Mountbatten called the undisciplined Dutch behavior "most reprehensible." And Sukarno warned that he could not be responsible for the hot-headed pemudas if Dutch provocation continued.

Trouble had already begun in late September 1945 at the naval base and port city of Surabaya, where street fights broke out between pemudas on one side and Eurasians and Dutch from the internment camps on the other. Tension rose when a Dutch Navy captain named P.J.G. Huijer, sent under British auspices to prepare for Allied occupation, conceived the idea of transferring weapons remaining in the Japanese garrison to the local republican government, in order to keep them out of the hands of the pemuda extremists. On October 3, he suggested this to the Japanese command-

er who—delighted to be relieved of responsibility—handed over his sword and his arms to Captain Huijer.

Huijer's action, though well intended, was a bad mistake. The weapons quickly found their way into a variety of eager hands—to men in the Republic's Army, to pemudas, to common thugs. Dutch, Japanese and Eurasian blood began to flow. Over the next three weeks whatever authority the republican government exercised in Surabaya virtually disappeared. A 25-year-old pemuda named Sutomo became the symbol of revolt for the surging masses in the city.

Vowing not to cut his hair or touch a woman until the Dutch were expelled, Bung Tomo, as Sutomo was called, played on all the emotional strings of the Javanese soul: Islam, tradition, independence, and hatred of the Dutch and Japanese. Another inciting influence was a middle-aged British woman who called herself K'tut Tantri. A former innkeeper on Bali who had taken up the nationalist cause, she had established her credentials among militant Indonesians by spending three and a half years in a Japanese prison. British soldiers who listened to her inflammatory radio broadcasts, exhorting Indonesians to rise and kill, called her Surabaya Sue—an epithet reminiscent of Japan's Tokyo Rose.

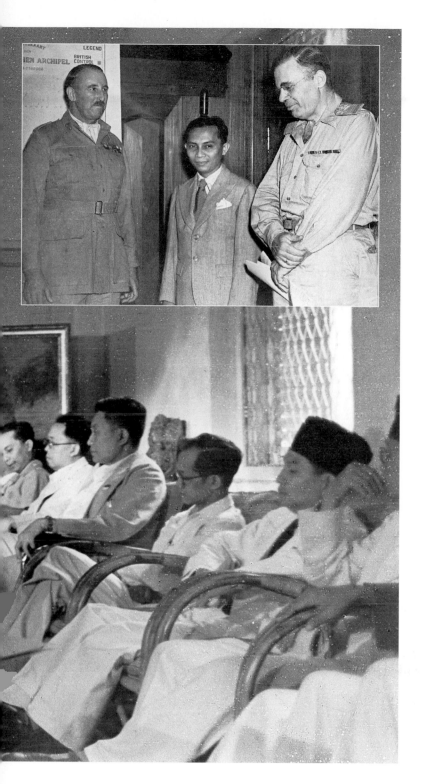

On October 25, British forces arrived in the strife-torn city: 4,000 mostly Indian troops commanded by Brigadier A.W.S. Mallaby. Greeted by representatives of the Indonesian Republic, Mallaby promised not to bring in Dutch forces. He assured his listeners that his only concern was to establish order and evacuate Dutch internees and Japanese troops. Tension eased, and Mallaby's men started moving cautiously from the dock area in the north through the restless heart of Surabaya to the internment camps in the southern quarter.

Then a shower of British leaflets, dropped from Royal Air Force planes, ordered the Indonesians to surrender all their arms within 48 hours. Mallaby himself was surprised by the leaflets, which had been disseminated on the orders of British headquarters in Djakarta. Pemudas were outraged by the ultimatum: They felt sure that the British wanted to disarm them in preparation for a Dutch landing. Even moderates lost faith in the British when Mallaby's troops set up roadblocks, started confiscating automobiles containing arms even before the 48 hours had elapsed, and occupied the railroad station and the telegraph office. The city was seething with fury.

On the night of October 28 a massive force of 120,000 armed pemudas attacked Mallaby's soldiers, who were divided between Surabaya's dock area and the internment camps. A number of Mallaby's troops, caught on the streets when the assault began, were literally hacked to pieces. It was clear that the vastly outnumbered British force would be wiped out unless someone could stop the mob. During the night, the British telegraphed Sukarno in Djakarta and asked for his help.

The next morning, Sukarno, Hatta and Sjarifuddin, the onetime underground leader who had joined the Republic's Cabinet as Minister of Information, flew to Surabaya and negotiated a cease-fire. Under its terms the British were to withdraw to their encampments, the Indonesians would permit the passage of the internees to the docks, prisoners taken by British and Indonesians would be exchanged, joint Indonesian and British patrols would keep the peace—and Surabayans would keep their weapons.

The compromise seemed to work; fighting died down and the Presidential party returned to Djakarta. But within hours the shooting broke out again, and when Brigadier

At his home in Djakarta, President Sukarno (center) presides over a pivotal meeting of his government in November 1945. The Dutch refused to deal with Indonesians who had collaborated with the Japanese, so Sukarno replaced the first nationalist Cabinet (seated, left) with a new one (right) more acceptable to the Dutch. Prime Minister Sutan Sjahrir (inset) then began talks with British Lieut. General Sir Philip Christison (left) and Hubertus J. van Mook, the acting Dutch Governor General.

Mallaby drove out under a white flag to stop it, he was killed. Mallaby's death changed everything. In a tough proclamation, General Christison warned Indonesians who had committed "unprovoked attacks" on British forces that he would crush them unless they surrendered. Then Cristison informed Sukarno that an entire division equipped with tanks was on its way by sea to Surabaya.

A plea broadcast by Sukarno calmed the situation long enough for the British to put the fresh division ashore and evacuate 6,000 to 8,000 internees. Then, on November 9, with all Dutch civilians who wanted to leave safely out of the city, the division commander, Major General E. C. Mansergh, issued an ultimatum. He demanded that any hostages being held by the Indonesians be released and that all weapons in pemuda hands be turned in by 6 p.m. that evening. If these orders were not obeyed, the general said, "I shall enforce them with all the sea, land and air forces at my disposal." He planned to move to occupy the town at 6 a.m. the next morning.

The British ultimatum had a significant effect: It united the pemudas and their moderate elders in the republican government. When Surabaya's leaders telephoned Djakarta to ask for a top-level decision about how to respond, Sukarno refused to intercede a second time. "We leave it to Surabaya," he said. That night, the republican governor of Surabaya broadcast a declaration that the city would resist to the last.

Early the next morning, as Bung Tomo went on the air and summoned the people to rise against the invasion, the British began to advance with infantry and tanks. They met stiff resistance and quickly called for air and naval support. RAF planes bombed the major buildings; British warships lying offshore shelled the city. The Indonesians refused to buckle, at first throwing themselves fanatically at the invaders, then regrouping and fighting in more organized fashion as the Japanese had taught them. The British had to shoot their way into every house in the center of the city in order to flush out the guerrillas.

A British officer later wrote that the battle of Surabaya represented revolutionary zeal run amok, an unmatched illustration of "hysterical ferocity" that was especially shocking to Europeans who had come to depend on the restrained attitude of the republican leaders in Djakarta. Indonesian and British sources alike reported atrocities against Europeans—wholesale slaughter, dismemberment and even ritual drinking of the blood of victims.

The British captured two thirds of Surabaya in the first three days of the battle, but it took three more weeks of hard combat before the city was entirely in British hands. The surviving insurgents dispersed into the countryside.

Surabaya opened the eyes of the British. Stunned by the self-sacrificial resistance they had encountered in the battle and aware that millions might die if such revolts took place all over Java, the British put new pressure on the Dutch to negotiate with the Republic. At the same time, Lieutenant Governor van Mook estimated that it would take at least 75,000 troops to restore Dutch authority, and The Hague would not be able to provide that many for at least a year. He began to look for ways to negotiate.

From the official Dutch viewpoint, Sukarno and Hatta were unacceptable as negotiators. But the Dutch were willing to talk with Sjahrir, who was a symbol of anti-Japanese resistance. On November 14, President Sukarno, committed to finding a diplomatic solution, installed Sjahrir as Prime Minister. On January 4, 1946, the bulk of the Republic's government moved to Jogjakarta, in central Java. It did so in order to decrease the risk presented by a growing Allied presence in Djakarta—including Dutch troops who were beginning to arrive in some numbers. Sjahrir, however, remained in Djakarta, where talks with Dutch representatives were to take place.

By now, Indonesian politics had become polarized between those leaders who believed that Indonesia's best hope was at the bargaining table, and the radicals who preferred armed struggle. The talks in Djakarta were destined to go on endlessly. Time and again, Sukarno managed to preserve his government's unity in the face of all those clamoring for power: the pemudas, the Army, the Muslims, conservatives, Socialists, Communists. Sukarno was the single great symbol of the struggle for independence, and his voice carried enormous weight. Although he himself could not negotiate, he translated the negotiators' compromises to the masses—and made them palatable.

The first compromise was offered by the Dutch. It grew out of recognition that the Republic controlled large areas of Java and Sumatra while the Dutch were dominant in the eastern part of the archipelago. In acknowledging this state of affairs, van Mook conceived the idea of a new political identity for the Indies—a sort of federation. The Republic would be one of its states and the others would be formed from areas held by the Dutch. The Netherlands government accepted the concept of "eventual" self-determination for the whole of Indonesia, with a van Mook-style federation as a first step. It was a grudging concession, but it opened the way for formal negotiations, mediated by the British, to begin in Djakarta in February of 1946. These talks were just starting to make some headway in May when the Dutch government, facing an electoral challenge from a

hard-lining opposition at home, broke off the negotiations.

Voters in the Netherlands, however, reelected a Parliament favoring a political solution for the Indies. The British also pushed for a solution before their final withdrawal, now planned for November 1946. Accordingly, the negotiators resumed their work by arranging for a cease-fire in October. The truce was needed to end sporadic fighting between Indonesian forces and the 55,000 Dutch troops who were replacing the British in Java.

Next the diplomats turned to a long-range settlement, and on November 12, at the resort town of Linggajati on Java's north coast, Dutch and Republic delegates initialed an agreement. Within the framework of an interim government

United Nations military observers talk with Indonesian soldiers in Jogjakarta, the temporary nationalist capital. The U.N. team was made up of observers from six nations and numbered 63 men at its peak. It was assigned in January 1948 to report on compliance with a U.N.-sponsored cease-fire and stayed on in Indonesia for three years.

run jointly by The Hague and the Republic, the Dutch recognized the Republic's de facto authority in Sumatra, Java and the small island of Madura off the east coast of Java. The Republic promised to cooperate with the Netherlands in establishing, by January 1949, "The United States of Indonesia." It would be a federation composed of the Republic, Borneo and a state of East Indonesia that would encompass all the remaining territory. The U.S.I., it was agreed, would have equal status under the Dutch crown with the kingdom of the Netherlands, in a union sharing mutual interests such as foreign relations and defense.

Left unsettled, however, were crucial questions about how all this would be accomplished—and about underlying assumptions. The Dutch expected to dominate the proposed federation, because they controlled both states outside the Republic. Leaders of the Republic, on the other hand, felt that cooperation meant mutual Dutch-Republic consultation in setting up the federation. Thereafter, the Republic saw nothing that would prevent it from dominating the federation, given its position as the wealthiest and most powerful part of the archipelago.

Without asking the Republic to participate, van Mook called a conference in Bali in December of 1946 to set up the state of East Indonesia. In the new state's territories—the eastern islands—the Dutch had been consolidating their control by arresting Republican leaders and deposing local nobles who sympathized with Sukarno. Pemudas in the Celebes retaliated by launching a guerrilla campaign that made it impossible for the Dutch to govern the region.

The Dutch responded with a three-month campaign of terror by commandos under Captain Raymond "Turk" Westerling. The commandos methodically went from village to village, rounding up the inhabitants and shooting them if they did not hand over the guerrillas assumed to be hiding nearby. Dutch officials claimed that the commandos killed a total of 3,000 people during the campaign; other estimates ranged much higher.

In the angry atmosphere created by such violations of the agreement's spirit, Sukarno felt compelled to go slow for fear of losing control of his government to extremists. As late as January 1947, the Republic's legislature still had not formally ratified the accord. Those opposed to the agreement had been indignant when Sjahrir had signed it in Novem-

ber, and opposition to ratification gathered momentum. Sukarno papered over this problem by packing the 200-member legislature with 314 new members, ensuring ratification on March 25, 1947.

By the time it was ratified, the accord was virtually dead. The Dutch had set up a naval blockade of the Republic, seizing vessels—including some that were flying Chinese, British and American flags—bringing war supplies to republican areas of Java and Sumatra or taking out goods for export. At the same time, the Netherlands reinforced its troop strength in the western islands; by late June 1947, al-

Accused killers are forced to dig up their victims in Balapoelang.

MASSACRE AT BALAPOELANG

The celebration on August 17, 1946, of the first anniversary of Indonesia's declared independence took an ugly turn in the Javanese village of Balapoelang. Eighteen Dutch civilians, some of them women and children, were made to bow before the nationalist flag. Then they were impaled on bamboo spears and bludgeoned. Months later, Dutch troops arrested five of the culprits and made them uncover the victims' remains before facing a firing squad.

The massacre at Balapoelang was one among many atrocities committed during Indonesia's long revolution. Some were politically motivated, but others were the work of out-and-out thugs in the lawless atmosphere of continuing warfare.

most 90,000 men awaited the order to march on Jogjakarta.

As the Dutch grew increasingly bellicose, Indonesian opposition mounted against continued accommodation. Resistance became overwhelming in late June after Prime Minister Sjahrir, seeking to avoid war, accepted what amounted to a Dutch ultimatum demanding expanded authority in the interim government—until the establishment of the Indonesian federation. In the uproar over this concession, Sjahrir was forced to resign. He was replaced as Prime Minister by Sjarifuddin.

The new government had barely taken over when the Dutch struck. At midnight on the 20th of July, spearheaded by tanks and supported by air bombardment, two strong Dutch divisions based in Djakarta and Bandung invaded western Java. Two additional brigades attacked out of Surabaya into eastern Java and Madura, while smaller units went into action in eastern Sumatra. According to a standing plan, Indonesian forces retreated into the countryside. Few men were captured.

One Dutch objective was simply to repossess the economic resources of Java and Sumatra. A renewed flow of commodities from the Indies was essential if the Dutch were

Dutch soldiers display the skulls and bones of civilians who were murdered at Balapoelang. The bamboo spear at center was one of the weapons used.

to solve their financial dilemma. It cost them an estimated one million dollars a day to maintain forces in the Indies, and nothing was coming out of the area to offset the expenditure. Accordingly, Dutch armored columns drove for economically strategic objectives: key roads, ports, storage areas, plantations, oil wells and mines.

At the start of the attack, The Hague dispatched a message to Trygve Lie, Secretary General of the United Nations, announcing that with "the utmost reluctance," the Netherlands had undertaken "police measures of a strictly limited character." The message blamed the Republic for destroying economic assets and asserted that it was incapable of maintaining law and order.

Meanwhile, Sjahrir had flown to New Delhi to rally international support for the Republic. As a result, Jawaharlal Nehru, Prime Minister-designate for the new nation of India, in conjunction with Australia, referred the matter to the

United Nations in New York. In a Security Council debate that began on July 31, the Dutch rejected U.N. jurisdiction, insisting that the fighting was an internal affair aimed at restoring order in their own territory, and therefore not a matter for international concern. The Security Council nevertheless passed a resolution on August 1 ordering a ceasefire—the first such resolution in the U.N.'s brief history. When both sides a few days later issued orders to their troops to stop fighting, the outcome was seen as a great victory for the U.N. and for international peace.

The Dutch had suffered a diplomatic setback, but in military terms their offensive had been a victory. It left them in possession of the richest parts of the Republic. All the seacoasts, the main roads and the major towns throughout western and eastern Java were in Dutch hands, leaving Republican territory in central Java isolated. The Dutch set to work to consolidate their gains. They called this action

An aerial photograph taken through scattered clouds immediately after the Dutch attack on Maguwo Airport in Jogjakarta shows the field dotted with the chutes of Dutch paratroopers and C-47s that landed later with reinforcements. The attack, on December 19, 1948, launched the second major Dutch offensive against the Indonesian nationalists.

"mopping up," asserting that they were not violating the cease-fire. The territory of the Republic was reduced to about one third of Java's 49,000 square miles and a large, impoverished section of Sumatra.

To enforce the cease-fire and try to settle the basic dispute, the U.N. set up a "Good Offices Committee," consisting of representatives from Belgium, Australia and the United States. The committee members arrived in October 1947, and after complex negotiations held aboard the U.S. Navy transport Renville, anchored off Djakarta, they managed to produce a new accord.

The Renville Agreement, signed in January 1948, confirmed the Dutch territorial gains and reserved sovereignty in all the Indies for the Dutch until a United States of Indonesia could be formed. But it held out the eventual possibility of plebiscites in which the people of the federated states might align themselves with the Sukarno government.

Prime Minister Sjarifuddin did not approve of the agreement, yet he feared the consequences of rejecting it: a renewed Dutch attack and a long, bloody guerrilla war. Moreover, the Republic desperately needed U.N. support. Dr. Frank P. Graham, head of the American delegation to the Good Offices Committee, promised Sjarifuddin that the United States would see that the plebiscites were held in areas outside the Republic. Graham's promise offered the Republic its only hope; Sjarifuddin signed, confident that if the plebiscites ever did take place the people would choose to affiliate with the Republic.

The Renville Agreement, however, cost Sjarifuddin his job as Prime Minister. This latest compromise was just the excuse that his opponents needed to force him from office, and the day after he signed, his government fell.

Three years after the end of World War II, Sjarifuddin's anti-Japanese credentials were no longer as useful to his country as they had been when he first entered the Cabinet in 1945. Preoccupation with Cold War politics increasingly dominated the deliberations of the U.N. What the Indonesian Republic needed, in order to obtain help in fending off the Dutch, was a clearly anti-Communist government. Sukarno named Vice President Hatta, valued for his pragmatic, unifying leadership, to form such a government, with Hatta himself as Prime Minister. To carry out his mandate, Hatta named a Cabinet made up largely of moderates; in doing so, he excluded men from the Leftist factions that had been part of the Republic's government. Thus isolated, these forces, which included Communists, formed an increasingly powerful coalition in opposition to the moderates.

Over the ensuing months, the Communists, for the first time in a generation, threatened to take over the nationalist ranks. A party member named Muso, who had been active in the failed Communist uprising of the 1920s, returned in 1948 from the Soviet Union, where he had spent the intervening decades. He soon found a way to exploit the discontent simmering in the Republic over the concessions made to the Dutch. In September 1948, a feud between two Republic Army units—one with Communist leanings—escalated into shooting near the city of Madiun in central Java. The city's government fell to the Communists.

Sukarno and Hatta saw the danger of a Communist resurgence and acted swiftly. On September 19, they ordered the arrest of all Communist leaders in Jogjakarta. That evening Sukarno broadcast a tough speech in which he declared that the revolt in Madiun was a plot intended to undermine the Republic's fight for independence.

For all Sukarno's display of resolve, his government was in trouble. Then Muso turned the tables on himself. His assertive reply to Sukarno's speech, delivered an hour later, has been called the worst piece of political psychology in Indonesian history. He attacked Sukarno and Hatta by name, calling them "slaves of Japan and America" and "evil men" who planned to sell out the people to American imperialism. In effect, Muso declared a civil war—and immediately lost it.

Under pressure from Sukarno loyalists, other Left-Wing groups disavowed the revolt. Puzzled and dismayed by Muso's call for a crusade against their hugely popular leaders, many soldiers in Communist-led units in Madiun and elsewhere mutinied and killed their commanders.

Loyal divisions of the Republic's Army converged on Madiun from several directions and chased the rebels from the city. As the hard-core Communists abandoned Madiun to take up guerrilla warfare, they murdered a number of non-Communist leaders whom they had captured in the first days of the coup. The discovery of these killings deepened popular hostility against the Communists, who became hunted men. On October 31, Muso was killed in a skirmish with government troops.

Throughout the non-Communist world, Sukarno's and Hatta's political reputations soared. Without help from the Dutch, the Republic had met and defeated a direct Communist challenge; the Indonesian revolution had turned to the right, and the U.S. State Department recognized in Jogjakarta a potential bulwark in Asia at a time when Communism was scoring victories in China and Indochina.

The Republic's triumph over the Communists was echoed by success against the Dutch. Despite the blockade, Republic armed forces had carried on guerrilla operations—and even occasional regular Army forays—against the colonialist troops. The Dutch public had reacted in elections held in the Netherlands in July 1948 by giving hard-liners control of their government; a new administrator, a former Dutch Prime Minister named Louis J. M. Beel, was sent to replace van Mook. In November, Beel canvassed his military commanders and was told that immediate offensive action was necessary even to hold existing positions. Informed of this, the Dutch Cabinet voted on December 13, 1948, to destroy the Republic by military action.

At 5:30 a.m. on December 19, the Dutch assaulted Jogjakarta. Planes bombed the airfield, strafed the streets and dropped paratroops. They were followed by transports car-

rying additional troops and supplies. Most of the Republic's leaders were caught in the city. Certain that international opinion—and the continuing presence of the U.N.'s Good Offices Committee—would protect them, they had stayed despite the worsening situation. Orders now went out to all Republic military units to retreat and commence guerrilla war. A dispatch was sent to Bukittinggi, a hill town in western Sumatra, instructing a Cabinet minister who was there to set up an emergency government.

By the afternoon of December 19, the capital of the Indonesian Republic had fallen to its former masters. Sukarno, Hatta, Sjahrir and half the Cabinet were taken prisoner. Sukarno was brought before the Dutch commander and told to order the surrender of the Republic's troops. As he recounted the confrontation in his autobiography, Sukarno replied: "General, is it that I am a prisoner or is it that I am a President? If I am a President I can negotiate. If I am a prisoner I cannot give that order." The meeting ended, and no order was issued. By the end of December, every sizable town in Java and all but a handful in Sumatra were in Dutch hands.

Although the emergency government in Sumatra presented a symbol of continuity to the outside world, all that effectively remained of the Republic was its Army and its people. The Army began a guerrilla war within Dutch territory, relying on local villagers for aid. Their resistance not only pre-

vented the Dutch from establishing complete control over their newly won territory, but would eventually loosen the Dutch hold on areas they had captured in 1947.

The military take-over of the Republic soon backfired in a staggering political defeat for the Dutch government. Some Dutch-sponsored officials in the eastern Indonesian islands resigned in protest. On Java, few Indonesian leaders could be found who were willing to cooperate with the Dutch. Indonesians everywhere increasingly identified their fate with that of the Republic, particularly as the guerrilla campaign continued to involve the populace in the day-to-day struggle, creating a bond between soldier and civilian that the Dutch were unable to break.

Ultimately, as Sukarno had hoped, world outrage provided the impetus that turned the Dutch adventure into disaster. In the days and weeks immediately following the attack on Jogjakarta, five Asian nations refused airport and docking facilities to Dutch planes and ships. Nehru convened a meeting of 19 Southeast Asian nations to propose recommendations to the U.N. for restoring the Republic's territories and calling for a final settlement. Moreover, the United Nations could not ignore the blatant Dutch action. A series of U.N. resolutions demanded a cease-fire and the release of Sukarno and his government.

It was pressure from Washington that finally forced the Dutch to back down. The Americans' leverage was the Marshall Plan, the U.S.-financed program for the recovery of Europe, which had gone into operation in April 1948. American reaction to the Dutch attack was swift: Three days after it was launched, Washington suspended direct Marshall Plan payments to the Dutch-administered East Indies government. In the U.N. Security Council, the U.S. representative denounced the offensive as a violation of both the *Renville* Agreement and the U.N. Charter itself. On January 28, 1949, the United States sponsored a tough new Security Council resolution. It called for the release of the Republic's leaders, the formation by March of an interim government for the Dutch-administered United States of Indonesia, elections for a constituent assembly by October and full sovereignty for Indonesia by July of 1950.

Although Dutch Foreign Minister Dirk Stikker denounced the resolution as "unacceptable," his cause was doomed. American newspapers had pointed out that the annual cost to the Netherlands of maintaining military forces in Indonesia nearly matched the $400 million that the Netherlands was receiving under the Marshall Plan, and the U.S. Senate debated whether to cut off funds to The Hague until the Dutch accepted the U.N. resolution.

The Truman administration, fearing to weaken the Marshall Plan, at first opposed the Senate's move. However, on March 31, 1949, Secretary of State Dean Acheson told Stikker that the administration would no longer fight Congressional efforts to cut the Dutch out of the Marshall Plan. Stikker saw the danger to his government, and three weeks later The Hague announced that it would restore the Republic's government if guerrilla warfare was stopped.

After complicated negotiations between Dutch and Indonesian representatives in Djakarta, an understanding was reached. The Dutch withdrew from the Jogjakarta area. On July 6, Sukarno and Hatta returned to their capital, and issued an order for the guerrillas to stop fighting. In August, a follow-up conference opened in The Hague.

At the conference, delegates from 15 Indonesian political units outside Java and western Sumatra that had been established under Dutch sponsorship aligned themselves with the delegates of the Republic. The Dutch accepted Indonesian sovereignty—with no supervised interim period. The Indonesian nation was to be a federation made up of the Republic and the other states. On December 27, 1949, the Dutch transferred full sovereignty to the new federation, named the Republic of the United States of Indonesia. It comprised all of the former Netherlands East Indies except West New Guinea, the status of which was to be negotiated over the following year. Although the constitution of the new nation gave two thirds of the seats in its legislature to representatives from the states outside the Jogjakarta Republic, Sukarno was elected President, Hatta was appointed Prime Minister and 10 of the 15 ministers chosen for the first Cabinet were former Republican leaders.

The next day, December 28, Sukarno returned in triumph to Djakarta, Indonesia's traditional capital. He was greeted by a sea of rejoicing people and an honor guard carrying the original proclamation flag his wife had sewed in 1945. Slowly Sukarno's car made its way to the palace. The man Indonesians called "brother" mounted the steps, turned to the crowd and exclaimed: "Thank God. We are free."

Crowds in Djakarta celebrate the fourth anniversary of Indonesian independence on August 17, 1949. A constitution drafted during the ensuing year provided for a parliamentary form of government, but in the decade that followed, regional resistance to central authority led President Sukarno to impose "democracy with guidance"—his way of describing his regime's increasingly authoritarian rule.

LAST DAYS OF COLONIALISM

At Djakarta's half-empty Harmonie Club, long a bastion of Dutch colonial social life, a few members in 1949 share a glass and memories of better times.

THE RELUCTANT RETREAT FROM SUPREMACY

The storied era of what Rudyard Kipling called "the white man's burden" was rushing to an end. In the romantic view articulated by Kipling, generations of Europeans had undertaken to lift up Asia's backward multitudes by exposing them to the institutions and the morality of the civilized West. Yet only by force had these colonialists made their word law, from the tea plantations of India and the rice paddies of Indochina to the tin mines of Malaya and the Indies. Over the years, they had exploited the region's natural riches, suppressed attempts at self-rule and for the most part stayed arrogantly aloof from the peoples they had mastered.

Europeans had developed an enormous social and economic stake in this far-ranging fiefdom. Many families had been entrenched there for decades, even for centuries. Perilously isolated early in the War, when Japan's armies swept through the Far East, thousands of them had suffered atrocity, internment and privation. Now, with the War won, they demanded a recapture of their privileged way of life—and many of them were willing to put their lives on the line to do it. But time was running against them.

White men had never ruled China. But their military and technological superiority had given them powerful leverage over a crumbling dynasty; they had established enclaves and trading privileges in China's most important cities. As many as 300,000 Europeans and Americans—missionaries as well as businessmen—lived in special settlements in 90 Chinese ports, protected by their own laws and police.

Such a system was anathema to the Chinese. Mao Tsetung's troops marched into Shanghai, the principal treaty port, in May 1949 and, through work stoppages and official harassment, the Communists began to make it difficult for foreigners to conduct business. They began to leave in droves and by August, according to one observer, Shanghai had taken on a "sick and ghostlike look." Yet some Westerners refused to acknowledge that times had changed. Membership in the Columbia Country Club, an exclusive American preserve, shrank drastically, but the club refused to change its policy and admit Chinese members.

French priests leaving Shanghai in 1949 carry their possessions aboard ship. Missionary work had been drastically curtailed by the government.

A Chinese soldier stands guard as residents of Shanghai's foreign settlements sail on the S.S. General Gordon in September 1949.

A relic of the British raj, the all-British Bengal Chamber of Commerce convenes in 1947.

British and Indian students attend chapel at a newly integrated private school in Simla.

A NEW ROLE FOR THOSE WHO STAYED

Of necessity, the British who had lived and worked in India accepted the end of the British raj in 1947 with resignation and good grace, even though for most it meant the end of a privileged way of life in a land many of them had come to love.

A few military men and civil servants remained at their posts at the request of the new governments of India and Pakistan. A handful of traditionally powerful British businessmen—notably, the members of the Bengal Chamber of Commerce (left), long entrenched as managers of industry and finance in India—also stayed on.

Those who remained had to cope with social as well as political change. No longer would they and their families be comfortably isolated in exclusive British preserves; instead they would live side by side with the people in whose land they were now guests.

For most Britons, Indian independence meant going home to a Britain made destitute by the War, where the future looked relatively bleak. Yet, as one civil servant later wrote, ''The prevailing thought was simply that we had done our part and that the time had come to go. It was over.''

At a rally at Peshawar, a British provincial governor who has been invited to stay on urges frontier tribesmen to accede to the new government of Pakistan.

127

Captured Vietminh insurgents are taken to prison under French guard in October 1945.

In La Pagode, a mirrored Saigon café, two young Frenchwomen pamper their pet dogs—one of which dines off its mistress's plate.

For a Spanish ball in 1950, with dinner and dancing outdoors till dawn for 1,000 guests, Saigon's Cercle Sportif erected a Moorish-castle backdrop.

A PARISIAN LIFE STYLE IN ISOLATED SAIGON

The French confidently expected to sweep all opposition aside when they returned to Indochina in 1945, and for a time it seemed that they had succeeded. True, Ho Chi Minh had established a Communist-dominated government in the north and was fighting to extend its power. But the French took the offensive and by late 1947 they had driven Ho's Vietminh forces out of every major Indochinese city.

Life for the French recovered some of its prewar glitter, and nowhere more than in beautiful Saigon, the "Paris of the East." Stylish shops lured fashionable women, and their menfolk joined them at the exclusive Cercle Sportif at the end of the day.

There were occasional moments of fear, when Vietminh guerrillas attacked isolated homes and farms or bombed a city café, killing Vietnamese as well as Frenchmen. But most colonialists, sheltering within the grenade-proof cages built around restaurants and cabarets, shrugged off the danger and clung determinedly to the old ways.

A FORTRESS MENTALITY IN MALAYA

British planters and mining engineers and their families were prime targets of the Communist uprising that erupted in Malaya in 1948 and continued until after Malaya became independent in 1957. The insurgents, bent on ruining the colony's economy, attacked its principal sources of wealth—tin mines and rubber plantations. In 1950 alone, more than 1,200 civilians were ambushed and murdered.

The sprawling plantations were harder to defend than the mines. Planters turned their remote homes into forts, surrounding them with barbed wire and floodlights; to venture just a few yards outside his compound, a typical planter carried a submachine gun and a pistol and hitched grenades to his belt. Even when visiting in Kuala Lumpur, Malaya's relatively secure capital, prudent Britons kept their weapons close at hand.

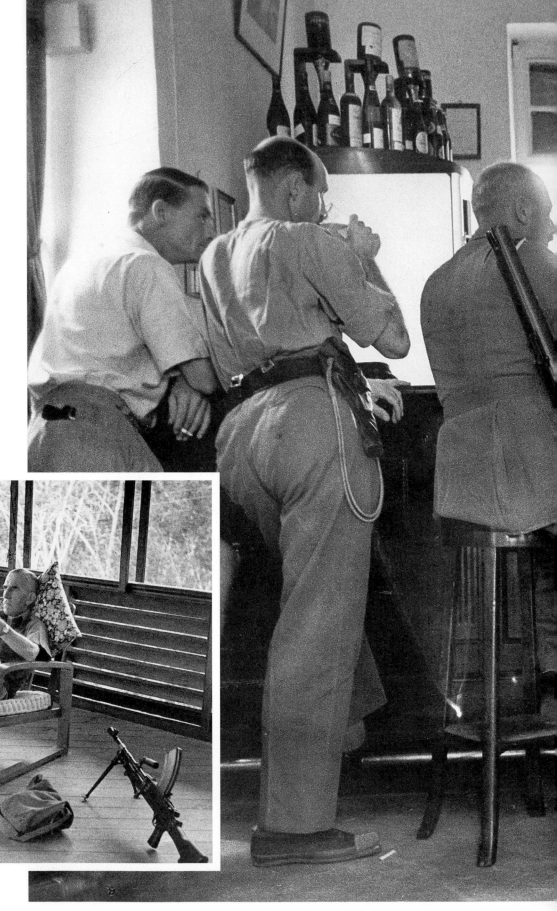

Safely indoors after a day's work, a planter relaxes with a newspaper—but keeps a loaded Bren gun and extra ammunition within reach.

Getting together in a favorite barroom in Kuala Lumpur for an early-afternoon drink in 1951, British planters keep their weapons visible and ready to be used.

5

Six weeks after the formal surrender of Japan, a contingent of the U.S. 6th Marine Division landed in the Chinese port city of Tsingtao to accept the surrender of Japanese forces in the region and to maintain order in the tumult caused by the War's sudden end. With the Marines was Navy Lieutenant Donald Keene, a 23-year-old language specialist who had been sent to interrogate suspected war criminals among the Japanese troops awaiting repatriation. In his free time, the visiting American explored the streets of Tsingtao, and his wanderings invariably attracted a crowd of curious Chinese. On one occasion, a man who spoke English emerged from the crowd and asked if Keene was hungry. Keene answered "Yes," and they headed for a café that displayed two flags out front, one Chinese and one American. An advertising card for the restaurant promised in English: "Open all night. Cold drinks and anything special you like." As they entered, the man took the young Navy officer by the arm and cried, "No British, no Russian, no goddamn Japanese. America and China, like brothers."

A bond of friendship between China and the United States was an old dream of many Americans and not a few Chinese. Nurtured during the War, often more as an act of political faith than as an effective military strategy, this dream of alliance was to be shattered in the postwar period. Its end came through the final unfolding of a Chinese revolution—a titanic struggle for power in the world's oldest, most populous nation—a contest in which the United States found itself on the losing side.

In late 1945, such an outcome was beyond perception—even though much of China was floundering in anarchy. The Nationalist government, headquartered in the remote western city of Chungking and led by the austere soldier-statesman Chiang Kai-shek, had been drained by eight years of war with Japan; the vigor of Chiang's regime was further sapped by more than 18 years of intermittent conflict with China's Communists, who had been led since 1934 by the shrewd, patient Mao Tse-tung. The United States and its wartime allies supported the Nationalists as the custodians of China's future. However, the Nationalists were seriously off balance—hardly capable of beginning the process of peacetime rebuilding that was the goal of U.S. policy.

The Japanese had ravaged large portions of China. An estimated 15 million Chinese had died since 1937, when the

CHINA'S WAR WITHIN

Japanese began to expand southward from their Manchurian colony. Cities were in ruins. River vessels, the mainstay of China's transportation system, lay on the bottom or were damaged and beached. Little could move on China's scanty network of railroads; war had destroyed rolling stock, bridges and tunnels. The highways were next to impassable; in any case, there were few vehicles to travel on them. Vast tracts of cropland had been put to the torch, and starvation and pestilence afflicted the populace.

The greatest devastation was in areas north of the Yangtze River, China's principal east-west artery and a traditional dividing line between north and south (map, page 134). In the far northeast, the Soviet Union, which had declared war on Japan on August 8, 1945, had occupied all of Manchuria.

Much of Chiang's Nationalist army of about 2.5 million men was concentrated in the southwestern provinces. At the conclusion of hostilities on August 15, they took over areas of central and eastern China south of the Yangtze from which the Japanese had retreated; Chiang's men were able to occupy these areas partly because of a cease-fire with the Chinese Communists that had begun just before the Japanese capitulated. The respite enabled the Nationalists to deploy men who would otherwise have been tied down in the Communist-dominated northwest. The Communist stronghold centered on Shensi province, a rugged region of deeply gullied hills; Communists held other inhospitable areas in the northwest, where there were no major cities. Although the Communists also controlled much of north-central and northeastern China, they had not penetrated the great urban areas such as Nanking and Shanghai, which the Japanese had turned into fortress enclaves. To forestall any move by Mao into these important cities, the United States quickly took steps to make sure that the Nationalists were in position to accept the Japanese surrender there.

During September and October, the Americans used a fleet of C-46 and C-54 transports to airlift about 80,000 of Chiang's best troops to Shanghai, China's largest city, and to Nanking, which had been Chiang's capital until it was overrun by the Japanese in 1937. Even before the airlift, which was organized by Lieut. General Albert C. Wedemeyer, the last wartime U.S. commander in China, Washington had been considering moves designed to bolster Chiang. They included an extension of wartime financial aid, which had

already amounted to several billion dollars, as well as the provision of arms and equipment for 39 divisions of troops. Washington also contemplated maintaining the Nationalist air force and supplying naval vessels to patrol the rivers and coastline. The 1,000 American servicemen who had spent the War in China training Chiang's forces would remain.

At the end of September came a direct application of American military power: 53,000 Marines, the first elements of an eventual force of about 100,000 men, began landing at ports north of the Yangtze. They spread out into a triangular area bounded by Peking, Tientsin and Chinwangtao in Hopeh province, setting up garrisons in the region's major population centers. The Marines also were ordered to guard the coal mines near Tangshan, which were the chief energy source for all of eastern China, and the railroad between Peking and the Yellow Sea port of Chinwangtao. Additional U.S. troops moved south into nearby Shantung province, where they garrisoned Tsingtao. Marine air bases were established in both Hopeh and Shantung provinces.

Only a token force of 1,500 Nationalist troops accompanied the Marines to the two provinces, where the Communists controlled almost all the countryside and some of the smaller cities as well. The Communists, choosing to avoid a confrontation, agreed to a temporary American occupation. Yet they were keenly aware of the Marines' purpose: to hold the area until the Nationalists could take over in force. Once the Marines were in position, American ships and aircraft summoned from all over the Pacific were assigned to the massive task of transporting Chiang's armies from southwest China to the north; eventually they moved several million Nationalist troops.

Official U.S. policy had long stated that the arms supplied to these forces were not for use against the Communists. Throughout the War, the Americans had been intent on concentrating all available Chinese power against the Japanese—and had been dismayed by the fact of Chinese fighting Chinese. Now Washington was anxious to reconcile the antagonists and guide the country along the road to recovery. But progress in that direction was far from smooth. The cease-fire signed in August soon broke down; clashes between Communist and Nationalist forces became more frequent and bloody during late 1945, and by early 1946 China was once again seething with civil war. And though the

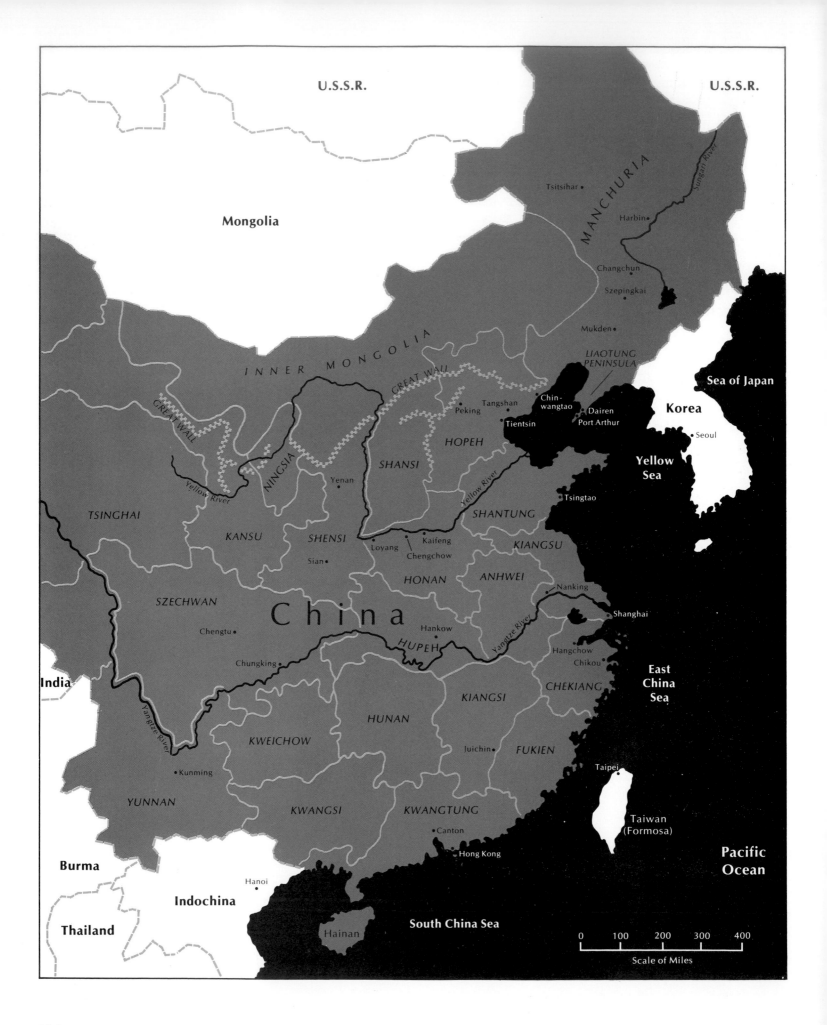

U.S.S.R.

U.S.S.R.

Mongolia

MANCHURIA

Tsitsihar •

Harbin •

Sungari River

Changchun •

Szepingkai •

Mukden •

INNER MONGOLIA

GREAT WALL

*LIAOTUNG
PENINSULA*

Sea of Japan

Korea

GREAT WALL

Tangshan • Chin-
wangtao •

Peking • Dairen
Tientsin • Port Arthur

HOPEH

Seoul •

Yellow
Sea

NINGSIA

Yenan •

SHANSI

Yellow River

SHANTUNG

• Tsingtao

Yellow River

TSINGHAI

KANSU

SHENSI

Loyang • Kaifeng
Sian • Chengchow

HONAN

KIANGSU

ANHWEI

Nanking •

Shanghai •

SZECHWAN

C h i n a

Chengtu •

Hankow •

HUPEH

Yangtze River

Hangchow •
Chikou •

East
China
Sea

Chungking •

Yangtze River

KIANGSI

CHEKIANG

India

HUNAN

KWEICHOW

Juichin •

FUKIEN

Taipei •

• Kunming

YUNNAN

KWANGSI

KWANGTUNG

Burma

• Canton

Taiwan
(Formosa)

Pacific
Ocean

Hanoi •

• Hong Kong

Indochina

Thailand

Hainan

South China Sea

0   100   200   300   400

Scale of Miles

Marines stationed in north China were a potential buffer between the warring factions, they were under orders to stand clear of the fighting.

Alternately raging and sputtering, China's civil war had been going on since the 1920s. Ironically, the conflict had originated during a period of cooperation between Nationalists and Communists, when each had needed the other. The Chinese Communist Party was organized in July 1921 in Shanghai, at a meeting attended by Mao Tse-tung and 12 other founding members. Among its earliest significant activities was participation in a struggle, initiated by the Nationalists, to modernize and unify China under a republican banner. Such a goal was the dream of Sun Yat-sen, father of the 1911 revolution that had overthrown China's last Imperial dynasty, the Manchu.

In the mid-1920s Chiang Kai-shek, Sun's military commander and devoted disciple, helped to reorganize the Nationalist Party, or Kuomintang. Inspired by Sun's admiration for the ideas of Karl Marx, and the recent success of the Russian revolution, the Nationalists used the Communist Party in the Soviet Union as a model. Beginning in 1923, Sun had political and military advisers from Moscow working with the Kuomintang. Borrowing from Soviet political techniques, the Kuomintang organized mass support through local cells that elected delegates to successively higher governing bodies, with a central executive committee at the top. In a move consistent with this political orientation, the fledgling Chinese Communist Party was brought into the government, which at that time was based in the southern port city of Canton.

A decade and a half after the onset of Sun Yat-sen's revolution, the Nationalists controlled only part of south China; the rest of the country was a sea of anarchy, broken here and there by islands of arbitrary power in the hands of so-called warlords—renegade military leaders who had staked out personal fiefs. From their southern base, Sun and Chiang were determined to launch what they called the Northern Expedition to wrest that part of China from the warlords, and they enlisted the Communists to fight alongside them.

Communist participation in the Nationalist government and in its military ventures gained Sun and Chiang a useful aura of national unity. But Communist involvement also made some Nationalist supporters nervous; Chinese businessmen were more interested in stabilizing the country than they were in the radical ideas that the Communists espoused. Chiang's Communist allies seemed intent on taking over the labor unions and instituting land and tax reform. Chiang himself felt uneasy over the Kuomintang's dependence on Red Chinese troops and Soviet advisers. Sun died suddenly in March 1925 and, with his mentor gone, Chiang's attitude toward the Communists hardened.

In April 1927, following the capture of Shanghai, which he had brought off with Communist help, Chiang ruthlessly struck out at his ally: He had more than 300 Communists rounded up and shot. Those who escaped went underground and organized a counterattack. The Kuomintang's Russian advisers fled, and the survivors of the Shanghai massacre regrouped in the hills of Kiangsi province, in south China. Mao gradually emerged as the political leader of the party's remnant, a collection of armed bands numbering about 10,000 men in all, which conducted intermittent raids for food and supplies and set ambushes for Nationalist troops.

Outraged by such depredations on the part of an enemy that he had considered crushed, Chiang mounted three largely unsuccessful anti-Communist drives that he called "bandit extermination" campaigns. The fourth was about to begin when the Japanese, on September 18, 1931, invaded Manchuria, China's massive northeast region. Launching their assault from mainland enclaves ceded to Japan by Russia after its defeat in the 1904-1905 Russo-Japanese War, the Japanese soon took over the entire territory.

Though the Communists were no longer in the government, they greeted this threat to China with an official declaration of war against Japan. Chiang, as head of China's government, issued no such declaration, feeling too weak to prevail against Japan.

Chiang had sent his Soviet advisers packing, but he still felt the need of advice from abroad. In 1933 he imported one of Germany's best-known strategists, General Hans von Seeckt, who had commanded the armed forces of the Weimar Republic in the 1920s. Seeckt discounted the possibility of mounting a guerrilla campaign against the Japanese and counseled Chiang to build up and perfect his regular forces before committing them to battle.

When the Japanese capitulated in August 1945, their 1.2 million troops in China occupied Nanking, Shanghai and most other ports, as well as large areas of Hopeh, Honan and Kiangsi provinces. About 2.5 million Nationalist troops were largely marshaled in the provinces of Yunnan, Szechwan and Kwangsi in the southwest; Chinese Communist armies held scattered bases in rural areas—mostly between Shensi province and the north bank of the Yangtze River near Nanking. In September, 53,000 U.S. Marines landed in such ports as Tsingtao, Tientsin and Chinwangtao and also set up a base in Peking. Soviet forces, having entered the war against Japan on August 8, had occupied Manchuria and parts of Inner Mongolia, taking 600,000 Japanese prisoners. By the end of August, the Russians controlled all major cities north of the Great Wall.

Believing that only an undivided China could withstand the Japanese, Chiang also redoubled his efforts to subdue the Communists, whose numbers continued to increase. After a yearlong campaign that may have cost both sides as many as one million dead—either killed in battle or victims of starvation and disease—Chiang's forces managed to surround a large number of Communists in and around the town of Juichin. Among those trapped were Mao and other leaders, including Chu Teh, the Communist military chief, and Chou En-lai, the descendant of a wealthy Chinese family, who was soon to become Mao's deputy.

By October 1934, facing slow death under the Nationalist siege, the Communist leaders elected to attempt a breakout; almost 100,000 men and a few hundred women fought their way out of the trap. Led by Mao, they then embarked on the harrowing 6,000-mile military pilgrimage that came to be known as the Long March. In the fall of 1935, a bare 7,000 to 8,000 survivors reached sanctuary of sorts in Shensi province, where they joined with other bands of Communists, numbering perhaps 13,000, who had also escaped the Nationalist purge.

The Communists chose as their capital Yenan, a pocket of green flatland nestled in a maze of hills, where they lived in caves burrowed into the slopes. "From the air," reported *Time* and *Life* correspondent Theodore H. White, "it had the look of a bandit's lair, hidden in the incredible fastnesses of the hills, with a note of incongruity touched in by a Tang pagoda perched atop a low peak, yellow and incredibly lovely against the blue sky."

Once firmly established in Yenan, the Communists carried out two decisions that had been made during the Long March: One affected the party's leadership for decades to come and permanently shaped its political direction; the other settled the question of how and when to defend against the Japanese.

During the Long March, Mao, by reason of his courage

and sagacity, had been elevated to the party chairmanship. And that in turn dictated the party's strategy. Mao believed in a revolution based on an agricultural proletariat—the peasantry. In this he differed radically from orthodox Communist thinking as formulated by Moscow. But the difference was an ideological refinement particularly suited to China, 80 per cent of whose people were agricultural laborers or tenant farmers clinging to a precarious subsistence in the countryside. Peasants far outnumbered the factory workers concentrated in industrial cities such as Shanghai and Hankow—the segment of the population that orthodox Marxism counted on to form the nucleus of a revolution.

In Mao's concept, the revolution was to be carried out by a guerrilla army made up of peasant soldiers. This army would be able to move undetected through enemy lines, attack without warning, then fade into invisibility among the rural population. "The Red Army," declared Mao, "lives among the people as the fish dwells in the water."

In the mid-1930s, the enemy against whom Mao's guerrilla tactics were directed was not Chiang, but the Japanese. Mao and his strategists believed that the foreign invaders had to be expelled before the Chinese could settle their internal quarrels. Mao was determined, however, that action against the Japanese should not expose his Communist forces to crushing defeat by a superior foe; he ordered that resistance take the form of attacks by small units whose mission was to harass rather than confront the enemy—at least, until the Red Army gained greater strength. Communist soldiers, meanwhile, were instructed to continue playing a political role—recruiting party adherents, as well as fighting men, from among the peasants.

At whatever level, resistance to the Japanese was not the most urgent priority of Chiang Kai-shek. The Generalissimo remained adamantly determined to wipe out the Communists before turning his attention to the Japanese. Specifically, he ordered Marshal Chang Hsüeh-liang, at the head of 100,000 Nationalist troops in Shensi province, to destroy the survivors of the Long March. But now Chiang faced the wrath of his own men.

Chang Hsüeh-liang and his soldiers were Manchurian. They had been driven from their homeland by the Imperial Japanese Army, and they were aching for a chance to avenge that defeat. Unable to comprehend why Chinese should fight Chinese while a foreign enemy ruled the northeast, Chang angrily protested his orders—and made clandestine contact with the Communists, hoping to establish a united front against the Japanese. Impatient to get on with his war against Mao, Chiang Kai-shek flew on December 4, 1936, to Sian, the capital of Shensi, to confront his subordinate. Marshal Chang's response was as bold as it was surprising: He kidnapped his own leader and refused to release him until the Generalissimo agreed to make the Japanese his first priority.

In the negotiations with the Communists that followed, Chiang gained—at least for the moment—much of what he had sought to accomplish by force: a country unified under his leadership. In return, the Communist forces, by now 85,000 strong, remained intact, though technically they were absorbed into the armies of the Kuomintang.

Six months after the kidnapping incident, the Japanese launched a major offensive, designed to subjugate China in one swift campaign. In July 1937, a provocation staged by Japanese troops at the Marco Polo Bridge outside Peking generated a skirmish with a local Chinese garrison; this minor fight was used in turn to justify a punitive expedition by Japan's North China Command against the Chinese troops deployed around Peking. The Japanese quickly captured Peking and swarmed southward as far as Tientsin, on the Yellow Sea coast, where their advance was slowed.

In this emergency, the Communists and Nationalists issued a joint announcement. The Red Army units that had been based in Shensi would become the Eighth Route Army, while Communist guerrillas operating farther east were designated the Fourth Army. They would operate as part of the Nationalist command.

Years of fighting would follow, in which the Red Army would prove itself as adept at politics as it was at guerrilla warfare. Though nominally allied with the Nationalists, the Communists never lost an opportunity to pursue their own ultimate objectives. As the Japanese advanced through the border regions east of Shensi and south of the Great Wall, they captured and fortified the major cities and towns, and established control of roads and railways. Communist forces in these areas gave ground but did not run away; after waiting for calm to return to an area following Japanese

An airport crowd greets an American C-54 transport carrying Nationalist Chinese soldiers to Shanghai. In September and October of 1945, the United States airlifted thousands of Chiang's troops to cities in the north and east in order to prevent the Communists from occupying them.

137

penetration, the Communists filtered back in to take control of the countryside. At the same time, the Communists assiduously recruited new party members. This pattern was repeated wherever the Red armies operated. Both the Japanese and Chiang knew what the Communists were up to—and each took action.

The Japanese, determined to end the Communists' guerrilla harassment, launched an operation in the early 1940s that they called the "three all" campaign—"Kill all, burn all, destroy all." This campaign of systematic terror and destruction was meant to cow the populace into rejecting the Communists; it achieved the opposite effect by fueling the peasants' hatred of the Japanese. Moreover, many landowners—whose fields the peasants tilled—collaborated with the Japanese in order to keep the invaders from burning their property. Since these landlords were usually supporters of the Kuomintang, the peasants increasingly came to regard the Communists as their protectors against both the Japanese and the Nationalists. Party rolls swelled.

In the meantime, Chiang once more had grown openly hostile to the Communists. Some years earlier, in 1938, Communist political activities had become so widespread in Chinese-held areas that the Nationalist high command nervously banned activities by Communist-sponsored youth organizations. In December 1938, the first of a series of armed clashes between Chiang's and Mao's forces occurred in the rural areas of Hopeh province (where the Japanese held Peking). As the fighting gained momentum, Chiang decided to go for the Communists' jugular. Mobilizing hundreds of thousands of his best troops from central and south China, he mounted what he hoped would be a climactic "extermination campaign" against the Reds' stronghold in the northwest. Chiang's method was simple but slow: Encircling Shensi, his forces pushed the Communists into an ever-smaller area, securing captured territory—and preventing escape—by erecting concentric circles of fortifications around the shrinking Communist redoubt.

The Communists, though at bay in the northwest, kept expanding their territory in the northern and northeastern parts of the country. In 1944 they succeeded in breaking Chiang's grip on Shensi, and were enlarging their holdings even in areas south of the Great Wall.

Wherever they gained ground, the Communists instituted moderate land reforms, such as reduced rent and taxes. Mao also insisted that members of the Red Army treat civilians with the greatest respect, and never take anything, not even a cigarette, without paying for it. By contrast, Chiang's armed forces often lived off the countryside, usually commandeering what they wanted from the people.

The behavior of Chiang's troops conformed to what was expected of soldiers in China. Fighting men had seldom been accorded high status. No one had ever doubted the ancient Chinese proverb that said, "Good iron is not used to make a nail; nor a good man to make a soldier." Despised as men and as soldiers, the troops acted accordingly.

The composition of the rival Chinese armies was another major difference between them. Chiang's troops were mostly conscripts, while Mao's men were volunteers. Moreover, Chiang's draftees could buy their way out. Wartime inflation had made corruption essential to survival in Chungking, and anyone with enough money could avoid military service. The conscripts who did serve tended to be poor and ill nourished, and they lacked motivation. Those who were healthy and aggressive were likely to be used against the Communists instead of the Japanese. Many observers, including Lieut. General Joseph W. Stilwell, the senior American commander in China until 1944, were outraged that Chiang did not throw his best men against the Japanese.

When Stilwell challenged him, Chiang responded frankly. "For me the big problem is not Japan," he is reported to have said, "but the unification of my country. I am sure that you Americans are going to beat the Japanese some day, with or without the help of the troops I am holding back for use against the Communists in the northwest. On the other hand, if I let Mao Tse-tung push his propaganda across all of free China, we run the risk—and so do you Americans—of winning for nothing."

In asserting that the Allies would win the War no matter what he did with his armies, Chiang turned out to be correct. Nevertheless, the War might have been shortened had Chiang pursued the Japanese more actively. As things were, it looked in 1944 as though the Japanese, while retreating across the Pacific, might still be victorious in China. In April the Japanese again launched a major offensive that quickly lived up to the ambitious image suggested by its code name,

Ichigo, or Number One. South of the Yangtze, the Imperial forces overran and destroyed the string of Nationalist air bases built by the Americans and operated by the U.S. Fourteenth Air Force.

Alarmed by the success of the Japanese drive, the Americans began the process that would culminate in their postwar intervention in China. Although Washington continued to favor the Nationalists for the long term, it perceived the immediate value of supplying arms to the Communists and of persuading the two Chinese factions to pool their resources against the Japanese—perhaps even in a coalition government.

The first step toward this goal was to make contact with Mao. With Chiang's reluctant consent, a United States delegation under Colonel David D. Barrett was dispatched to Yenan in the summer of 1944. Barrett was an old China hand. He had learned Chinese in Peking in the 1920s, had served with a U.S. infantry detachment in Tientsin in the early 1930s, and from 1936 until the United States entered the War he had been an assistant military attaché in Japanese-occupied Peking.

The Barrett delegation, which included 18 military and State Department officials, was known as the "Dixie Mission," a nickname inspired by a popular song about the American South, "Is It True What They Say about Dixie?" Yenan, like Dixie, was rebel territory; not much was known about it, and little of that was considered true. Because the Nationalists refused to sanction trips by Western correspondents to Yenan, reliable information about the Communist stronghold was virtually nonexistent.

Colonel Barrett's basic assignment was to open a dialogue with the Communist leaders that would lead to further contacts. He and his group were to size up the Red Army's effectiveness and estimate what kinds and amounts of arms they needed to press the fight against the Japanese. And in the face of nearly two decades of hostility between Nationalists and Communists, the mission was supposed to find a way to resolve the enmity between the two sides and explore the possibilities of Communist participation in a postwar Chinese government.

The Dixie Mission received a cordial welcome in Yenan. The Chinese invited Barrett's group to frequent dinner parties. As Barrett later recalled, the food at these banquets was always excellent; but the liquor, called Mao Tai, was terrible—a powerful concoction "with a definite flavor of coal oil" that "could make you terribly drunk, for it had a kick like a mule."

Dances, held outdoors in a grove of pear trees, were another favorite form of recreation. The music, Barrett wrote, was provided by "a battered phonograph playing scratchy records of ancient vintage." Mao and other top Communists invariably attended these dances, Mao graciously responding to invitations from pig-tailed girls who approached him and said, "Chairman, please dance with me."

During business hours, according to the reports that Barrett filed by courier, the Chairman talked at length about how he looked forward to cooperating with the United States after the War. But for now, Mao urged that the Americans strike in force at China's mainland; he predicted that he could easily push to the coast to link up with the invading Americans. But he could only do this, Mao declared, if he was supplied with American arms.

The time seemed right for a visit by an envoy more senior than Colonel Barrett. On the bright, sunny afternoon of November 6, 1944, a C-47 that had been escorted by American fighter planes from Chungking landed unannounced on an airfield in Yenan. Its principal passenger was Patrick J. Hurley, a tall, extroverted man with a bristling white mustache, resplendent in the beribboned uniform of a U.S. Army major general.

Hurley, in his early sixties and bursting with vitality, was an Oklahoman, a former coal miner and cowboy who had become wealthy dealing in oil and real estate. He was, in addition, shrewd enough to work both sides of the political street. He had served a Republican President, Herbert Hoover, as Secretary of War, and had come to China as the personal emissary of President Roosevelt, a Democrat. Roosevelt had selected him in a wartime gesture of bipartisan solidarity, and because of Hurley's reputation as an effective trouble shooter.

Hurley was unacquainted with Chinese culture or language, and knew nothing at the outset about Chinese politics beyond what he had absorbed from hasty State Department briefings before his departure from Washington. He had spent two months in China, mainly in Chungking, before flying to Yenan. The experience so far had not shaken his vociferous self-assurance; the keystone of his optimism was the conviction that the Communist-Nationalist quarrel was no different from the rivalry between Democrats and Republicans back home.

Learning of Hurley's arrival, Mao and other leaders hastily emerged from their cave dwellings and piled into a battered ambulance; the ambulance was the Chairman's official vehicle, donated—according to the sign on its side—by the New York Laundrymen's National Salvation Association. At the airfield, they jumped out and hurried to the plane to welcome Hurley—by far the highest-ranking foreigner ever to visit the Communist base. The tall American responded by slapping backs and shouting ''Yahoo!''—a Choctaw Indian war whoop that he had learned in Oklahoma—and soon everyone was laughing. With Mao, Chou En-lai and the others, Hurley squeezed into the ambulance for the bumpy ride back to headquarters.

As they drove past a shepherd, Mao, with Colonel Barrett translating, related how he had tended flocks himself as a boy in south China; Hurley countered with stories of life on the range in America. When they crossed a shallow river called the Yen, Mao told how it rose in spring and went dry in summer; Hurley spoke of rivers in Oklahoma so dry that a traveler could spot the fish by the dust they stirred up; the puzzled Chinese laughed politely. That evening Hurley attended a gala banquet (given to celebrate the November 7 anniversary of the Bolshevik Revolution) and the festive air prevailed for the rest of his three-day visit.

Before he left Yenan for the return flight to Chungking, Hurley made up his mind to recommend that Mao be sent American arms and equipment. Moreover, he promised Mao personal mediation to bring the warring factions of China together. Mao and the general put their signatures to a proposal for a joint Communist-Nationalist government. The new united front, Hurley hoped, would not only finish off the Japanese but prevent a new outbreak of internal strife. To the accompaniment of Choctaw battle cries, the most ambitious intervention in Chinese affairs ever undertaken by a Western power had begun.

The American involvement was intense and enduring. It lasted two full years after V-J Day, and well after the Chinese countryside had become a fratricidal killing ground.

For much of this time, the Russians also urged reconciliation between Chiang and Mao. Yet rarely did the Chinese parties vying for mastery bend to the wishes of outsiders. Mao, staunch revolutionary and believer in class struggle, and Chiang, stern traditionalist intent on reviving the values of old China, marched to their own martial hymns.

The positions of the antagonists in 1945 were clear enough. As the year opened, the Japanese drive in the south began to run out of steam, leaving Chungking safely beyond its reach. Chiang saw ever fewer reasons to cooperate with the rival Communists, and he refused to sign the agreement Hurley brought back from Yenan. Thus Hurley was forced to choose between Mao and Chiang and, in a decision of lasting import, he found it far easier to back away from the Yenan agreement than to challenge Chiang.

Hurley soon found himself in opposition to a group of young Foreign Service officers from the U.S. Embassy in Chungking who had visited Yenan as members of the Dixie Mission. They had become convinced that it would be wise for the United States to support the Communists as well as the Nationalists in the war against Japan. In an independent report cabled to Washington in February 1945, this group declared that there existed "tremendous internal pressure in China for unity based on a reasonable compromise with the Communists." They argued that "such a policy would be greatly welcomed by a vast majority of the Chinese people, although not by the very small reactionary minority in control of the Kuomintang."

Hurley, who was visiting Washington shortly after the cable arrived, felt betrayed. He decided that those in the Embassy who endorsed the idea of shared power—even though Hurley himself had signed the proposal in Yenan—were conspiring against their own country as well as against the Kuomintang. On his return to Chungking, Hurley arranged to have everyone who had signed the cable transferred out of China. Indeed, when Hurley left China for good later that year he charged that "a considerable section of our State Department is endeavoring to support Communism generally as well as specifically in China."

In Yenan, Mao Tse-tung learned soon enough of Hurley's disaffection. He concluded that he could no longer rely on the United States for support. As the War drew to a close, he took a harder line than ever against Chiang, and he added the Americans to his roster of enemies.

The Seventh Congress of the Chinese Communist Party, the first such gathering in 17 years, convened in Yenan in the spring of 1945 and stretched into the summer. Only six months had passed since the gala reception for Patrick Hurley, but the political winds had changed dramatically. The United States was now a target of Communist rhetoric, and the party congress made it clear that the Communists had finally resolved to go it alone: "The United States government's policy of supporting Chiang Kai-shek against the Communists shows the brazenness of the U.S. reactionaries," Mao told the 752 delegates who had come from all across China.

At the same time, in Chungking, Chiang was speaking of his cause—meaning personal control of China—as a sacred trust left to him by Sun Yat-sen. To Yenan Radio, however, he was a "lunatic," and the people around him were "gangsters."

Then portentous events began to unfold at a dizzying pace. On August 2, the Potsdam Conference, setting conditions for an end to the War in the Pacific, came to an end. Throughout the conference, Stalin had reiterated his position on China: He would support any American attempt to unite the country under Chiang. On August 6, the United States dropped the atomic bomb on Hiroshima. On the 8th, the Soviet Union announced that it was entering the war against Japan, and hordes of Russian troops began pouring across the Manchurian border. On the 9th, another atomic bomb was dropped, and much of Nagasaki was obliterated. A day later, word reached both Chungking and Yenan that the Japanese were suing for peace. August 14 became the occasion not only of the Japanese capitulation but also of the signing, in Moscow, of a Chinese-Soviet friendship agreement that reaffirmed Soviet backing for Chiang as China's recognized leader.

The announcement of the treaty staggered the Chinese Communist leadership. Convinced that Soviet support for Chiang made confrontation too dangerous, Mao's Central Committee performed a complete about-face. All criticism of either the Nationalists or the United States was prohibited, and at the end of August, Mao—who under normal circumstances entrusted such missions to Chou En-lai—flew

Though implacable foes, Mao Tse-tung and Chiang Kai-shek manage to force a smile as they toast each other during reconciliation talks convened in Chungking in August and September of 1945 at the urging of the United States. It was the first time the two enemies had met since the Kuomintang-Communist break in 1927, and it would be the last.

to Chungking for a series of talks aimed at achieving unity.

Mao was playing for time. All along, he had spoken of ultimate Communist victory, yet he clearly assumed that such a victory would take decades to achieve. He foresaw a Communist government emerging after a lengthy period of jockeying within the framework of a coalition with the Nationalists. Just before leaving for Chungking he told his closest associates that international pressures made it prudent to agree to new talks with the Kuomintang. "At present, the Soviet Union, the United States and Great Britain all disapprove of civil war in China," Mao explained, adding that "if the Kuomintang still wants to launch civil war, it will put itself in the wrong in the eyes of the whole nation and the whole world."

In his analysis, Mao overestimated the British. Their day in Asia was done, and they had neither the force nor the will to influence events. But Mao clearly understood the power of the other two Allies. It was the presence of American and Soviet armed forces, which had moved in to fill the vacuum left by the Japanese, that effectively kept Communists and Nationalists from each other's throats.

The Russians entered the picture first. By V-J Day, less than a week after the Soviets had started across the Manchurian border, their presence was formidable. A 300,000-man force commanded by Marshal Rodion Y. Malinovsky moved like a juggernaut across northern Manchuria toward the city of Harbin. Within two weeks, Malinovsky's army had taken all of Manchuria, from the Soviet border through Tsitsihar and Harbin in the north, to Dairen and Port Arthur on the southern tip of the Liaotung peninsula.

Soon the Chungking government was bitterly protesting what it called the Rape of Manchuria. During their 14 years in the northeast, the Japanese had built Manchuria almost from scratch into China's only large industrial region. Manchuria had received limited attention from American bombers, and when Japan surrendered, the priceless industrial complex was still largely intact. It boasted nearly every kind of industry needed by a modern nation—factories for aircraft and automobiles, aluminum mills and steel furnaces, plants to turn out rubber products and munitions, even giant breweries and the largest complex of cigarette factories in the Far East. In all, Manchuria contained 70 per cent of China's industry.

Such, at any rate, was the case until the Soviet Army

moved in. Observers who toured Manchuria after the Russians had been there a while were in for a shock. In February 1946, George Moorad, an American reporter, visited the city of Mukden, the provincial capital and formerly Manchuria's most important industrial center; he reported seeing "mile after mile of skeletons and emptiness, shells of buildings, frameworks of factories in which great holes had been gouged to permit the exit of machinery. Mukden looked as if a horde of steel- and concrete-eating termites had passed through." The Russians had methodically uprooted and shipped home Manchuria's industry for use in rebuilding their own devastated economy.

Observing the pillage of Manchuria, Mao Tse-tung was careful not to echo the protests of Chiang. Although the Soviet friendship pact had forced him to return to a conciliatory line with Chungking, the Soviet presence in Manchuria also offered immediate opportunities for Communist cooperation and expansion. General Chu Teh quickly ordered units of the Chinese Red Army to move north of the Great Wall and link up with the Soviets.

The first encounters between Chinese and Soviet soldiers were not particularly auspicious. The two nations traditionally had little liking for each other, and a Soviet commander, getting his first look at the Chinese, described them as a "people of low culture." American newsmen who witnessed the early meetings reported that the Russian officers did not consider the Chinese true Communists because their revolution was rooted in the peasant rather than the urban working class. The Chinese, according to one newsman, were embittered by such treatment, angered by the dismantling of the factories, and "plainly dubious about their well-muscled allies."

The Soviet attitude reflected ancient Russian prejudices toward the Chinese. Yet overriding the ethnic rivalry was a powerful ideological kinship: Russians and Chinese acknowledged that they were soldiers together in a common cause. When a Chinese force commanded by General Lin Piao began to advance through Manchuria in September of 1945, the Russians did not attempt to stop it. Within weeks, 100,000 Chinese Communist soldiers and no fewer than 50,000 political officers, or cadres, had moved into the northeast. There they launched a massive recruiting campaign among the populace, and by early 1946 the Communists claimed 300,000 men under arms in Manchuria.

Like the basic Soviet empathy for fellow Communists, the assistance the United States gave to Nationalist China was rooted in ideological kinship. Although the United States insisted that it would not help Chiang eliminate Mao and his followers, the Americans could no more resist providing support to Chiang's "Free China" than the Soviets could resist aiding fellow Reds.

In the immediate postwar years, the United States would consistently come down on Chiang's side. Lines to Mao were not completely cut, however. Some members of the Dixie Mission remained in Yenan until the spring of 1946. Their continuing presence was an indication of Washington's willingness to compromise. General Wedemeyer, the U.S. military commander in China, repeatedly tried to persuade the Nationalists to come to terms with Yenan. Yet none of these efforts were sufficient to convince Mao of American good will.

One factor that caused Mao to lose faith in the Americans was the political downfall of a Dixie Mission diplomat: In June 1945 news had reached Yenan of the arrest on espionage charges of John S. Service, the son of a China missionary and one of the Foreign Service officers whom Hurley had sent home. Service was accused of leaking to a Leftist American magazine classified State Department documents that presented Mao in a favorable light and recommended that the United States support him. The grand jury that heard the case refused to indict Service. But Mao was right about the overall political implications of the incident: Eventually Service and all his colleagues who had disagreed with Hurley would be forced out of public life. David Barrett of the Dixie Mission, denied his general's star, wound up as a teacher of Chinese at the University of Colorado.

Even as the political situation moved inexorably toward a break in relations with Mao, Washington made one more major effort to help unite China. President Truman summoned out of brief retirement General of the Army George C. Marshall, one of the United States' most respected military leaders and a major architect of the Allies' World War II victory. On the 21st of December, 1945, Marshall arrived in Chungking with a presidential mandate to seek—yet again —a Communist-Nationalist accommodation.

Victorious Russian soldiers, who entered the war against Japan in its final week, mingle with Manchurian civilians — including a farmer who balances baskets overflowing with cabbages on his shoulder. The Nationalist Chinese flag displayed by the man at left was still an appropriate symbol of welcome in 1945, when the Soviet Union recognized Chiang Kai-shek's regime as China's legitimate government.

On January 10, Marshall did manage to get both sides to agree to a formal truce. A complex, multitiered system of three-man committees, each with a representative of the Kuomintang, the Communists and the United States, was set up to enforce the pact. A Political Consultative Conference was convened with the hope that it would be the forerunner of a broadly based parliament for a reconstituted coalition government.

As the machinery for unity was being set in place, however, Mao came under intense pressure from within his own party; his most trusted lieutenants urged him to draw back from a coalition with the Nationalists. Communist field commanders, continuing to gain ground in their recruiting efforts outside the cities, urged Mao not to make peace. Chiang was under similar pressure from within the Kuomintang. Mass meetings, called by the three-man committees to explain the truce, were broken up by Nationalist thugs. The Kuomintang ordered its own mass meetings, os-tensibly to protest the Soviet looting in Manchuria, but these meetings were easily turned into demonstrations against home-grown Communists.

By the end of February 1946, the Marshall-sponsored truce agreement was breaking down, and progress toward a coalition government was stalled. In north China and Manchuria, where the people had suffered severely at the hands of the Japanese and their Manchurian puppets, the demand for revenge was fierce. In the Communists' expanding ''liberated areas,'' people went about settling old scores. Punishments were extreme: One man accused as a ''people's enemy'' was hitched to a plow like a draft animal and lashed to death with whips.

At the same time, some of the worst elements in Chinese society followed the Nationalist troops who were reclaiming villages below the Yangtze. Correspondents who traveled with the Nationalists cabled back stories of ghastly atrocities. Men, women and even children suspected of

being pro-Communist were hurled into pits and trenches and buried alive.

As the forces of Nationalism and Communism became more violently polarized, the military barriers erected by the United States and the Soviet Union to keep the two Chinese adversaries apart began to crumble. Under pressure to bring war veterans home, the United States began withdrawing seasoned Marine units and replacing them with young men who had never seen battle. Ostensibly serving in peacetime, they were reluctant to risk their lives in someone else's fight. And in April of 1946, the Marines began withdrawing units without replacing them at all.

A month earlier the Soviets had begun to pull out of Manchuria. General Malinovsky had never made good on his government's promise to Chungking to transfer control of Manchuria to the Kuomintang. The Chinese Communists who controlled the Manchurian countryside—in part because of Soviet cooperation—rushed in to take the cities as

Malinovsky's troops abandoned them. In response, the Nationalists pushed to the northeast in strength to challenge the Chinese Red Army.

Mao had often predicted that China's cities would fall to the Communists indirectly, after a take over of the countryside. But the indirect method took time; it was quicker to conquer cities directly, although a head-on conventional assault required more numerous, better-armed forces than the Chinese Red Army had usually enjoyed. Recently, however, Mao had been saying that the time was nearly ripe for a switch of strategies—"from the country to the city"—and his army was growing strong enough to fight pitched battles rather than hit-and-run guerrilla engagements. At the end of March came the first test of whether that time had come. The Communists decided to do battle at Szepingkai, the southernmost Manchurian city under Communist control.

During the next two weeks Lin Piao, the Communist commander in Manchuria, concentrated 40,000 men and engaged an advancing Nationalist division 40 miles southwest of Szepingkai. An observer later described in horror the "human sea" with which the Nationalists were confronted: Communist units of company size, he wrote, assaulted single Nationalist machine-gun positions. "No matter how many of them got killed, there was always another horde coming behind them."

The Nationalists, however, stood fast. Both sides committed reinforcements, and soon 140,000 men were slugging it out in the largest battle in China since the Japanese invasion of 1937. Although not lacking in manpower, the Communists were inferior to the Nationalists in heavy artillery and air power. In May, Lin Piao abandoned Szepingkai and withdrew his army to the north, giving up city after city as he retreated.

Chiang Kai-shek, who had proudly reestablished his capital at Nanking on May 1 after an absence of nine years, went to the northeast front himself to direct the pursuit of an apparently beaten enemy. General Marshall urged Chiang to call off the offensive and return to Nanking, but the Generalissimo refused. He pushed his campaign until early June, when the last Communist troops were driven across the Sungari River in central Manchuria.

During the rout, statements emerged from Yenan hinting that the Communists were ready to talk peace—or at least a

In a rare moment of accord in March of 1946, Communist and Nationalist leaders stand side by side with American mediator General George C. Marshall, during an airport ceremony at Yenan in the mountainous province of Shensi. From left are: future Communist Premier Chou En-lai, General Marshall, Communist General Chu Teh, Nationalist General Chang Chih-chung and Communist Party Chairman Mao Tse-tung.

British troops sent to garrison Hong Kong following the Japanese surrender in 1945 man artillery emplacements that guard the 404-square-mile colony.

THE RECLAIMING OF HONG KONG

A priority for Britain in 1945 was to reoccupy Hong Kong, its prosperous colony on China's southeast coast—despite American urging that it be returned to China.

When Japan capitulated, Britain moved swiftly and in strength, dispatching a Royal Navy task force to Hong Kong. For appearances' sake, the surrender of Japanese forces there was accepted in the names of both Britain and China; but the British had no intention of sharing power. Nor were they seriously challenged: Chiang Kai-shek was too preoccupied with the Communist threat to his regime to take on the British too.

When the Communists came to power in 1949, they saw Hong Kong as a valuable commercial and financial pipeline to the world, and allowed the colony to remain an imperialist enclave.

Refugees, at right, stream into Hong Kong from China in 1950, passing some going the other way.

cease-fire. Mao's deputy, Chou En-lai, let General Marshall know that a halt in the fighting might be possible, even though the Communist leaders disagreed among themselves on the issue and were becoming increasingly bitter toward the United States for providing Chiang with the tools of war. Marshall, the persistent mediator, succeeded by early June in persuading the antagonists to sign another temporary cease-fire. In the north, the agreement confirmed the separation of the Communist and Nationalist forces by the Sungari River. Elsewhere, however, the Communists soon broke the truce; in areas between the Great Wall and the Yellow River, where the Communists had controlled the countryside throughout the War, they intensified their attacks on Nationalist strongholds in the towns and cities.

These renewed hostilities were in step with increasing Communist bellicosity toward the United States. In late July of 1946, a unit of the Red Army—now called the People's Liberation Army, or PLA—ambushed a U.S. Marine supply convoy southeast of Peking, killing three uniformed Americans and wounding another 12. The Communists claimed that the Marines were fighting side by side with Nationalists. The United States angrily denied the charge, and warned that in the future Marines would retaliate if fired upon.

In Nanking, John Leighton Stuart, the American Ambassador to Chiang's government, who had spent half a century in China with the missionary movement, issued a press release indicating that American mediation between Nationalists and Communists was coming to an end. In mid-August George Marshall threw in his hand. He told an aide, "This is it. It's all over. We're through in China."

The U.S. never formally abandoned its role as mediator. Marshall remained in Nanking until January 1947, when he was recalled to Washington to become Truman's Secretary of State. As soon as he was installed at the State Department, however, Marshall saw to it that the last of the Marines were withdrawn. That same January, Truman sent one more team, led by General Wedemeyer, to attempt further negotiations between the warring sides. But Marshall had been right; the effort was in vain.

In mid-July, Chiang ordered a massive sweep through the north of China designed to destroy the Communists there. Once again the Nationalist strategy was to surround and squeeze the main Communist base area. This campaign, combined with the earlier victory in Manchuria, created a picture of Nationalist predominance. Chiang's forces controlled all of China south of the Yangtze River as well as the provinces of China's far west, all the major cities of the north, and the entire seacoast. By American estimate, the Nationalists had three million men under arms at the beginning of 1947, compared with one million for the Communists. The Communists had only one fifth as many small arms as their adversaries, and nothing to balance the Nationalist tanks, aircraft and heavy artillery. Although a third of the Chinese people were living in areas directly administered by the Communists, the PLA's territory was confined exclusively to poor and rural China.

Such were the visible facts. They did not, however, tell a complete story. Mao's men, after the lesson learned at Szepingkai, were again practicing infiltration rather than head-on conflict; they continued to hit and run, still able to blend into a countryside in which the people were their friends.

Although the Nationalists appeared to have gained thousands of square miles of territory, they suffered from the same problem that had afflicted the Japanese in China a few years earlier. Whenever the Nationalists established a front, the PLA moved in behind it. Recruiting in such areas swelled the Communist ranks—often at the direct expense of the Nationalist armed forces. Many individual soldiers deserted to the Reds, and in one spectacular defection in January of 1947, Chiang's entire 26th Division—8,000 men—switched sides, taking their arms and equipment with them. The division's leaders had decided that their future lay with Mao.

Such blatant disloyalty aroused a violent paranoia in Chiang. Increasingly he came to see disagreement of any kind as treason. His police harassed anyone whose reliability was questioned. Many thousands of Chinese in Nationalist areas were officially labeled as suspect; hundreds were jailed and executed.

Mao's strategy, by contrast, was to keep his position flexible. He had no qualms about relinquishing territory temporarily, if such a move seemed to be strategically necessary and if it would contribute to his long-term objectives. In March of 1947 the Nationalist forces in the northwest captured Yenan itself, but Mao was unruffled. "Empty cities don't matter," he declared. "The aim is to destroy the enemy's army." Far from being sentimentally attached to Yenan, he added that the longtime Communist base was, "after all, only caves."

The Nationalists proclaimed the capture of Yenan a resounding victory. But it was a hollow one. Communist forces in other parts of the country had already launched operations that would seize the initiative from the Kuomintang. The primary target was Manchuria.

In January 1947, Lin Piao launched a campaign to neutralize the region's extensive rail system and defeat the well-equipped Nationalist troops defending it. Four Communist offensives in four months were beaten back at great cost, but in May a fifth attack succeeded in encircling Szepingkai, the battleground of a year earlier, and capturing a key airfield near the rail center of Changchun. By June 10, the PLA had also cut off Changchun, interrupting rail traffic throughout the region.

Fighting raged in Manchuria until July, when rains made offensive operations impossible. The opposing forces took stock: Chiang's armies had surrendered half the territory they had occupied in 1946; they had also lost two thirds of their rail mileage and enormous quantities of equipment and matériel; and their combat strength had been drained by defections. The Communist troops were still woefully short of heavy weapons, and their casualty rate early in the campaign had been painfully high. But they had withstood the setbacks well, maintaining discipline and high morale in the ranks.

In September, Lin Piao renewed the offensive. His men succeeded in shutting down what remained of Manchuria's railroad system and laid siege to Mukden. By the end of the year, 250,000 of Chiang's best troops had been pinned down in various Manchurian cities.

To the south, the Communists were also on the move. Beginning in mid-August, twin PLA columns swept southward 300 miles from the Yellow River, advancing at a rate of 30 miles a day against weak resistance. Not until their advance units reached the north bank of the Yangtze did the Communists pause to consolidate their gains.

As 1948 began, the once-dominant Nationalists were clearly on the defensive. Their troops were defecting in

The Communist Eighth Route Army parades through Peking on February 3, 1949, their trucks adorned with propaganda posters depicting Chinese Nationalists in craven flight from the Red Army. Many heavy vehicles in the procession had been captured by the Communists two months earlier when they intercepted six trainloads of supplies shipped from the United States and intended for the Nationalist forces.

ever-increasing numbers. Logistics were so poor that few units were adequately fed, and some were left to fend entirely for themselves. Enlisted men were routinely beaten with bamboo cudgels and iron bars for minor infractions. Chiang did not help matters when he began ordering the execution of officers who he felt had failed him in combat.

Chiang clung with a desperate grip to what was left of Manchuria, even though abandoning the isolated territory would have freed several hundred thousand men for operations elsewhere in China. They were soon needed. At the end of February 1948, the Communists recaptured Yenan. In March, they took Loyang, a strategically important rail center in central China; possession of Loyang enabled the Communists to link their newly established bases in Honan province with their strongholds in the north.

In May, the Red Army commanders felt secure enough to concentrate their forces in numbers greater than at any time since their 1946 reverse at Szepingkai.

Committing 200,000 regulars, supported by guerrillas and a number of captured tanks, the Communists engaged 250,000 Nationalist troops between Kaifeng, the capital of Honan province, and the nearby railroad town of Cheng-chow. Part of the Communist force, under General Ch'en I, captured Kaifeng, stripped its depots of tons of supplies, then slipped out of the city. Nationalist troops pursuing Ch'en collided with the main Communist force south of Kaifeng. A set-piece battle ensued. After two weeks of fighting in which both sides sustained terrible losses, the Nationalists drove their enemy from the field. But the People's Liberation Army had demonstrated that it could engage in, and survive, a major confrontation.

Just as significantly, when the Nationalists reentered Kaifeng, they found the provincial capital not only bare of supplies, but well seeded with Communist agents. Even the Kuomintang propaganda chief of Kaifeng, it turned out, had been converted. In other parts of China, the Communists were gaining strength without even having to fight. Governors of provinces, mayors of cities and division commanders began deserting the Nationalist cause in the face of what they perceived as a Communist tide.

By the autumn of 1948, the People's Liberation Army outnumbered the Nationalist forces by 2 to 1. All through the north, white flags were being waved by Nationalist units. During September and October alone, Chiang lost 300,000 troops in battle and to defection. By November, the Communists controlled Manchuria and almost all of north China, including, for the first time, the major cities.

The Kuomintang's treatment of the people still under its control grew increasingly harsh. Police raided the universities and arrested students; many were beaten and some died. The authorities drew up lists of the government's ever more numerous enemies, both real and imagined. Chinese intellectuals, who generally had tried to keep aloof from the struggle and had stayed in Nationalist-controlled cities, now fled in fear to Communist territory.

In Nationalist areas, inflation ran wild, entrenching corruption and hardship. In 1937 the Chinese dollar had been exchanged at the rate of two to the American dollar; by June of 1948 the exchange rate had become 2 million to 1; by August it was 11 million to 1. The situation was reminiscent of Germany in the 1920s: On paydays, Chinese workers stuffed gunny sacks full of their nearly worthless currency and exchanged it as quickly as they could for food, cooking oil or coal before the passage of a few more hours debased the money's value even more. Even sackfuls of money did not go far. A pound of rice now cost well over a quarter of a million Chinese dollars.

Chiang tried desperately to stem the ruinous inflation through currency reform. On the 19th of August he ordered the Chinese dollar converted to a so-called gold yuan, whose worth the government guaranteed at the rate of 4 to 1 U.S. dollar. Citizens were required to turn in their old currency—along with all of their gold, silver and foreign currency—in return for the appropriate sums of gold yuan. But soon even the new currency began to lose value. As it plummeted, it wiped out the savings of the middle class—and also destroyed the remnants of any confidence they had retained in Chiang's rule.

Communist areas were relatively better off. China's rural system of cottage industries provided such basics as clothing and cooking utensils; those items that could not be made locally could frequently be acquired in barter with Nationalist-controlled areas—with the transactions closely supervised by party officials. In return, the Communist areas supplied food, which was badly needed by people living under the Kuomintang.

Chiang, seeking a respite, broadcast a New Year's message in 1949 that he described as an "appeal for peace." Mao responded that he would make no agreements; the PLA, he said, was in a position to crush the Nationalist apparatus "into dust and extinction."

The surest symbols of Communist ascendancy were the two Chinese capitals: Peking, the ancient Imperial seat, and Nanking, Chiang's government stronghold. Peking had been surrounded for weeks by the Communists when, at the end of January 1949, units of the old Eighth Route Army entered the city without firing a shot—following negotiations with the local Nationalist commander, who surrendered rather than subject the city to destruction. The Communists then put on a victory procession that featured students and workers performing traditional dances of China, and displays such as stilt-walking along the parade route. A contemporary note was struck by what a Western observer called "cheerleaders"—young people who enthusiastically led groups of spectators in chanting the political slogans of Chairman Mao.

Thousands of veterans of the Eighth Route Army dominated the parade, described by one witness as "probably the greatest demonstration of Chinese military might in history." What made it so impressive, he said, was the amount of American military equipment on display—he counted 250 heavy vehicles in an hour, along with "innumerable jeeps and other smaller vehicles," and weapons ranging from rifles to heavy artillery. Nearly all of it had been taken, in one way or another, from the Nationalists.

The last great campaign of the civil war had begun late in 1948 in the region north of Chiang's capital, Nanking. Over a period of 65 days, half a million men were committed on each side. The Communists' strategy evolved in two stages: First they cut the Nationalists' communications with the surrounding areas; then they maneuvered to separate Chiang's units from one another and proceeded to defeat them piecemeal. Before the campaign was over, most of the Nationalists' remaining military strength—including the last of their tanks—had been captured or destroyed. Two of their senior generals had been killed, and two others had been taken prisoner.

In April of 1949 the PLA occupied Nanking. Chiang's government fled south to Canton. The Communists crossed the Yangtze in massive waves and went on to overrun south China. U.S. Ambassador John Leighton Stuart, the former missionary-educator, somewhat sadly explained the dramatic turn of events. Mao's cause, he said, had proved to be "a dynamic movement fostering among millions those qualities of which China had stood so palpably in need, qualities which Christian missions and other forces had been slowly inculcating among so pitifully few."

As the year wore on, the Nationalist government stayed constantly on the move, retreating westward as it had during the Japanese war—pausing only briefly in Chungking, the wartime capital, before moving still deeper into Szechwan province. At Chengtu, late in the year, the government announced a dramatic decision: A new capital would be established at Taipei on the island of Taiwan, a former Japanese colony known to Westerners as Formosa, 100 miles from the mainland. Many Kuomintang officials, officers and men, and other Nationalist supporters had already fled there from the coastal ports. Eventually two million mainlanders migrated to the island. Chiang joined them by plane on December 10 and resumed command of what remained of his government.

Mao Tse-tung had already established himself in Peking, moving into comfortable quarters within the complex of ornate palaces called the Forbidden City, the historic home of China's Emperors. On October 1, 1949, with the civil war as good as over, Mao appeared in the vast T'ien An Men Square outside the palace walls. Standing with Chou En-lai, Chu Teh and others who had been with him since his days as an outlaw in the hills, he formally proclaimed the People's Republic of China.

IMAGES OF CIVIL WAR

Shanghai citizens struggle desperately to exchange their plummeting currency for gold in this picture by famed French photojournalist Henri Cartier-Bresson.

EYEWITNESS TO A COMMUNIST TRIUMPH

Ma Hung-kuei, a powerful warlord and Nationalist ally, sits for Cartier-Bresson beneath scrolls describing the responsibilities of a good general.

Late in 1948, *Life* sent French photographer Henri Cartier-Bresson *(above)* to cover the dramatic events unfolding in China. He arrived in Peking as the civil war was entering its climactic phase, and after spending several days in the besieged Nationalist stronghold, he caught the last plane out just as Communist soldiers came pouring onto the airfield.

Cartier-Bresson's next stop was Shanghai, where the population of five million had been swollen, in his words, "by thousands upon thousands of refugees who settled like crows in any available space, exhausted and famished." From Shanghai the photographer ranged through China's eastern provinces, rushing in mid-April 1949 to Nanking, the Nationalists' capital, where he witnessed the collapse and flight of the remnants of Chiang Kai-shek's government.

Cartier-Bresson left China in September 1949 on a ship carrying refugee foreigners from Shanghai to Hong Kong. What perhaps impressed him most during his 10-month stay were the signs of permanence and continuity that provided a backdrop to the violent upheaval at center stage. Religious pilgrims, he noted, still visited the Buddhist shrines in Hangchow; traditional woodcuts remained on exhibit in Shanghai; and in Peking he could still photograph an old man walking alone in front of the Imperial Palace, "looking very small," he reported, "in the midst of all this history."

Youngsters in Shanghai watch parading Communist soldiers after the city's fall. The portraits are of Mao (right) and General Chu Teh.

Seemingly oblivious to the conflict raging outside the city's gates, workers in Peking weed a palace lawn on a misty morning in December of 1948.

THE CALM BEFORE PEKING'S FALL

Though war often raged within earshot, many aspects of Chinese life seemed impervious to disturbance. Farmers tended their fields; markets hummed with commerce in many cities; old men took their seats each day at favorite teahouses.

Cartier-Bresson marveled at the calm detachment of the Chinese. In the days before Peking fell, he watched its citizens gather at bulletin boards to read the war news. "Judging from their dispassionate attitudes," he wrote, "they might have been looking at real estate ads or want-ad notices. Everyone must have been aware that the Kuomintang government was losing rapidly in the face of the determined People's Liberation Army. But the course of history would not interrupt their lives."

An elderly former retainer (right) of the imperial court gossips with a friend on a Peking street.

In an open-air market in Peking, barbers do a brisk business, and at a table in the background a policeman has his fortune read.

Conscripts for the Nationalists' last-ditch defense of Peking wait to receive their orders in a courtyard of the Imperial Palace.

RELUCTANT RECRUITS FOR A LAST STAND

The war beyond Peking's walls became a hard reality in December 1948 for the men who were called up at the last minute to defend the ancient capital. The Nationalist command asked for 10,000 fresh troops. Despite the promise of gifts and special privileges for those who enlisted, only 14 men volunteered. The rest were rounded up from among Peking's remaining young men—and from among the city's shopkeepers and businessmen.

As the new recruits assembled one cold morning in the courtyard of the Imperial Palace, Cartier-Bresson noted their mood: "Resigned, impassive, they had no illusions about their capacity to change history's course." The photographer's assessment was correct: In a matter of weeks, Mao Tse-tung's troops would invest Peking without firing a shot.

Standing before gift boxes for the few volunteers, a Nationalist general addresses his green troops.

Anxious women look for sons and husbands among the recruits, who were conscripted so hastily that some of them were unable to notify their families.

159

Beneath a portrait of Sun Yat-sen, the Nationalist parliament ends its final session in Nanking in April 1949, shortly before the Communists took over the city.

A GOVERNMENT IN FLIGHT

Nanking in the spring of 1949 seemed almost in a trance. The parliament continued to meet and Nationalist soldiers lolled about Hsuan-Wu Lake Park, even though a few miles away Communist troops were battering at the city's defenses.

When word came that the Communists had broken through, there ensued a mad scramble to evacuate the capital. Legisla-

tors fled by plane—some, noted Cartier-Bresson, carrying their tennis rackets. Army officers and their families crowded the southbound trains. Most troops were left to flee on foot, or on any available vehicle—trucks, jeeps, pedicabs, bicycles.

The last retreating soldiers left Nanking on April 23. At 7 a.m. the next day, the People's Liberation Army marched in.

Demoralized Nationalist soldiers wait near
a railroad crossing for transportation out
of Nanking—and away from the shooting.

Two Nationalist soldiers—one of them
already out of uniform—leave Nanking with
their belongings piled in a pedicab. Much
of what the retreating soldiers took with them
had been looted from homes and shops.

Shouldering a sack of looted flour, a woman attracts little notice as she runs across a Nanking street. Civilians took the things they needed most: food and fuel.

Nanking citizens get their first look at the soldiers of the victorious Red Army.

NEW MASTERS IN CHIANG'S CAPITAL

Except for a brief outbreak of looting, Nanking's transition from Nationalist capital to provincial Communist city was peaceful. The fighting had taken place outside the city, and when Mao's Army marched in, people greeted the Communists with curiosity. There was no resistance.

In the days that followed, in fact, a holiday mood took hold. Cartier-Bresson reported that the city's walls blossomed with victory posters, shops closed up, people filled the streets and the young among them staged impromptu dances. When the celebrating was finished, the pace of life returned to its familiar beat, almost as though there had never been a civil war.

Cartier-Bresson captures the peaceful mood in Hangchow, where a child stands beneath a laundry pole and a barber plies his trade.

A youngster browses at a sidewalk bookstall before a poster exhorting workers to greater productivity.

6

The prospect of better times that beguiled most people around the world with the coming of peace was a dream whose fulfillment eluded millions of Asians. Few were more frustrated than the peoples of Korea and Indochina: Long held in thrall by alien colonizers, they had hoped that the Allied victory would end the domination of their countries by foreigners. But it was not soon to be.

True, the Japanese were expelled from Korea, which they had ruled with an iron fist since 1905. But two new sets of outlanders—Americans and Russians—took their places, confronting each other on Korean territory in deepening antagonism. Indochina for almost a century had been a French preserve, and the guns of war were barely silenced when the French moved to regain their colonial eminence there —in the face of an independence movement dominated by home-grown Communists.

On a night late in August of 1945 two clusters of three parachutes each blossomed over Vietnam. Clinging to the shroud lines were the advance guard of France's bid to re-establish control in Indochina. Three of the chutists landed in a rice field in the southern part of Vietnam, which the French called Cochin China. Their leader, Colonel Henri Cédile, had been appointed Commissioner of Cochin China by Charles de Gaulle's provisional government. Cédile's first encounter that night with the people he had come to preside over was not encouraging: The Vietnamese delivered Cédile and his companions to the Japanese, whose troops had entered the country in 1940 and still controlled it, since no Allied force had yet arrived to take their surrender. Cédile was stripped and forced to kneel before a Japanese soldier who held high a sword; after an agonizing wait, Cédile heard the Japanese around him laugh, and he realized that his life would be spared. Instead of killing Cédile and his men, the Japanese took them to Saigon, the capital of Cochin China, as their prisoners.

The other three parachutists, jumping from a second plane, came down in northern Vietnam. They were led by Major Pierre Messmer, who had been appointed French Commissioner in Hanoi, and their treatment paralleled that of their comrades in the south. Captured by Vietnamese, Messmer and his men were imprisoned and given poisoned food; one man died. After several weeks, Messmer and

CONTESTS WITH COMMUNISM

the other survivor escaped and made their way to China.

At the end of September the French tried again, appointing diplomat Jean Sainteny, a wartime Resistance hero who was head of the French military mission in southern China, to replace Messmer. Sainteny was allowed by the Vietnamese to take up residence in Hanoi. Nevertheless, the treatment given the vanguard group of Frenchmen would have been unthinkable in the long era of French domination that World War II had interrupted. During the War years, seismic political changes had transformed the safe colonial world of French Indochina forever and had convinced many Vietnamese that French rule was a thing of the past.

The first visible upheaval had come harshly and without warning in March 1945, when the Japanese moved aggressively to obliterate the French colonial regime that was still effectively operating in Indochina. France's capitulation in 1940 to Germany, Japan's ally, had left a French colonial garrison 50,000 strong under the nominal control of the new French government at Vichy. Japanese forces had moved into Vietnam without a fight, and thenceforth the two powers coexisted. The Japanese left administration and law enforcement to the French, while they used Vietnam as a base to stage invasions of other parts of Southeast Asia.

The men of the two armies got along rather well. Over the years a pattern of small, genial gestures evolved; French officers gave ceremonial cocktail parties for their Japanese counterparts to mark such occasions as the arrival of a new unit commander. And the hospitality was returned. Once France was liberated in mid-1944, however, the Japanese grew wary, fearing French collaboration with American forces in the Philippines, only 700 air miles away.

On the 9th of March, 1945, all still seemed well: A French captain was refereeing a basketball game between Japanese soldiers and local residents of Hacoi, about 130 miles northeast of Hanoi; French and Japanese officers were pouring *apéritifs* for one another at various garrisons and headquarters.

Then the Japanese struck. Senior French officers were arrested—in their quarters or while guests of the Japanese. The basketball referee at Hacoi was told to order his men, in writing, to surrender; when he refused, he was tortured and he later died. Japanese troops attacked French garrisons, in some cases with extraordinary ferocity. At Hagiang, on the Chinese border, the Japanese used French women and children as shields as they advanced. At Fort Brière de l'Isle, another northern post, captured French troops were lined up and machine-gunned; the men sang the ''Marseillaise'' as they died. At Langson, Japanese soldiers took two French officials to the fort's gate; when the men refused to plead with the fort's defenders to surrender, they were beheaded on the spot. Then the fort was overrun and its defenders massacred; the only survivor was a soldier who was thrown into a ditch filled with corpses and left for dead.

Elsewhere, French troops were treated less brutally, but all those who survived the fighting—except for 6,000 who escaped to China—were herded into prisons or fenced compounds. France's grip on Vietnam had been broken.

Under France, which had completed its conquest of Indochina in 1888, Vietnam had been administered in three segments, all of them relatively rich in rice and sugar cane. They were Cochin China in the south, with its capital at Saigon and rubber plantations in the Mekong River delta; Tonkin, in the mineral-rich north, whose chief city, Hanoi, was capital of all Indochina; and the large area in the center of the country called Annam, with the ancient city of Hue as its capital. Hue had been the seat of the area's rulers since 1635, and an imperial capital since 1802. The French had shrewdly maintained the forms of imperial rule while stripping the throne of Annam of all real power. Also left nominally intact were the neighboring kingdoms of Laos and Cambodia, although the French had taken control as effectively there as in Vietnam.

Since 1932, a husky 5-foot-10-inch-tall aristocrat named Bao Dai, who had been educated in France and kept a villa on the French Riviera, had reigned at Hue on behalf of the French as Emperor of Annam. His duties were almost entirely ceremonial.

The Japanese, after wiping out all French control in March 1945, offered to keep Bao Dai on the throne of Annam and to add Tonkin to his domain. Bao Dai accepted the offer, even though it was tendered only on condition that his realm become part of the Greater East Asia Coprosperity Sphere, as the Japanese called their wartime empire. Bao Dai thus became a puppet of the Japanese as he had been of the French. But he was ambitious. In the War's last days he pressed the Japanese to add Cochin China to his domain and they agreed, chary of provoking the Emperor's subjects.

Bao Dai took his role seriously. When first enthroned, he had eliminated customs that he considered outdated, such as the rule requiring persons addressing the Emperor to touch their foreheads to the ground. "A country that does not change is a dead country," he had said, while pledging to strive for progress in cooperation with the French. In 1945 he adopted the same attitude toward the Japanese; at the same time, he looked around for fellow Vietnamese to serve as ministers in what he hoped would become the independent government of his enlarged domain. His search had only scant success; men willing to serve in such uncertain circumstances were few and unreliable.

Unfortunately for Bao Dai, most able Vietnamese had decided to fight the Japanese rather than make deals with them. Their resistance movement was led by Ho Chi Minh, a frail man in his midfifties whose wispy hair was turning white. Ho had spent three decades in exile, mostly in Europe where he had shaped a career as a revolutionary. In 1920 he had been present at the founding of the French Communist Party at Tours; in Canton, China, in 1930 he had organized the Vietnamese Communist Party, which that same year had led a bloody uprising against the French in northern Annam. Suppressed at a cost of 10,000 Vietnamese lives, the rebellion had nevertheless established the Communists as the most formidable anti-French force in Indochina. Ho returned to Vietnam in 1941 and immediately began assembling an organization called the Vietminh (Vietnamese Independence League), which was controlled by Communists but included many non-Communist nationalist parties and individuals.

During the final year of the War a strong relationship developed between the Vietminh and the United States when the American Office of Strategic Services (OSS) looked for ways to assist anti-Japanese guerrillas in Indochina. Vietminh guerrilla fighters, commanded by General Vo Nguyen Giap, were the only effective source of intelligence about Japanese movements inside Vietnam. The OSS also asked the Vietminh to help American fliers who were forced down in territory controlled by the Japanese—a service the Vietminh performed effectively. All along, the Vietminh avoided close combat with the Japanese, believing that it was

foolish to suffer casualties fighting against an enemy who would be soon defeated anyway. Nevertheless, General Giap's forces provided the OSS with information and, in return, received some American weapons and equipment, airdropped into the jungle.

The Vietminh spread its influence throughout northern Vietnam, and as the War drew to a close it took control of the disparate forces there that hoped to make Vietnam independent. On August 16, 1945, one day after Emperor Hirohito called on the Japanese people to lay down their arms, a provisional Vietnamese government was formed with Ho at its head; the Vietminh took over Hanoi. On August 25, Bao Dai—abandoned by his advisers and pressured by the Vietminh to step down—abdicated the imperial throne. However, Bao Dai did not withdraw completely from public life; he offered to support the Vietminh as he had supported the French and then the Japanese, by assuming the post of "Su-

Vietnam's Emperor-in-exile, Bao Dai, fondles a pet terrier in Hong Kong in 1948, three years after he abdicated. In 1949 he returned to Saigon in a French-inspired effort to form a new non-Communist government.

preme Adviser" to Ho's government. Glad of any assistance at this point, Ho accepted the offer.

The Vietminh soon controlled all major population centers in the north; in the south, political groups that were eager for independence, following the Vietminh lead, took over Saigon and several lesser cities. On September 2, the provisional government in Hanoi was succeeded by the Democratic Republic of Vietnam (DRVN). The proclamation declaring the new state was read by its President, Ho Chi Minh, to one half million supporters assembled in front of Hanoi's French-built opera house. Vietnam, for the first time in the 20th Century, appeared to be substantially under the control of the Vietnamese.

But the appearance was misleading. Ho was stronger in the north than in the south, where a splintered array of political and religious groups were united only in their desire for independence. And the French were planning a comeback. General de Gaulle, in addition to dispatching the ill-fated advance guard of parachutists, had appointed a fire-breathing admiral named Georges Thierry d'Argenlieu to be High Commissioner for Indochina. D'Argenlieu's orders were to restore French sovereignty in Indochina at whatever cost. The admiral had every intention of carrying out these orders, but the substantial contingents of fresh troops he needed would not arrive before October. In the meantime, armed Japanese soldiers remained in Saigon and Hanoi.

The tenuous nature of Vietminh power became evident within a week of Ho's proclamation. In early September there arrived in Hanoi and Saigon the first of a new wave of foreigners—Chinese and British—who were to serve as occupation troops and take the surrender of the Japanese forces. Under agreements reached by the Allied powers at the Potsdam Conference in July, Indochina had been divided across the 16th parallel, with the Chinese Nationalists of Chiang Kai-shek responsible for the area north of the line and the British in charge of the south.

Despite the controlling influence of Communists in the new Democratic Republic of Vietnam, the Chinese Nationalists maintained an official neutrality toward Ho's government. At the grass-roots level, however, the ancient enmity between China and Vietnam—part of which had been a Chinese colony for 1,000 years—short-circuited any real possibility of friendly relations.

The 150,000 troops of the Chinese occupation swarmed over northern Vietnam like an army of locusts; although they disarmed the Japanese in rapid order, their only other motive for being in Indochina seemed to be personal profit. Gold and jewelry turned in by northern Vietnamese during a Vietminh-sponsored "Gold Week" in September was traded to Nationalist soldiers in return for some of their American-made weapons. More often, the Chinese took what they wanted without giving anything in exchange.

In those turbulent days, the few Americans in Hanoi, mainly OSS officers, generally sympathized with the Vietnamese as a colonial people trying to achieve independence. Their sympathy was not shared in Washington, however, where there was no official support for—and in fact no visible interest in—the Hanoi regime. Repeated appeals for aid and recognition of Vietnamese independence made by Ho to President Truman and other officials went unheeded; the response to one such appeal, made by Ho on the 17th of October, was typical: a terse State Department notation in an internal memo dated November 15, that "no action" should be taken.

In the south, the attitude of the British toward the Vietnamese was colored by a deep colonialist bias. Their franchise was to establish order, disarm and evacuate the Japanese as well as Allied prisoners of war, and then withdraw—turning over administration to the French. The British commander, Major General Douglas D. Gracey, was ordered to occupy no more of southern Vietnam than was necessary to ensure control over the 60,000-man Japanese force that was still there; he was to avoid intervention in local political affairs. Gracey flew into Saigon on September 13 to join an advance contingent from the 20th Indian Division, made up of tough, professional Gurkhas, Punjabis and Rajputs. These troops, who would eventually number no more than 1,600, had arrived a day earlier along with a company of French commandos.

The atmosphere of Saigon was thick with tension, and General Gracey, a longtime colonial officer, soon took action that went beyond his mandate. On September 21 he declared martial law in all of Indochina south of the 16th parallel. Then he openly sided with the French against the self-proclaimed Vietnamese government that was trying to establish control in the southern capital. On September 22, Gracey's men began releasing—and arming—1,400 ragged, angry French troops who had been locked up in March by the Japanese. Civilian French government functionaries, unemployed since the Japanese coup, came back to work. That night, with British consent, the French ousted the Vietnamese who had occupied Saigon's city hall and took over other public buildings.

To help keep order, the British used Japanese soldiers, who remained fully armed but under Gracey's orders. But the Japanese were loath to turn against fellow Asians on behalf of either the British or the French. On September 25, Vietminh guerrillas attacked a French residential district in a section of Saigon where the Japanese were responsible for keeping order; the guerrillas tortured, killed and kidnapped men, women and children while Japanese troops stood by, doing nothing. The British, desperately short of troops, contented themselves with reprimanding the Japanese commander; thereafter, his men, reluctant but generally faithful to their Emperor's mandate to obey the Allied victors, fought alongside Indian and French troops against the Vietminh guerrillas.

The conflict widened, and additional Japanese troops who had stacked their weapons in expectation of being repatriated were ordered back on a war footing. In areas such as Dalat, 140 miles northeast of Saigon, that were beyond direct control by British headquarters, Japanese garrisons were told to hold their districts against the Vietminh. The Japanese complied, and earned the admiration of their British overseers, who mentioned them in military communiques. A typical brief dispatch, giving no clue that Britain and Japan had ever been enemies, recounted action in a Saigon suburb: "Japanese troops supported by armored cars of the 16th Cavalry extended the perimeter west of Cholon against slight opposition."

Even Japanese air units were enlisted in the campaign against the Vietminh: According to British reports, in the first month of operations Japanese crews manning Japanese planes flew 100,000 miles, carried 45,000 pounds of supplies and ferried 1,000 Indian and French troops. So indispensable had the Japanese ground and air contingents become that, eight weeks after Gracey's arrival in Saigon, only one out of 20 Japanese had been disarmed.

Meanwhile, the French government hastened to pour troops into Indochina. On October 5, General Philippe Leclerc arrived with 1,000 men—the vanguard of a force that was soon to number 25,000. Leclerc launched what he called a campaign of "pacification," occupying towns and cities and occasionally fighting sharp local battles with guerrillas. The French usually won these engagements—the guerrilla groups were small in size, poorly armed and generally ineffective—and Leclerc was sure that he was making progress. By December 1945, most of the towns in the south were in French hands.

But the French success was illusory because the opposition was so weak. Unlike the Vietnamese in the north, where the independence movement was centralized under Ho, the Vietnamese in the south were fragmented and at war with one another. Arrayed against the few Vietminh guerrillas were scores of small nationalist political parties, some with armed auxiliaries. More formidable were politically oriented religious sects such as the Hoa Hao, a Buddhist group with a 20,000-man militia, and the Cao Dai, which boasted a private army of 25,000. The Vietminh and the religious sects were savagely antagonistic. Prisoners taken by either side were subjected to a treatment called "crab fishing"; the hapless captives were tied together in bundles like so many logs and thrown into the Mekong, Indochina's great river, to float downstream and slowly drown.

The chaotic situation in Vietnam was aggravated during the last months of 1945 by the movement of hundreds of thousands of refugees in both directions across the 16th parallel. Many southerners headed north to live under the new independent state; and as many northerners, rejecting a future under the Communist Vietminh, traveled south to seek French protection.

By early 1946, despite the French Army's apparent success in the south and Ho's sense of strength in the north, neither the French nor the Vietminh felt committed to an all-out war. Nor were they strong enough to fight one. The first months of the new year were a period of negotiation. In January, General Gracey and the British ended their occupation in the south, having finally repatriated the Japanese forces there. While the French and the Vietminh tried to reconcile their conflicting goals at the conference table, talks

A Japanese soldier in Saigon, pressed into service by the short-handed British, posts Proclamation No. 1, declaring martial law in three languages—English, French and Vietnamese—in September of 1945.

between the French and Chiang Kai-shek's government led to the end of Chinese occupation of the north. By October 1946, the last Chinese had departed.

Many among the Chinese occupiers had made fortunes from their control of the harvest of opium poppies in Laos. This windfall came as a reward of sorts: The Chinese had helped the Laotians by preventing the French from reasserting themselves in Laos. The British, by contrast, had sent Indian troops into Cambodia, which was included in their southern occupation zone, to stifle Cambodian independence on behalf of the French.

The departure of the Chinese was a mixed blessing for the Vietnamese; glad as they were to see the backs of the occupiers, the Vietminh were deprived of the screen that the Chinese had afforded against growing French power, now more than ever bent on asserting itself.

Yet Ho Chi Minh continued to reject the prospect of full-scale war. Instead he pursued negotiations, believing that the French, risen from the humiliation of their defeat by Nazi Germany, might change their ideas about colonialism. Moreover, he hoped—mistakenly as it turned out—that French Socialists and Communists, who he believed sympathized with Vietnamese nationalism, would come to power in the next French elections.

Talks in Hanoi between Ho and Jean Sainteny, who was France's negotiator, produced an accord, subject to final negotiations in Paris, that seemed to bear out Ho's optimism. Signed on March 6, 1946, the agreement decreed that France would recognize Ho's Hanoi regime as a "Free State having its own government, parliament, army and treasury." Although the brief agreement did not specify borders for the new state, Ho could—and did—interpret the agreement as covering all of Vietnam. The new state was to be part of the French Union, an association similar to the British Commonwealth. In return for this recognition, the French would be allowed to station 15,000 troops above the 16th parallel. Under the agreement, these forces would be relieved over a five-year period by Vietnamese soldiers whom the French would supply and train.

Part of the accord was a truce in the guerrilla warfare that so far had left 1,200 French soldiers dead and 3,500 wounded—with an unknown number of Vietnamese casualties. However, the French, returning in force to Laos after the Chinese withdrew, soon found themselves fighting Laotians determined to win their own independence.

The March 6 agreement between Paris and Hanoi was a child of necessity. General Leclerc was aware by now that his capture of southern towns had meant little; he had begun to doubt whether any military venture in Vietnam could overcome its people's desire for independence. Leclerc's superiors in the French government nevertheless wanted to establish a foothold in the north. Ho simply wanted recogni-

tion of independence and a pause in the fighting to consolidate his power and begin rebuilding the economy.

Though he regarded these aims as essential, Ho had a hard time selling the March accord to the Vietnamese people. Many of them felt that the presence of foreign troops in their midst—where no Frenchman had gone armed since the Japanese coup the year before—fatally compromised the recognition of their independence. Among many Frenchmen, there was a different kind of rejection: Such diehard colonialists as Admiral d'Argenlieu could not understand the need for even talking to the Vietnamese. "France has such a fine expeditionary corps in Indochina," wrote d'Argenlieu in disgust, "and yet its leaders prefer to negotiate rather than to fight."

Ho was still on very shaky ground with his own constituency when he traveled to France at the end of May 1946 to negotiate the final settlement that was to confirm the March accord. No sooner had Ho left Vietnam than d'Argenlieu moved to erode Ho's position—and undermine the intent of the March agreement. Without authority from Paris, the admiral recognized a separate pro-French puppet regime in the south, called the Cochin China Republic. By August, ignoring the Hanoi government, d'Argenlieu was presiding over meetings of republic officials and French-sympathizing representatives of Cambodia and Laos as if they truly represented the people of Indochina.

Ho stayed on at the talks in France, which continued through the summer. In September he reluctantly signed yet another interim agreement that he found deeply unsatisfactory because it failed to deal with such basic issues as independence and the status of Cochin China. Even this accord came too late to abate the country-wide fighting that sputtered anew despite the truce.

In October 1946, the future of Ho's republic suffered a further shock when France adopted a new constitution that provided no place for truly independent nations within the French Union; members of the union were to have no control, for example, over their foreign policies. For Ho and his colleagues, this was one rebuff too many. On November 9, without consulting the French, they published their own constitution; it described the northern regime as the government of all Vietnam and did not mention any ties to France.

Events now moved toward outright war. The Vietminh mustered about 60,000 men who for more than a year had been undergoing intense training—much of it supervised by Japanese who had deserted their units rather than go home in disgrace. The French for their part had slightly inferior numbers—50,000 ground troops. But they were well enough equipped with tanks, planes and naval craft suitable for use on coastal and river missions to convince many observers that they were capable of wiping out the relatively ill-equipped Vietminh.

On November 20, the tension in the north was broken by a series of shooting incidents in the seaport of Haiphong. By themselves, they were insignificant. But by November 23, great throngs of city dwellers, frightened by the sporadic gunfire, had left their homes and were hurrying along the coast in the direction of a French air base at Cat-Bi. The captain of the French cruiser *Suffren,* in Haiphong harbor, was unaware that the refugees were unarmed and he may have feared that they were on their way to attack the air base. He opened fire on the crowd and some 6,000 Vietnamese were killed by the shells or were trampled to death in the panic that followed. Both sides now girded for a serious fight.

At precisely eight o'clock on the evening of the 19th of December, bombs exploded at the electric power plant in Hanoi. The city was plunged into darkness and waves of Vietminh militia descended on French military installations and attacked French civilians in their homes. Within hours, French garrisons throughout Vietnam had come under similar assaults. The vicious French-Indochina War, which would last for more than seven years and take an estimated 600,000 lives, had begun.

The French expected to achieve a rapid victory by combining the maneuverability of their mobile columns with support from stationary units holding such essential positions as highway junctions. Tanks, artillery and naval units on rivers and coasts were the bludgeons of this strategy. But the war did not go as planned. Despite the ability of the French to control towns and major roads, and notwithstanding some skillful use of gunboats and lighter craft on the rivers, French superiority in armor and artillery was not enough to make a real difference. Moreover, the French lacked the manpower required to fight a successful counterguerrilla war. In such a war, a 10-to-1 ratio is considered minimum, but the French

THE EMERGENCE OF HO CHI MINH

In July 1945, the first of several American OSS agents parachuted into northern Vietnam to make contact with anti-Japanese guerrillas there. Though the Japanese surrender in August cut short their mission, the Americans came away impressed by the guerrilla chieftain—a slight, middle-aged Vietnamese with a high forehead and a wispy goatee; the OSS leader described him as "a brilliant and capable man."

The man, known to his followers as Ho Chi Minh ("He who enlightens"), was born Nguyen That Thanh in 1890 near the central Vietnamese city of Vinh. His father was a dedicated nationalist who soon enlisted his son in the cause; as a schoolboy Ho began running messages for the local anti-French underground.

Ambitious and curious, Ho left for Europe when he was 21. After World War I

Ho Chi Minh addresses the 1920 meeting at which the French Communist Party was born.

he adapted his ardent nationalism to the rising new discipline of Communism, attracted by its call for the immediate liberation of colonial lands. In 1920, Ho became a founding member of the French Communist Party, and over the next two decades his crucial contribution was to organize a unified Indochinese Communist Party, a feat he accomplished from a base in China, recruiting fellow exiles and filtering them across the border into Vietnam.

In 1941, Ho Chi Minh went home himself after an absence of 30 years. His goal had not changed. From an underground hideout, he organized resistance to Japan's occupation of Vietnam and built a political coalition that became known as the Vietminh. Plans carefully laid during the War culminated in the Vietminh's swift takeover of Hanoi in August of 1945.

Ho (fourth from right) and his military aide, Vo Nguyen Giap (far left), meet with OSS agents in 1945 to coordinate harassment of the Japanese.

Seizing power was a modest challenge compared to holding it in the face of resurgent French colonialism. Aware of his regime's economic and military weakness, Ho began bargaining with the despised French. Like the Americans, the French agents who dealt with Ho in Hanoi and during a summer-long conference at Fontainebleau in 1946, came to respect him. Jean Sainteny, a key French negotiator, praised his "stamina and self-control."

Ho sensed that France had no intention of allowing an independent Vietnam. Publicly, he remained eminently reasonable, but secretly his guerrillas girded for war. When open rebellion erupted on December 19, 1946, Ho once more went underground—this time not merely as a jungle chieftain, but as the focus of national hope for many of his 24 million countrymen.

Ho shares a plane in 1946 with Commissioner Jean Sainteny, who later said that Ho "had the look of a hunted animal ready to spring."

Accorded a VIP welcome to Paris in June 1946, Ho receives a bouquet and the banner-waving support of Vietnamese living in France.

In a cave northwest of Hanoi that served as his headquarters after the war with France began, Ho conducts a meeting of the Vietminh's governing council. At left hang Ho's picture and the Vietminh flag.

were fighting on even terms at best and often were outnumbered in local engagements.

Vietminh operations followed classic guerrilla models: They were willing to give up cities, even Hanoi, in order to control the countryside. This strategy left the French, like the Nationalists in China, isolated in fortified or built-up areas. By late 1949, although the war was far from over, the French were on the defensive.

The French had also lost the initiative on the political front; they were increasingly isolated from the Vietnamese people, many of whom became willing allies of the Vietminh. Looking for a way to involve anti-Communist Vietnamese in the struggle against the Vietminh, the French turned once more to Emperor Bao Dai.

The former Emperor was no longer in Vietnam. Early in 1946, before the last hope of peace had evaporated, and while Ho and Sainteny were still negotiating, Bao Dai had left Hanoi. His announced mission was to seek aid from the Nationalist government in Chungking. Instead, he went into self-imposed exile—first in the British colony of Hong Kong, later in Europe. The royal expatriate led a playboy's life, idling away his days at the movies and his evenings at restaurants and cabarets, gaining a label he would never shake off: "the nightclub Emperor." But Bao Dai's imperial lineage still endowed him with prestige among the French and among many Vietnamese, and by the end of 1947 the French were trying to woo him back to his homeland.

From his home of the moment in Geneva, Switzerland, Bao Dai negotiated cleverly with the French: He would not admit he was even considering a comeback unless France solemnly recognized Vietnam's independence.

In June 1948, the playboy monarch had seemed to get what he wanted—including acknowledgment, on paper, of a Vietnam including Cochin China as well as the other regions that had long been a part of his papier-mâché empire. Bao Dai was to be head of this new "entity," though without retracting his abdication as Emperor. But in truth the new government was little more than a camouflage for continued French rule. France would control the Army and foreign relations and in other important respects would continue to dominate government operations through French officials, just as it had in colonial times.

A so-called Central Provisional Government based on the June accord was formed—though Bao Dai, in the end, remained aloof from it. Another year of negotiations dragged by, producing yet another written agreement that contained nothing more advantageous to Bao Dai than the previous one. Bao Dai nevertheless decided that it was the best he was likely to get and agreed to return to Vietnam. When he entered Saigon on June 13, 1949, flags flew everywhere—the French tricolor and the Vietnamese banner (three horizontal red stripes on a yellow field). But apart from functionaries and officials, almost no one turned out to welcome the former Emperor home.

True popular support for the Bao Dai administration never materialized. The French recognized this lack of backing in their own disparaging way: They continued to occupy the vast, ugly—but prestigious—palace that had for so long been the residence and seat of power for the colonial rulers of Indochina. Bao Dai and his ministers had to make do with lesser quarters.

Formal acknowledgment of the South Vietnamese government came in more satisfactory measure from abroad, however. In February 1950, the United States and Great Britain recognized the new state and established legations in Saigon. And that August, under the shock of the Communist victory in China, the first 35 men of an American military assistance advisory group (MAAG) arrived in Saigon. Their mission was to supervise delivery of military equipment to the French Union forces, made up of Vietnamese, Cambodians and Laotians as well as Frenchmen, Foreign Legionnaires and French African troops.

With increasing American support—by 1952 the United States was bearing one third of the War's cost—the troops of the French Union would campaign with rising frustration during the next four years against the elusive and determined Vietminh. Then in 1954 the French suffered a decisive and humiliating defeat at the valley fortress of Dienbienphu. Cut off and besieged, almost 11,000 French Union soldiers surrendered to the guerrilla army of General Giap. After eight years of struggle to regain their colonial empire, the French withdrew from Indochina. But peace in the region remained tragically elusive. Ho Chi Minh had prevailed in the north. The French legacy in the south, however, was a rival government, supported now by the United

States, which was determined to keep at least that portion of Vietnam free of Communist rule.

But the fact that a few American military men returned to Vietnam in the summer of 1950 was lost in the uproar over a more urgent drama. At that time most of the world was anxiously watching the emergency American intervention in another troubled spot on the Asian mainland—Korea.

Korea is a mountainous peninsula that hangs like a stubby udder from the long underbelly of China. In 1945, most of its heavy industry—which had been developed by the Japanese during their 40 years of occupation—was in the northern half of the peninsula; most of the arable land, sown to rice, barley, cotton and tobacco, was in the south. As a result of the talks at Potsdam in July 1945, Korea had been divided at lat. 38° N., about 40 miles north of the capital at Seoul. The Soviet Union, with 120,000 men commanded by Colonel General Ivan M. Chistyakov, occupied the territory north of the line, where nine million Koreans lived; the U.S. XXIV Corps, 50,000 men under Lieut. General John R. Hodge, occupied the south, which was the home of 19 million people. The United States had proposed the 38th parallel as a dividing line because it was far enough north to ensure that Seoul was in the U.S. zone, and the Soviets had accepted it without argument.

The Soviets took firm hold in the northern part of the country, disarming and interning Japanese soldiers and colonial government officials—many of whom they deported as prisoners to Manchuria and the Soviet Union. Along with their own troops, the Soviets brought in a contingent of 300 Korean soldiers, plus an unknown number of Korean Communist political cadres, who had been trained in the Soviet Union. As an additional security measure, the Russians froze the 38th parallel as a permanent border between the two military control zones, denying virtually all outsiders entry to the northern area. Beyond that, the Soviet occupiers often blocked the transit of goods and services that normally flowed from north to south. Such actions effectively disrupted the administrative and economic unity of the country. Although neither the United States nor the Soviet Union had mentioned the 38th parallel as a permanent dividing line at the outset, it soon became a symbol of the increasing contention between the two great powers, and a serious obstacle to the Koreans' drive toward independence.

In their planning for the postwar period, the Allies had regarded the Koreans as a people unfortunately lacking experience in self-rule. Indeed, Korea's history of subjugation was a long one. Although once independent, Korea had spent 10 centuries under Mongol, then Chinese, domination—so isolated from other foreign influences that it was called the Hermit Kingdom. Korea therefore needed time, in the Allied view, to generate a supply of leaders. Also, Korea's economy had long been linked to that of Japan, and the Japanese defeat was certain to create economic chaos that would take time to alleviate.

Nevertheless, self-rule for Korea was an avowed goal of the Allies. At a conference in Moscow in December of 1945 the Western Allies apparently succeeded in getting Soviet agreement to a scheme for turning that goal into reality: A joint U.S.-Soviet commission was to work out a plan for setting up a provisional all-Korean government; for a maximum of five years, this government would function under a trusteeship formed by the Soviet Union, Britain, China and the United States.

Despite the agreement, however, the 38th parallel remained a hostile border. Americans south of the line could get very little hard information about what the Soviets were doing in their zone; sightseers even made Sunday afternoon forays from Seoul to the line just to try to get a glimpse of the Russians—almost invariably without success.

In the south, meanwhile, the Americans were beset with problems. Chief among them was the physical prostration of Korea. Although no fighting had taken place there, the Japanese had exploited the economy—straining Korea's capacity to produce food and timber; the Japanese defeat had wrecked the machinery of trade and commerce and helped push the country to the brink of collapse. Now mineral resources, the wealth of the north, were withheld from the south; power stations in Soviet territory that fed current across the 38th parallel often were shut down, blacking out southern homes, offices and factories. Even in the agricultural south, food was desperately short. Fertilizer that was manufactured in northern plants did not make it across the parallel, and as a result the southern rice harvest declined. During the winter of 1945-1946, average daily food consumption dropped to 900 calories per person.

Korea's economic crisis was made worse by inflation, which multiplied the cost of rice tenfold between 1945 and 1948. A thriving black market soon took hold, fueled by the tons of military equipment that the Americans brought with them into Korea. In a single year, 2,000 jeeps were reported missing from American motor pools, and more than one American official found it easier to get spare parts through the black market than through official U.S. Army channels.

Many of southern Korea's problems were generated—or worsened—by the occupying Americans. Inflation, for example, was stimulated by well-meaning Army paymasters who recognized that their Korean employees' salaries were being eroded to the equivalent of three dollars per month. Out of generosity, and to control the theft of American property, they padded payrolls and paid for unearned overtime. The head of one military government office sold lumber from supply packing cases and cigarettes from a nonsmoking American staffer's tobacco ration—and added the proceeds to the payroll fund.

Other Americans were neither so generous nor so pragmatic. Many GIs, eager to get home, confused by the unfamiliar ways of an Asian country and unable to speak its language, hated Korea and disliked its people. Even General Hodge and his staff were far from adequately briefed or equipped to operate in Korea. Hodge's orders, in fact, were woefully misconceived; they had been adapted from those issued for Japan, on the assumption that the two nations were comparable. The instructions stated that order should be maintained by keeping local officials on the job and by working through them. This was a sensible policy in Japan, but not in Korea, where the local official was usually a hated Japanese, aided by despised Korean collaborators. Hodge tried to get his orders changed, but his superiors—notably General MacArthur—let them stand.

Hodge, a bluff, capable infantry commander, tried hard to do as he was told. Upon arriving at Seoul, he had duly ordered Japanese officials, including the police, to retain their arms and maintain order. Some Japanese Army units also were employed to keep the peace, briefly wearing USMG (U.S. Military Government) arm bands and riding in trucks bearing explanatory signs. (One sign, displayed on a vehicle in Seoul, read: "Japanese Army Detachment: Understood by U.S. Army.")

The antagonism generated among Koreans by the continued employment of their former oppressors was made worse by stiff regulations against fraternization. American personnel were not allowed to visit Korean homes or hotels, or to eat in Korean restaurants. Such constraints were enormously frustrating for the Koreans, for whom the end of the War had seemed to promise so much.

By the middle of October 1945, the American command had begun the repatriation of Japanese troops to their home islands; but much damage had been done. Although the Koreans had embraced the Americans as liberators, the relationship now seemed to be one of conqueror to subject people. The result was violent unrest: Strikes, riots, banditry and sabotage became normal events in southern Korean life. Civilian political leadership was fragmented and, as the Allies had feared, inexperienced. The police came increasingly under control of Right-Wing forces, and the hard times grew worse.

The situation was ripe for exploitation by the Communists, and they soon moved to take advantage of it. Party members already in place in the cities spread anti-American propaganda. An armed force of 5,000 guerrillas, who infiltrated from the north or were recruited locally, took hold in Korea's mountainous southwest. The Communist political organ was the South Korean Workers' Party, which was twin to a so-called Workers' Party in the north. The two, maintaining close touch, worked for a common goal: a Korea unified under Communism.

Non-Communist Koreans, angered at the continued pres-

A youthful Kim Il-sung attends a session of the Soviet-U.S. Joint Commission on Korea's future in 1947, the year after he became chairman of the provisional government in the Soviet zone. Born Kim Song-ju to a farming family near Pyongyang in 1912, he adopted the name Kim Il-sung from a legendary Korean freedom fighter of the early 1900s.

ence of a foreign army on their soil, added to the political turmoil in the American zone. A remarkable number of Koreans reacted to the prospect of liberty by anointing themselves to lead their new nation; between 1945 and 1947, more than 200 political parties sprang up. Sometimes a "party" (with a name like "The Full Moon Meeting Society") represented no more than one man and his family group. Others were more substantial; an example was the organization founded by a nationalist named Lyuh Woon Hyung, who put together an entire governmental structure, ready to take power as the "Korean People's Republic."

In American eyes, the energy behind this political ferment was not matched by equivalent expertise. The proud Koreans, however, rejected the idea that they were unable to run their own affairs. They considered it a humiliating paradox that the Americans were encouraging self-government in Japan, a beaten enemy, but were reluctant to allow the Koreans, victims of Japan, to take more than nominal charge of their country, ruling instead through a military government.

The Japanese were chiefly to blame for the Koreans' stunted development. Under their harsh rule even the important nongovernment jobs were off limits to Koreans: For example, 67 per cent of all teaching positions in Korean colleges and universities, and all the top college-level administrative jobs had been reserved for Japanese. It was therefore difficult to find people with the background to handle the many administrative jobs that became available in the American military government. General Hodge, who was learning his job, tried to delegate to Koreans as much re-

sponsibility as possible. But often the appearance of power did not match the reality: American advisers stood behind each Korean functionary and in fact ran such important institutions as hospitals and the school system directly.

Unable to find even enough administrators to go around, the Americans despaired of finding the caliber of political leaders who might be trusted to guide Korea toward a stable, democratic future. Among the very few who even began to meet the test of leadership was Syngman Rhee, a 70-year-old zealot who had devoted his life to the cause of Korean independence. As early as 1897, Rhee had gotten in trouble with the authorities for leading independence demonstrations. As a result he had spent most of his years in exile; he had not set foot in Korea since 1912. Rhee lived for many years in Hawaii and for a quarter of a century had vainly sought recognition for a provisional government of which he had been elected head—though he was not present at a 1919 meeting of Korean nationalists in Seoul. When the American Occupation began, Rhee was waiting in Washington, where he had spent the War. The crushing of the Japanese Empire was a moment of personal triumph for him. Yet his waiting was not over.

As Koreans at home watched a new occupation force replace the old, Rhee was making the rounds of State Department offices. Rhee stood five feet five inches tall and was unprepossessing in appearance. As before, he met a succession of rebuffs. During the War, Stanley Hornbeck, who headed the State Department's Far Eastern desk, had dismissed Rhee's provisional government as a "self-constituted club with limited membership among a group of expatriates." As recently as June 1945, in response to a letter from Rhee, the State Department had stated that the United States was not ready to recognize Rhee's government or any other group in Korea; such recognition, the statement asserted, "might compromise the right of the Korean people to choose the ultimate form and personnel of the government which they may wish to establish."

Yet Rhee was the one person who could claim a semblance of organized backing by Korean nationalists, and he had proved his will and mettle by the years of struggle in exile. He began to grow in stature in American eyes.

On October 16, 1945, Syngman Rhee returned to his

South Korea's 70-year-old Syngman Rhee convalesces in Seoul after a bout of pneumonia in 1946, following his return to Korea from a 33-year exile. Age did not deter the staunchly anti-Communist Rhee from creating the most potent coalition in the U.S. Occupation zone, and in 1948 he was elected President of an independent Republic of Korea.

THE HARDENING LINE AT LATITUDE 38° NORTH

A sign at an American outpost warns passersby that they are approaching the line that separates South and North Korea.

From their observation post on a mountain ridge, South Korean guards keep watch along the border. To the right and rear is Communist territory.

The 38th parallel, destined to become the frontier of the Cold War in Asia, was born in a spirit of cooperation at the Potsdam Conference in the summer of 1945, when the Soviet Union agreed to declare war on Japan. To prevent accidental clashes between Russian and American planes and ships in areas bordering Korea, the Allied negotiators divided the Sea of Japan into separate operational zones. The line drawn between the zones intersected the Korean coast at about latitude 40° N.

After the Japanese surrendered a few weeks later, the United States proposed a land boundary somewhat farther south, at latitude 38° N., as a line of demarcation between Soviet and American occupation forces. The plan apportioned Korea's land area about equally, but favored the Americans by placing the capital, Seoul, in their zone. Despite this apparent geopolitical disadvantage, the Russians agreed.

Neither side asserted, at first, that the line was to be more than a temporary expedient. However, as relations between the former Allies soured, the 38th parallel became a closed, hostile border bristling with checkpoints and bunkers.

Since the course of the parallel was nothing but a straight line on the map, it made a highly impractical border. It ran through the northern edge of the city of Kaesong and also bisected several smaller towns. In the west it sliced off the southern tip of the Ongjin peninsula, isolating it from overland supply from the south—except for a weekly convoy that the Russians grudgingly allowed to pass through their zone. The line also cut across the grain of such natural barriers as the mountain ranges of eastern Korea, making the line militarily all but indefensible.

Manning a rampart of crude sandbags on the isolated Ongjin peninsula, South Koreans stand armed and dressed in a mix of American and Japanese uniforms and civilian clothes.

American GIs question a Korean traveler at a checkpoint on the 38th parallel in January of 1946. The Korean carries his possessions on a versatile carryall frame called a jige.

homeland for the first time in 33 years, a passenger on a U.S. military plane. On the following day, learning that he had come home, 50,000 of Rhee's fellow Koreans lined the streets of Seoul to welcome him as he was driven to a press conference arranged by General Hodge. Each succeeding day, people gathered in front of his hotel, hoping for a glimpse of him. And it was not long before Rhee established himself as the man with whom the Americans would have to deal. Speaking for his countrymen, he warned in his first public appearance that, "through the years of Japanese oppression we remained unconquered and undivided. We intend to remain so even at the cost of our lives. The Allied Powers might as well know that now."

But Rhee had little chance of leading an undivided Korea. From the moment of their arrival, the Soviets had begun organizing a rival regime north of the 38th parallel, and from it emerged the man who would challenge Rhee for the leadership of all Koreans. He called himself Kim Il-sung, a name he was said to have adopted from a legendary guerrilla who fought against the Japanese early in the 20th Century. Kim had spent the War as part of a Communist-oriented guerrilla group fighting the Japanese in Manchuria. He was 33 years old when he returned with the Russian occupation and began building a power base as leader of the North Korean Workers' Party. In November of 1946 he was installed as Chairman of the Interim People's Committee of northern Korea. The Russians supported him grandly; his picture appeared, along with Josef Stalin's, on posters throughout the north, resplendent in Soviet medals.

The Interim People's Committee ran northern Korea as an instrument of the Soviet Union's policy. Since land reform, to redress the grievances of a nation of tenant farmers, was a demand of both northern and southern Korean political groups, the People's Committee proclaimed a land-reform plan even before Kim became chairman. It later sponsored the nationalization of industries and laws designed to improve the lives of industrial workers—acts that generated enthusiasm on both sides of the 38th parallel.

South of the line, Syngman Rhee lobbied hard with the Americans, asserting total opposition to Communism and repeating the demand that his country be unified and set free. Washington applauded Rhee's anti-Communism and continued to express hope for a peaceful and unified Korea.

At the same time, the Americans deplored Rhee's evident inability to work with moderate and liberal Korean groups, which as a result coalesced to oppose him. Rhee's fiery rhetoric did nothing to bolster Korean popular confidence in the United States, which, he intimated, favored a permanent division of the country. Koreans in the south continued to demonstrate against the American Occupation.

The first open displays of anti-American feeling had erupted in December of 1945, when the Moscow plan for international trusteeship over Korea was announced. Rioting broke out when the southern Koreans learned that the United States had proposed the plan, which to many seemed a prescription for keeping their country divided and occupied. The only groups that were not involved in the rioting were those controlled by the Communists, whose leaders calculated that the years of trusteeship would give them time to build their power in the south.

Whether or not they acted independently, the south Korean Communists' support of the plan proved convenient for the Soviets. When the joint panel met for the first time on March 23, 1946, the Soviet delegation demanded that in preparing the country for trusteeship, the commission negotiate only with groups that had not opposed the Moscow agreements. The Americans rejected the demand because it obviously would have limited the commission to transactions with Communists. That issue and almost every other still remained unsettled when the commission adjourned on the 6th of May. Far from being able to reach agreement on broad issues of national unity, it could not even arrive at a consensus on such matters as a uniform currency or a north-south telephone system.

The commission reconvened in June of 1947, but by autumn the United States had become convinced that it would never contribute substantively to the cause of Korean independence. Moreover, the Truman Administration, under intense lobbying pressure for independence by Koreans in Washington, and determined to cut its military budget, was increasingly anxious to end the Occupation and pull American troops out of Korea. The United States turned its back on the trusteeship commission and took the matter to the United Nations. It pushed a resolution through the General Assembly calling for elections throughout Korea in the

A white-jacketed orchestra and the flags of the Soviet Union, Korea and
the United States brighten up an otherwise drab session of the Joint
Commission in Pyongyang in July of 1947. The Soviet and American
delegations, headed by General Terenty F. Shtikov (left) and Major
General Albert E. Brown, had resumed their meetings after a year's recess
in an attempt to work out a plan for the reunification of Korea. The
commission finally dissolved in frustration a few months after this session.

spring of 1948 to establish a unified government. The elections were to be supervised by a special U.N. commission.

The Soviet Union refused to allow the U.N. observers to move north of the 38th parallel, but in the south U.N.-sponsored elections for a constituent assembly went ahead on May 10. Eighty-six per cent of the adult population went to the polls; women were allowed to vote for the first time. Rhee's supporters and other conservatives won a majority of seats in the new National Assembly, and Rhee carried his district in Seoul with 9 out of every 10 votes cast.

The National Assembly moved quickly. By July of 1948 it had written a constitution and elected Rhee the first President of the Republic of Korea, which was formally proclaimed on August 15. In addition to being recognized by the U.N. General Assembly, the new Korean state underwent a change in its relationship with the United States. Ambassador John J. Muccio replaced General Hodge as the highest-ranking American in Korea and overall head of the U.S. Mission there.

North of the 38th parallel, the Communists responded on September 9, 1948, by proclaiming their own new nation: The Democratic People's Republic of Korea, with Kim Il-sung as Premier. Kim's regime was immediately recognized by the world's Communist nations. On January 1, 1949, the Soviets announced the withdrawal of the last of their occupation troops. It was a moment they had been preparing for since 1947, when Soviet officers began recruiting and training an indigenous force of impressive size, stocked at first with Japanese and later with Soviet arms. When the Red Army pulled out, a strong North Korean Army was ready to take its place.

The Americans also withdrew their occupation forces—but without replacing them by a Korean force comparable to that in the north. By the end of June 1949, the last 7,500

U.S. troops had departed, leaving behind a 500-man Military Assistance Group to operate under the supervision of Ambassador Muccio. Also left behind was $110 million worth of equipment. The matériel included rifles, some machine guns, light mortars and bazookas, and more than 40,000 vehicles—but no artillery or tanks, and no combat aircraft. This array was considered enough to equip 50,000 of the 65,000 troops of the South Korean Army, a force intended to deal only with the guerrillas who were still a problem in the south.

North Korea, in stark comparison, boasted heavy artillery, tanks, about 110 fighter planes and fighter-bombers—and an Army of 150,000 to 200,000 men. Its ground forces included as many as 40,000 Koreans who had fought in the Chinese Communist Army of Mao Tse-tung. The South Korean forces, which gradually built up to about 100,000 men, had no such backbone of veterans.

Aware of this imbalance, Syngman Rhee urgently sought guarantees that in an emergency the United States would come to his defense. In May of 1949 he had demanded, in exchange for his acquiescence in the withdrawal of U.S. troops, an American-supported Pacific pact similar to the North Atlantic Treaty in Europe. As alternatives, he asked for a bilateral mutual-defense treaty, or at least a "public pledge by the United States to defend a reunited, democratic, independent Korea" against Communist aggression.

In Washington, defense officials were leery of making any agreement with Rhee that might eventually commit American ground forces to fight in Asia. Most Americans had a visceral dislike for such an involvement. As early as January of 1947, Secretary of War Robert P. Patterson had spoken of Korea as a "strange land, with strange-looking people," from which the United States should withdraw. Working with a shrunken postwar budget, the Joint Chiefs of Staff had chosen to emphasize the defense of Europe and repeatedly issued statements expressing their conviction that Korea was of "little strategic interest." They did, however, oppose abandoning Korea to Communism.

The Joint Chiefs' stance evolved into basic U.S. military doctrine, supported by General MacArthur in Tokyo. MacArthur defined the limits of the basic American defense perimeter as "the chain of islands fringing the coast of Asia." On January 12, 1950, this doctrine became public policy, expressed in a speech by Secretary of State Dean Acheson at the National Press Club in Washington. In the speech, Acheson described a Pacific defense line that ran from the Aleutian Islands to Japan, then south from Japan to the Ryukyu Islands and the Philippines. If any country west of this line was attacked, Acheson said, it was the responsibility of the people under assault to defend themselves, with help from the United Nations.

South Koreans publicly expressed confidence in their ability to defend themselves, notwithstanding the disparity between northern and southern forces. In late spring of 1950, Brigadier General William Roberts of the U.S. Military Advisory Group in Seoul declared that the South Koreans had "the best doggoned shooting army outside the United States." Harold Noble, First Secretary of the American Embassy in Seoul, was reported as saying that the Republic of Korea, or ROK, Army was capable not only of defending

In May 1948, South Koreans taking part in United Nations-sponsored elections—the first secret ballot in their country's history—study posters illustrating how to vote. Despite a Communist boycott, almost 90 per cent of the registered voters south of the 38th parallel went to the polls.

South Korea against attack but of moving north of the 38th parallel and capturing the Communists' capital at Pyongyang within two weeks' time.

The first rains of the season were drenching the rice fields near Seoul at 4 a.m. on Sunday, June 25, 1950, when the North Korean Army hurled itself across the 38th parallel. For the first few hours there was scant contact between northern and southern armies and the invading tanks rolled forward at will. Russian-built Yak fighter-bombers began bombing and strafing Seoul on the first day. ROK units stationed between Seoul and the border were no match for the invaders and within 60 hours of their initial assault the

North Koreans had reached the outskirts of the capital.

Ambassador Muccio already had ordered an evacuation of American women and children. But he scrapped a long-standing air-evacuation plan for fear that Communist aircraft might shoot down the evacuation planes. On the 26th of June, 682 people, mostly American civilians, boarded a Norwegian fertilizer ship in Inchon harbor that had accommodations for 12 passengers; when they arrived in Japan after three miserable days at sea, 50 of them had to be removed from the ship on stretchers.

On June 27, most of the remaining 2,200 Americans in Seoul were evacuated, this time by air. Among other items, the Americans left behind 22,000 gallons of gasoline in the

Gesturing in the direction of Communist positions, a South Korean general explains the tactical situation to U.S. envoy John Foster Dulles, who visited the 38th parallel in mid-June of 1950. When the North Koreans struck across the parallel a few days later, Dulles urged President Truman to commit American troops and matériel to stem the invasion.

Embassy motor pool and $40,000 worth of liquor in the Embassy itself. Personal effects valued at $4.5 million were abandoned. Also inadvertently left intact—and available for study by North Korean intelligence officers and political police—were the personnel records of the South Koreans on the Embassy staff.

The U.N. Security Council condemned the North Korean invasion as a "calculated attack prepared and launched with secrecy." (The Soviet delegate, who might have vetoed the resolution, did not attend; he was boycotting the Council at the time to protest the presence on it of the Nationalist Chinese instead of the Chinese Communists.) The United States was convinced that the invasion had been instigated by the Soviet Union. Despite the earlier pronouncement that mainland Asia was outside the primary American defense perimeter, the United States saw the move as a challenge to its power and prestige that had to be resisted. It moved quickly to provide the South Koreans with naval and air support. President Truman also ordered the U.S. Seventh Fleet to take up station between Communist-held mainland China and Taiwan, where the government of Chiang Kai-shek had taken refuge, in order to forestall any resumption of the war between Communist and Nationalist Chinese.

Backed by a second U.N. resolution calling on members to furnish South Korea with assistance to repel the attack, Truman on June 29 ordered U.S. troops dispatched from Japan. The reinforcements began arriving on July 4. Fed piecemeal into battle as they arrived, the Americans suffered 6,000 casualties, including 1,884 dead. The retreating ROK forces lost 50 per cent of their strength. But by August 4 the combined American and South Korean Armies had stopped the Communist advance. And none too soon. When the retreat ended, 45,000 GIs and their ROK allies were defending a perimeter only 50 miles wide and 80 miles long around the port of Pusan at the southeastern tip of the Korean peninsula.

The perimeter at Pusan would hold, and after three years of costly fighting, South Korea would be saved. But the conflict in Korea and its deadlocked conclusion reflected a pattern of international confrontation that was perhaps the most perilous legacy of World War II.

The War had wrought change almost beyond measure.

Some of it was grimly actuarial: An estimated 50 million lives were lost, and much of the physical and economic structure of Europe and Asia lay shattered. A fact equally dramatic was the stunning shift in the relative strength of nations. Most of the prewar powers, Axis and Allied, that had fought longest and hardest were major powers no more. In their place, two rival superpowers had emerged.

The United States, in gearing up for war, had discovered the great depth of its resources; its overall industrial production nearly doubled during the War years. The American aircraft industry, alone, increased its output from 6,000 planes a year in 1940 to a wartime peak of more than 9,000 a month. The United States had also created and used the atomic bomb, a fearsome weapon that gave its owner a decisive edge in the early postwar years and would change military concepts forever. But mobilization on an enormous scale had also produced a troublesome side effect. Government spending ballooned so rapidly that only two fifths of the $387 billion expended during World War II was covered by tax revenues. The consequence was a greatly increased national debt.

The Soviet Union, though its western lands were ravaged and 20 million of its people had perished, found its own wellsprings of strength. It emerged as a military colossus, shielded on its western border by an Iron Curtain of subservient satellites. While the United States demobilized all but about one million of the 12 million men and women it had under arms when the War ended, the Soviet Union chose to maintain its armed forces at a postwar level of nearly three million, backed by an arsenal of 50,000 tanks and 20,000 aircraft. Thus, even before the Russians developed their own atomic weapon in 1949, they presented a formidable challenge to the United States and its allies.

The result was an uneasy parity that has since tolerated, and survived, many localized wars while helping to prevent any new worldwide conflict. In 1950, Winston Churchill offered his assessment of the standoff: "Another world war would begin by fearful cataclysms," he said. "Moralists may find it a melancholy thought that peace can find no nobler foundations than mutual terror. But for my part I shall be content if these foundations are solid, because they will give us the extra time and the new breathing space for the supreme effort that has to be made for a world settlement."

A NEW KIND OF WARFARE

On a marshy plain west of Saigon, a French patrol searching in vain for Vietminh guerrillas manages only to burn one of the insurgents' storage huts.

A lookout climbs to his loft atop an immense tree at a French outpost near Hanoi. He was watching for Vietminh, who controlled the vicinity.

A JUNGLE FILLED WITH INVISIBLE TIGERS

The European colonialists who in 1945 expected to resume control of their Asian possessions shared a common error: They had scant respect for the Asians' ability to fight for independence. As one Frenchman in Saigon said of the Vietnamese insurgency: "It's nothing—some agitators bought by the Japanese. We'll kill them off. It won't take long."

Such monumental arrogance led to some mighty falls. In Malaya, the British read local conditions correctly and instituted such measures as the massive resettlement of civilians in time to defeat a Communist uprising. But the French in Indochina and the Dutch in Indonesia repeatedly misjudged their own weaknesses and their adversaries' strengths. The results were years of stalemate and eventual defeat.

To reclaim their colonies, the French and Dutch arrived brandishing the kind of arms that had won World War II. They assumed that their aircraft and artillery gave them an overwhelming edge on the ragtag cohorts of Ho Chi Minh in Indochina and Sukarno in Indonesia. By contrast, these nationalist rebels initially had only what they had been able to steal or barter from the occupying Japanese, or buy from Chinese Nationalists.

Yet the Europeans' advantages were illusory: Cannon and armored cars whose mobility and firepower had been effective on the paved roads and open terrain of Europe ground to a halt in the jungles of Asia. Guerrilla warfare became the ideal strategy—one the rebels were forced into by their very lack of heavy arms. Maneuvering without front lines and avoiding set battles, the guerrillas used their flexibility as a weapon. They knew the land and lived off it; they chose their targets with care, struck by surprise, then faded back into terrain that made counterattack almost impossible.

In 1946, Ho Chi Minh characterized the opposing forces in Vietnam in a prophetic parable: "If the tiger ever stands still," he said, "the elephant will crush him. But the tiger will not stand still. He will leap upon the back of the elephant, tearing huge chunks from his side; then he will leap back into the dark jungle. And slowly the elephant will bleed to death."

A group of captured Malayan Communists—including three women—are guarded by a British soldier after a raid in which their leader (right) was killed.

Dutch marines board a landing craft at Surabaya in July 1947. By such means, the Dutch occupied large coastal areas of Java and all its major ports, before a U.N.-sponsored cease-fire halted their operation against the Indonesian nationalists.

Dutch infantrymen struggle to move their bicycles inland from a riverbank in Sumatra.

THE LIMITS OF MODERN MOBILITY

For the most part, the coastlines and rivers of the contested lands belonged to the Europeans. Equipped with versatile landing craft and amphibious vehicles of a kind that had proved effective from Normandy to Iwo Jima, they were able to patrol shallow waters and move men and supplies with relative dispatch.

On land, however, the story was different. In most places, roads were poor or nonexistent. Overgrown jungle trails made difficult going even for troops on bicycles. Motorized columns, when the Europeans tried to use them, moved slowly and predictably along the few available roads, and presented easy targets for the well-informed guerrillas lying in ambush.

Foreign Legionnaires assemble in amphibious vehicles, dubbed "crabs," in Vietnam's Mekong delta.

Trucks filled with French troops stop on a jungle track during a sweep against the Vietminh. Such missions had to be completed by dark to avoid counterattack.

HOME AND BATTLEGROUND IN THE BUSH

For the Asian guerrilla, the villages that dotted the landscape were places to capture arms, destroy vehicles and intimidate government loyalists. Usually the guerrilla's home was the bush, an ideal environment for his kind of fighting, with ample cover and an abundant supply of the bamboo stalks needed to fashion mantraps of deadly poisoned shafts called punji sticks.

But not every rebel was at home in the jungle. A guerrilla leader in Malaya noted rather poignantly that one of his men was sometimes "fearful" in the jungle, and that another was "not hygienic enough."

Barely visible in the undergrowth, Vietminh guerrillas wait to ambush a French column in 1948.

Indonesian nationalists in a motley array of uniforms triumphantly wave their rifles after capturing a town. A helmeted rebel (foreground) holds a machine gun.

Their weapons slung from bamboo poles, members of a Vietminh light artillery unit push through the bush.

In the wake of a 1947 Vietminh mortar attack in Cochin China, civilian vehicles burn and survivors run for cover.

ASIAN LOYALISTS WHO FOUGHT ASIANS

Like the Gurkhas of Nepal and the Indians who long had served the British Empire with valor, thousands of Asians enlisted in the fight against the insurgents in their countries. The pay was meager, but the men were attracted in many cases by long-standing ties with the colonial administrators: Before the War began, Malays, for instance, had served on police forces under the British and had been accorded relatively favored status.

In Indochina, large numbers of Vietnamese and Cambodians willingly joined the French Union forces. Some did so simply to be on what they believed would be the winning side. Others—such as the hill tribesmen—joined the French out of fear and hatred of the Communist Vietminh.

Lieut. General Sir Harold Briggs, the British commander, inspects a Malay jungle patrol in 1950.

A combined patrol of French and Indochinese soldiers returns to the village of Dai Mo, 15 miles from Hanoi. Barbed wire and bamboo pickets guard the village perimeter.

Searching for Communists in 1949, a team from a Malay-British police task force checks the identity of a farmer in Malaya's interior.

Indochinese sentries, members of a unit armed and commanded by the French, man a guard tower overlooking a rural thoroughfare 10 miles from Saigon.

As night approaches, French troops cluster in the relative security of a landing craft on an Indochinese river. After dark, much of the jungle belonged to the Vietminh.

Bayonets at the ready, Dutch marines wade cautiously through waist-high rice plants in east Java during a mission to root out Indonesian insurgents in mid-1948.

A FRUSTRATING CAMPAIGN OF "SEARCH AND DESTROY"

Western soldiers detested the jungle battlefield. The French called their struggle in Vietnam the "dirty war"—and grimly fought on against malaria, leeches and primitive booby traps.

Unable to find a massed enemy, the Europeans used the "search-and-destroy" tactic in which patrols methodically swept an area clear of rebels. Yet the colonialists' task was insuperable; they were aliens fighting indigenous enemies. Only in Malaya did the British overcome this hurdle in part: They resettled thousands of Malayans in areas where they could be protected—and kept apart—from the guerrillas.

For even battle-hard European troops, the psychological burden grew heavy. In 1950 a French noncom summed it up: "There are ten thousand Vietnamese for every hundred Frenchmen."

British military planners in Kuala Lumpur, Malaya's capital, plot counterinsurgency-patrol routes.

Carrying a captured guerrilla bound hand and foot over a pole, British soldiers in Malaya return to their base following a fire fight in the jungle.

199

As their unit presents arms, French marines in 1947 inter a comrade in a patch of friendly soil—the garden of a French official's residence in a village where

they had just fought off an attack. By the time they had lost the War in 1954, French Union forces had suffered 140,992 casualties, including 75,867 killed.

BIBLIOGRAPHY

Acheson, Dean, *Present at the Creation: My Years in the State Department.* W. W. Norton, 1969.

Allen, Charles (ed.), *Plain Tales from the Raj: Images of British India in the Twentieth Century.* London: André Deutsch, 1975.

Allen, G. C., *The Japanese Economy.* St. Martin's Press, 1981.

Allen, Louis, *The End of the War in Asia.* London: Hart-Davis, MacGibbon, 1976.

Anderson, Benedict R. O'G., *Java in a Time of Revolution: Occupation and Resistance, 1944-1946.* Cornell University Press, 1972.

Ashe, Geoffrey, *Gandhi.* Stein and Day, 1968.

Barrett, David D., *Dixie Mission: The United States Army Observer Group in Yenan, 1944.* University of California Center for Chinese Studies, 1970.

Beals, Carleton, *Great Guerrilla Warriors.* Prentice-Hall, 1970.

Beasley, W. G., *The Modern History of Japan.* Praeger, 1974.

Bedlington, Stanley S., *Malaysia and Singapore: The Building of New States.* Cornell University Press, 1978.

Belden, Jack, *China Shakes the World.* Monthly Review Press, 1970.

Benedict, Ruth, *The Chrysanthemum and the Sword: Patterns of Japanese Culture.* New American Library, 1974.

Bisson, T. A., "Japan: Recovery and Reaction." *The Nation,* February 2, 1952.

Blair, Clay, Jr., *MacArthur.* Nelson Doubleday, 1977.

Bolitho, Hector, *Jinnah: Creator of Pakistan.* London: John Murray, 1955.

Borton, Hugh, *Japan's Modern Century: From Perry to 1970.* Ronald Press, 1970.

Buhite, Russell D., *Patrick J. Hurley and American Foreign Policy.* Cornell University Press, 1973.

Bullitt, William C., "The Saddest War." *Life,* December 29, 1947.

Burks, Ardath W., *Japan: Profile of a Postindustrial Power.* Westview Press, 1981.

Busch, Noel F., "A Report on Japan." *Life,* December 2, 1946.

Buss, Claude A., *Asia in the Modern World: A History of China, Japan, South and Southeast Asia.* Macmillan, 1964.

Cady, John F., *A History of Modern Burma.* Cornell University Press, 1958.

Caldwell, John C., *The Korea Story.* Henry Regnery, 1952.

Calvocoressi, Peter, and Guy Wint, *Total War: Causes and Courses of the Second World War.* Penguin Books, 1979.

Campbell-Johnson, Alan, *Mission with Mountbatten.* E. P. Dutton, 1953.

Cartier-Bresson, Henri, and Barbara Brakeley Miller, *China: Photographed by Henri Cartier-Bresson.* Bantam Books, 1964.

Cary, Otis (ed.), *War-Wasted Asia: Letters, 1945-46.* Tokyo: Kodansha International, 1975.

"Challenge Accepted." *Time,* July 3, 1950.

Chassin, Lionel Max, *The Communist Conquest of China: A History of the Civil War, 1945-1949.* Transl. by Timothy Osato and Louis Gelas. Harvard University Press, 1965.

Clubb, O. Edmund:
 China & Russia: The "Great Game." Columbia University Press, 1971.
 20th Century China. Columbia University Press, 1978.

Coast, John, *Recruit to Revolution: Adventure and Politics in Indonesia.* London: Christophers, 1952.

Collins, Larry, and Dominique LaPierre, *Freedom at Midnight.* Simon and Schuster, 1975.

Coughlin, William J., *Conquered Press; The MacArthur Era in Japanese Journalism.* Pacific Books, 1952.

Crockett, Frederick E., "How the Trouble Began in Java." *Harper's Magazine,* March 1946.

Crozier, Brian, *The Man Who Lost China: The First Full Biography of Chiang Kai-shek.* Charles Scribner's Sons, 1976.

Dahm, Bernhard:
 History of Indonesia in the Twentieth Century. Transl. by P. S. Falla. London: Praeger, 1971.
 Sukarno and the Struggle for Indonesian Independence. Transl. by Mary F. Somers Heidhues. Cornell University Press, 1969.

Das, Durga, *India from Curzon to Nehru and After.* John Day, 1970.

Davies, John Paton, Jr., *Dragon by the Tail: American, British, Japanese and Russian Encounters with China and One Another.* W. W. Norton, 1972.

Day, Beth, *The Philippines: Shattered Showcase of Democracy in Asia.* M. Evans, 1974.

Decker, Benton Weaver, and Edwina Naylor Decker, *Return of the Black Ships.* Vantage Press, 1978.

Donnison, F.S.V., *British Military Administration in the Far East, 1943-46.* London: Her Majesty's Stationery Office, 1956.

Doyle, Edward, Samuel Lipsman and the editors of Boston Publishing Company, *The Vietnam Experience:*
 Setting the Stage. Boston Publishing Company, 1981.
 Passing the Torch. Boston Publishing Company, 1981.

Doyle, Robert, "Report on Communist Shanghai." *Life,* October 17, 1949.

"Editorial: Gandhi." *Life,* February 9, 1948.

Edwardes, Michael:
 British India 1772-1947: A Survey of the Nature and Effects of Alien Rule. Taplinger, 1968.
 The Last Years of British India. World Publishing Company, 1963.

Fairbank, John K., *China Perceived: Images and Policies in Chinese-American Relations.* Alfred A. Knopf, 1974.

Fairbank, John K., Edwin O. Reischauer and Albert M. Craig, *East Asia: Tradition & Transformation.* Houghton Mifflin, 1978.

Fairbank, John K. (ed.), *The Cambridge History of China.* Vol. 10, *Late Ch'ing, 1800-1911, Part I.* Cambridge: Cambridge University Press, 1978.

Fall, Bernard B.:
 Last Reflections on a War. Doubleday, 1967.
 Street Without Joy: Indochina at War, 1946-54. Stackpole, 1961.
 The Two Viet-Nams: A Political and Military Analysis. Frederick A. Praeger, 1968.

Feis, Herbert, *The China Tangle: The American Effort in China from Pearl Harbor to the Marshall Mission.* Princeton University Press, 1953.

Fifield, Russell H., *Americans in Southeast Asia: The Roots of Commitment.* Thomas Y. Crowell, 1973.

Fischer, Louis:
 The Life of Mahatma Gandhi. Harper & Row, 1950.
 The Story of Indonesia. Harper & Brothers, 1959.

Fitzgerald, Charles Patrick, *Revolution in China.* Frederick A. Praeger, 1952.

Fontaine, André, *History of the Cold War: From the Korean War to the Present.* Transl. by Renaud Bruce. Pantheon Books, 1969.

Forbis, William H., *Japan Today: People, Places, Power.* Harper & Row, 1975.

Frank, Isaiah (ed.), *The Japanese Economy in International Perspective.* Johns Hopkins University Press, 1975.

Fryer, Donald W., and James C. Jackson, *Indonesia.* Westview Press, 1977.

Gandhi, M. K., *An Autobiography: Or the Story of My Experiments with Truth.* Transl. by Mahadev Desai. Ahmedabad: Navajivan Publishing House, 1969.

Gibney, Frank, "The Birth of a New Japan." *Life,* September 10, 1951.

Gopal, Sarvepalli, *Jawaharlal Nehru: A Biography:*
 Vol. 1. Harvard University Press, 1976.
 Vol. 2. Harvard University Press, 1979.

"The Great Migration." *Life,* November 3, 1947.

Greene, Graham, "Malaya, the Forgotten War." *Life,* July 30, 1951.

Gunther, John, *The Riddle of MacArthur: Japan, Korea and the Far East.* Harper & Row, 1951.

Hadley, Eleanor M., *Antitrust in Japan.* Princeton University Press, 1970.

Halle, Louis J., *The Cold War as History.* Harper & Row, 1967.

Hammer, Ellen J., *The Struggle for Indochina, 1940-1955.* Stanford University Press, 1968.

"Heavy Industry for Japan." *Business Week,* March 26, 1949.

Heijboer, Pierre, *De Politionele Acties.* Haarlem: Fibula-Van Dishoeck, 1979.

Hough, Richard, *Mountbatten.* Random House, 1981.

Htin Aung, *A History of Burma.* Columbia University Press, 1967.

"An Incident in Malaya." *Life,* August 2, 1948.

"India Loses Her 'Great Soul.' " *Life,* February 9, 1948.

"India's Leaders." *Life,* May 27, 1946.

Isaacs, Harold R., *No Peace for Asia.* M.I.T. Press, 1967.

Jack, Homer A. (ed.), *The Gandhi Reader: A Source Book of His Life and Writings.* Indiana University Press, 1956.

"Japan Blames U.S. For Troubles." *U.S. News & World Report,* April 28, 1950.

Japanese Government Ministry of Transportation, *Quarterly Bulletin of Transportation.* Tokyo, January-March 1954.

"Japan's Economic Recovery." *The World Today,* September 1952.

Johnson, U. Alexis, *The Memoirs of U. Alexis Johnson.* Unpublished manuscript (to be published 1983).

Jones, Howard Palfrey, *Indonesia: The Possible Dream.* Harcourt Brace Jovanovich, 1971.

Kahin, George McTurnan, *Nationalism and Revolution in Indonesia.* Cornell University Press, 1952.

Kawai, Kazuo, *Japan's American Interlude.* University of Chicago Press, 1960.

Kirby, S. Woodburn, *The War Against Japan:* Vol. 5, *The Surrender of Japan.* London: Her Majesty's Stationery Office, 1969.

Klein, Lawrence, and Kazushi Ohkawa (eds.), *Economic Growth: The Japanese Experience since the Meiji Era.* Richard D. Irwin, 1968.

Kublin, Hyman, *India.* Houghton Mifflin, 1973.

Kulkarni, V. B., *The Indian Triumvirate: A Political Biography of Mahatma Gandhi, Sardar Patel and Pandit Nehru.* Bombay: Bharatiya Vidya Bhavan, 1969.

Kurian, George Thomas, *Historical and Cultural Dictionary of India.* Scarecrow Press, 1976.

"Labor Policies and Programs in Japan Under the Occupation." *Monthly Labor Review,* February 1947.

The Labor Union Movement in Postwar Japan. Tokyo: Daily Labor Press, 1954.

Legge, J. D., *Sukarno: A Political Biography.* Praeger, 1972.

"Life in Tokyo." *Life,* December 3, 1945.

Livingston, Jon, Joe Moore and Felicia Oldfather (eds.), *The Japan Reader:*
 Imperial Japan, 1800-1945. Pantheon Books, 1973.
 Postwar Japan, 1945 to the Present. Pantheon Books, 1973.

Lord, John, *The Maharajahs.* Random House, 1971.

Lumby, E. W. R., *The Transfer of Power in India 1945-7.* Frederick A. Praeger, 1954.

MacArthur, Douglas, *Reminiscences.* McGraw-Hill, 1964.

McAlister, John T., Jr., *Vietnam: The Origins of Revolution.* Alfred A. Knopf, 1969.

McMahon, Robert J., *Colonialism and Cold War: The United States and the Struggle for Indonesian Independence, 1945-49.* Cornell University Press, 1981.

Manchester, William, *American Caesar: Douglas MacArthur, 1880-1964.* Little, Brown, 1978.

Mao Tse-tung, *Mao Tse-tung on Guerrilla Warfare.* Transl. by Samuel B. Griffith II. Anchor Press, 1978.

Mao Tse-tung, *Selected Works,* Vols. 4 and 5. International Publishers, 1956.

Maraini, Fosco, *Meeting with Japan.* Transl. by Eric Mosbacher. Viking Press, 1960.

Martic, Milos, *Insurrection: Five Schools of Revolutionary Thought.* Dunellen, 1975.

May, Brian, *The Indonesian Tragedy*. London: Routledge & Kegan Paul, 1978.

May, Ernest R., and James C. Thomson Jr. (eds.), *American-East Asian Relations: A Survey*. Harvard University Press, 1972.

Mears, Helen, "Our Far-flung Correspondents: Tokyo Revisited." *The New Yorker*, October 19, 1946.

Mehrotra, S. R., *India and the Commonwealth, 1885-1929*. Frederick A. Praeger, 1965.

Mehta, Ved, *Mahatma Gandhi and His Apostles*. Viking Press, 1977.

Mende, Tibor, *South-east Asia between Two Worlds*. London: Turnstile Press, 1955.

Menon, V. P.:
The Story of the Integration of the Indian States. Macmillan, 1956.
The Transfer of Power in India. Princeton University Press, 1957.

Miller, Harry, *A Short History of Malaysia*. Frederick A. Praeger, 1967.

Millis, Walter, *Arms and Men: A Study in American Military History*. G. P. Putnam's Sons, 1956.

Moon, Penderel, *Divide and Quit*. University of California Press, 1962.

Moorad, George, *Lost Peace in China*. E. P. Dutton, 1949.

Moraes, Frank, *Jawaharlal Nehru: A Biography*. Macmillan, 1958.

Mosley, Leonard, *The Last Days of the British Raj*. Harcourt, Brace & World, 1961.

Mountbatten, Vice Admiral the Earl Mountbatten of Burma, *Post Surrender Tasks: Section E of the Report to the Combined Chiefs of Staff by the Supreme Allied Commander, South East Asia, 1943-1945*. London: Her Majesty's Stationery Office, 1969.

Murphy, Robert, *Diplomat Among Warriors*. Doubleday, 1964.

Nanda, B. R., *Mahatma Gandhi. A Biography*. New Delhi: Allied Publishers Private Limited, 1968.

Neville, Robert, "The Princes of India." *Life*, April 21, 1947.

Oliver, Robert T.:
Syngman Rhee: The Man Behind the Myth. Dodd Mead, 1960.
The Truth about Korea. London: Putnam, 1951.

"Pakistan Struggles for Survival." *Life*, January 5, 1948.

Palmier, Leslie H.:
Indonesia. Walker, 1966.
Indonesia and the Dutch. London: Oxford University Press, 1962.

Patrick, Hugh, and Henry Rosovsky (eds.), *Asia's New Giant: How the Japanese Economy Works*. Brookings Institution, 1976.

Patti, Archimedes L. A., *Why Viet Nam? Prelude to America's Albatross*. University of California Press, 1980.

Payne, Robert, *The Life and Death of Mahatma Gandhi*. E. P. Dutton, 1969.

"The Peace City: Hiroshima Celebrates Day of Atomic Bomb." *Life*, September 1, 1947.

Pelissier, Roger, *The Awakening of China, 1793-1949*. Transl. and ed. by Martin Kieffer. G. P. Putnam's Sons, 1967.

Penders, C.L.M., *The Life and Times of Sukarno*. Fairleigh Dickinson University Press, 1974.

Perry, John Curtis, *Beneath the Eagle's Wings: Americans in Occupied Japan*. Dodd, Mead, 1980.

Petillo, Carol Morris, *Douglas MacArthur: The Philippine Years*. Indiana University Press, 1981.

Philips, C. H., *The Evolution of India and Pakistan, 1858 to 1947*. London: Oxford University Press, 1964.

Reardon-Anderson, James, *Yenan and the Great Powers: The Origins of Chinese Communist Foreign Policy, 1944-1946*. Columbia University Press, 1980.

Reid, Anthony, *The Indonesian National Revolution, 1945-1950*. Hawthorn, Victoria, Australia: Longman, 1974.

Reischauer, Edwin O.:
Japan: The Story of a Nation. New York: Alfred A. Knopf, 1981.
The Japanese. Belknap Press of Harvard University Press, 1981.
The United States and Japan. Harvard University Press, 1965.

"Revolt in Java." *Life*, January 28, 1946.

Rose, Lisle A., *Roots of Tragedy: The United States and the Struggle for Asia, 1945-1953*. Greenwood Press, 1976.

Ryan, N. J., *A History of Malaysia and Singapore*. Kuala Lumpur: Oxford University Press, 1976.

Sainteny, Jean, *Ho Chi Minh and His Vietnam: A Personal Memoir*. Transl. by Herma Briffault. Cowles Book Company, 1972.

Schuman, Frederick L., *International Politics: The Western State System in Mid-Century*. McGraw-Hill, 1953.

Sebald, William J., and Russell Brines, *With MacArthur in Japan: A Personal History of the Occupation*. W. W. Norton, 1965.

Shaplen, Robert, *The Lost Revolution: The U.S. in Vietnam, 1946-1966*. Harper Colophon Books (Harper & Row), 1966.

Shaw, Henry I., Jr., *The United States Marines in North China, 1945-1949*. Washington: Historical Branch, G-3 Division, Headquarters, U.S. Marine Corps, 1968.

Sheridan, James E., *China in Disintegration: The Republican Era in Chinese History, 1912-1949*. The Free Press, 1975.

Shewmaker, Kenneth E., *Americans and Chinese Communists, 1927-1945: A Persuading Encounter*. Cornell University Press, 1971.

Shirer, William L., *Gandhi: A Memoir*. Simon and Schuster, 1979.

Singh, Rajendra, *Post-War Occupation Forces: Japan and South-East Asia, Official History of the Indian Armed Forces in the Second World War, 1939-1945*. Kanpur, India: Combined Inter-Services Historical Section, India & Pakistan, 1958.

Singhal, Damodar P., *Pakistan*. Prentice-Hall, 1972.

Sjahrir, Soetan, *Out of Exile*. Transl. by Charles Wolf Jr. John Day, 1949.

Smail, John R. W., "Bandung in the Early Revolution, 1945-1946: A Study in the Social History of the Indonesian Revolution." Monograph Series, Modern Indonesia Project, Cornell University Department of Asian Studies, 1964.

Smith, Vincent A., *The Oxford History of India*. Ed. by Percival Spear. Oxford: Clarendon Press, 1967.

Snow, Edgar, *Red Star Over China*. Grove Press, 1977.

Spear, Percival:
India: A Modern History. University of Michigan Press, 1972.
The Oxford History of Modern India, 1740-1975. Delhi: Oxford University Press, 1978.

Spencer, Cornelia, *Chiang Kai-shek: Generalissimo of Nationalist China*. John Day, 1968.

Stueck, William Whitney, Jr., *The Road to Confrontation: American Policy toward China and Korea, 1947-1950*. University of North Carolina Press, 1981.

Suh, Dae-Sook, *The Korean Communist Movement, 1918-1948*. Princeton University Press, 1967.

Sukarno and Cindy Adams, *Sukarno: An Autobiography*. Bobbs-Merrill, 1965.

Sunderman, James F., *World War II in the Air: The Pacific*. Van Nostrand Reinhold, 1981.

Taylor, Alastair M., *Indonesian Independence and the United Nations*. London: Stevens & Sons, 1960.

Terrill, Ross, *Mao: A Biography*. Harper & Row, 1980.

Thomson, James C., Jr., Peter W. Stanley and John Curtis Perry, *Sentimental Imperialists: The American Experience in East Asia*. Harper & Row, 1981.

Tinker, Hugh, *The Union of Burma: A Study of the First Years of Independence*. London: Oxford University Press, 1967.

Toland, John, *The Rising Sun: The Decline and Fall of the Japanese Empire, 1936-1945*. Random House, 1970.

Torrens, James G., "Japan's Textile Industry." *Far Eastern Survey*, June 4, 1947.

Townsend, Peter, *The Last Emperor: An Intimate Account of George VI and the Fall of his Empire*. Simon and Schuster, 1976.

Trager, Frank N., *Burma from Kingdom to Republic: A Historical and Political Analysis*. Frederick A. Praeger, 1966.

Tregonning, K. G., *A History of Modern Malaya*. David McKay, 1964.

Trumbull, Robert, *The Scrutable East: A Correspondent's Report on Southeast Asia*. David McKay, 1964.

Tuchman, Barbara, *Stilwell and the American Experience in China, 1911-45*. Macmillan, 1971.

"Two-Billion Dollar Failure in Japan." *Fortune*, April 1949.

U.S. Department of State:
Foreign Relations of the United States: Diplomatic Papers 1945, Vol. 6, *The British Commonwealth: The Far East*. Government Printing Office, 1969.
Foreign Relations of the United States 1949, Vol. 7, *The Far East and Australasia*, Part 2. Government Printing Office, 1976.

U.S. Military Academy, *Revolutionary Warfare, South Korea 1948-1954*. Department of Military Art and Engineering, Notes for Instructors, HM 486, Lesson 34.

U.S. Senate, Subcommittee to Investigate the Administration of the Internal Security Act and Other Internal Security Laws of the Committee on the Judiciary, *The Amerasia Papers: A Clue to the Catastrophe of China*, Vol. 1. Government Printing Office, 1970.

U.S. Strategic Bombing Survey, *The Strategic Air Operation of Very Heavy Bombardment in the War Against Japan (Twentieth Air Force), Final Report*. Government Printing Office, 1946.

Van Mook, H. J., *The Stakes of Democracy in Southeast Asia*. W. W. Norton, 1950.

Vlekke, Bernard H. M., *The Story of the Dutch East Indies*. Harvard University Press, 1945.

Wehl, David, *The Birth of Indonesia*. London: George Allen & Unwin, 1948.

White, Theodore H., *In Search of History: A Personal Adventure*. Harper & Row, 1978.

White, Theodore H., and Annalee Jacoby, *Thunder Out of China*. William Sloane Associates, 1946.

Whitney, Courtney, *MacArthur: His Rendezvous with History*. Alfred A. Knopf, 1956.

Williams, Justin, Sr., *Japan's Political Revolution under MacArthur: A Participant's Account*. University of Georgia Press, 1979.

Willoughby, Charles A., and John Chamberlain, *MacArthur: 1941-1951*. McGraw-Hill, 1954.

Wittner, Lawrence S., "MacArthur and the Missionaries: God and Man in Occupied Japan." *Pacific Historical Review*, February 1971.

Wolf, Charles, Jr., *The Indonesian Story: The Birth, Growth and Structure of the Indonesian Republic*. Greenwood Press, 1973.

Wolpert, Stanley:
India. Prentice-Hall, 1965.
A New History of India. Oxford University Press, 1982.

Woodruff, Philip, *The Men Who Ruled India: The Guardians*. London: Jonathan Cape, 1963.

Yamamura, Kozo, *Economic Policy in Postwar Japan: Growth Versus Economic Democracy*. University of California Press, 1967.

Yano, Tsuneta, and Kyoichi Shirasaki, *Nippon: A Charted Survey of Japan, 1936*. Transl. by Z. Tamotsu Iwado. Tokyo Kokusei-Sha, 1936.

Yano, Tsuneta, Memorial Society, *Nippon: A Charted Survey of Japan, 1955*. Tokyo: Kokusei-Sha, 1955.

Yim, Louise, *My Forty Year Fight for Korea*. A. A. Wyn, 1951.

Yoshida, Shigeru, *The Yoshida Memoirs: The Story of Japan in Crisis*. Transl. by Kenichi Yoshida. Houghton Mifflin, 1962.

Zainu'ddin, Ailsa, *A Short History of Indonesia*. Praeger, 1970.

Zinkin, Taya, *India*. Walker, 1966.

PICTURE CREDITS

Credits from left to right are separated by semicolons, from top to bottom by dashes.

COVER and page 1: Margaret Bourke-White for *Life*.

"ASIA FOR THE ASIANS"—8, 9: Map by Leonard Vigliarolo and Diana Raquel Vazquez. 10: U.S. Army. 12, 13: Johnny Florea for *Life*. 15: Wide World. 16: Imperial War Museum, London. 18: Wide World.

A FRIENDLY CONFRONTATION—22-25: U.S. Army. 26, 27: U.S. Army(2); UPI. 28, 29: Wide World; U.S. Army—U.S. Marine Corps. 30, 31: Wide World(2)—U.S. Army. 32, 33: George Silk for *Life*; Johnny Florea for *Life*; U.S. Army—Joe Scherschel for *Life*. 34-37: U.S. Army.

A BENIGN INVASION—40: UPI. 42: National Archives (Neg. No. 306-NT-1147-F9). 44-46: U.S. Army. 47, 49: Wide World.

JAPAN REBORN—52-54: U.S. Army. 55-57: Wide World. 58, 59: Johnny Florea for *Life*; Carl Mydans for *Life*. 60, 61: U.S. Army—Carl Mydans for *Life*. 62, 63: Wide World(2)—Joe Scherschel for *Life*. 64, 65: Wide World.

INDIA'S VIOLENT DESTINY—69: Wide World. 72: Jack Birns for *Life*. 73: BBC Hulton Picture Library, London. 75: Margaret Bourke-White for *Life*. 77: Wide World. 80, 81: Margaret Bourke-White for *Life*; Popperfoto, London—Central Press Photos Ltd., London; Margaret Bourke-White for *Life*. 83: Map by Diana Raquel Vazquez. 84, 85: Hunnar Stronachs Ltd., Bombay.

THE APOSTLE OF FREEDOM—88, 89: Margaret Bourke-White for *Life*. 90: Gabriel, Durban, South Africa. 91: BBC Hulton Picture Library, London. 92, 93: BBC Hulton Picture Library, London; Wide World; Camera Press, London. 94: Udit Gopal, Bombay—David Douglas Duncan for *Life*. 95: UPI. 96, 97: Wide World; Margaret Bourke-White for *Life*. 98: Wide World—Henri Cartier-Bresson from Magnum. 99: Henri Cartier-Bresson from Magnum. 100, 101: Henri Cartier-Bresson.

DEFEAT FOR THE DUTCH—104: Information Section, Consulate General of Indonesia, New York. 108: Government Institute for War Documentation, The Hague. 109: Dutch Institute for Military History, The Hague. 111: Imperial War Museum, London. 112, 113: Johnny Florea for *Life*, inset, Wide World. 115: National Archives (Neg. No. 306-NT-1120-X2). 116, 117: Government Institute for War Documentation, The Hague. 118: UPI. 120: National Archives (Neg. No. 306-NT-1120-8).

LAST DAYS OF COLONIALISM—122, 123: Magnum. 124, 125: Henri Cartier-Bresson from Magnum. 126, 127: David Douglas Duncan for *Life*(2); Margaret Bourke-White for *Life*. 128, 129: UPI; Carl Mydans for *Life*—Jack Birns for *Life*. 130, 131: BBC Hulton Picture Library, London; Howard Sochureck for *Life*.

CHINA'S WAR WITHIN—134: Map by Leonard Vigliarolo. 136, 140: UPI. 142: Fotokhronika-TASS, Moscow. 144, 145: Wide World. 146: National Archives (Neg. No. 306-NT-1330-B1)—Wide World. 148, 149: Jim Burke for *Life*.

IMAGES OF CIVIL WAR—152, 153: Henri Cartier-Bresson from Magnum. 154: Henri Cartier-Bresson from Magnum; Magnum. 155-165: Henri Cartier-Bresson from Magnum.

CONTESTS WITH COMMUNISM—168: Jack Birns for *Life*. 171: Imperial War Museum, London. 173: Edimedia-Snark, Paris—Alan Squires. 174, 175: Jean-Loup Charmet, Private Collection, Paris—Parisien Libéré, Archives Tallandier, Paris; Ngo Vinh Long Collection. 178: East-West Photo Agency. 179: Alfred Eisenstaedt for *Life*. 180: U.S. Army—Wide World. 181: National Archives (Neg. No. 306-NT-1001-D11)—Alfred Eisenstaedt for *Life*. 183: East-West Photo Agency. 184, 185: Carl Mydans for *Life*. 186: U.S. Army.

A NEW KIND OF WARFARE—188, 189: Carl Mydans for *Life*. 190, 191: Jack Birns for *Life*. 192, 193: National Archives (Neg. No. 306-NT-1120-X16); E.C.P. Armées, France—Keystone; E.C.P. Armées, France. 194, 195: Viet Nam Information Service, Hanoi; Sovfoto—National Archives (Neg. No. 306-NT-1120-X1); Viet Nam Information Service, Hanoi. 196: BBC Hulton Picture Library, London—Carl Mydans for *Life*. 197: BBC Hulton Picture Library, London—Jack Birns for *Life*. 198: Carl Mydans for *Life*—Koninklijke Marine Afdeling Maritieme Historie, The Netherlands. 199: BBC Hulton Picture Library, London—Graphic Photo Union, London. 200: E.C.P. Armées, France.

ACKNOWLEDGMENTS

For help given in the preparation of this book, the editors wish to express their gratitude to Henri Cartier-Bresson, Paris; George Chalou, Assistant Chief, Modern Military Field Branch, The National Archives, Suitland, Maryland; Jeannette Chalufour, Archives Tallandier, Paris; Chandra, Bank Indonesia, New York City; T. Charman, E. C. Hine, J. W. Pavey and M. J. Willis, Imperial War Museum, London; Colonel Maurice Courdesses, Curator, Fonds Historique Général Leclerc, Saint-Germain-en-Laye, France; Rear Admiral Benton W. Decker, USN (Ret.), San Diego, California; F. De Rochemont, Indonesian Department, Dutch State Institute for War Documentation, Amsterdam; V. M. Destefano, Chief, Reference Library, U.S. Army Audiovisual Activity, The Pentagon, Washington, D.C.; Philippe Devillers, Paris; Julie Fischer, Boston Publishing Co., Boston, Massachusetts; Général Fonde, Ville-d'Avray, France; Margaret Gayle, Librarian, British Information Service, New York City; Mary Greene and Jo Ann Ollman, Corporate Affairs Research, RCA, New York City; Chia-Yaung Hu and Deborah White, Harvard-Yenching Library, Cambridge, Massachusetts; Susan Jonas, New York City; Brooks Kleber, Deputy Chief Historian, William Mossman and Hannah Zeidlik, U.S. Army Center for Military History, Washington, D.C.; Narenda Kumar, Consul for Press and Public Relations, Consulate General of India, New York City; Steven Levine, American University, Washington, D.C.; Françoise Mercier, Institut d'Histoire du Temps Present, Paris; Uhnsook Park, Oriental Division, New York Public Library, New York City; Connie Pender, Corporate Communications, Sony Corporation of America, New York City; Jerry Phillips, New York City; Amin Rianom, Consul for Press and Public Relations, Consulate General of Indonesia, New York City; Claude Sainteny, Paris; John S. Service, Berkeley, California; Whitney Smith, Flag Research Center, Winchester, Massachusetts; Toshiko Takahara and Roger Van Damme, Japan Information Center, New York City; John Taylor, Modern Military History Branch, National Archives, Washington, D.C.; Raymond "Turk" Westerling, Amsterdam; Marjorie Willis, BBC Hulton Picture Library, London.

The index for this book was prepared by Nicholas J. Anthony.

INDEX

Numerals in italics indicate an illustration of the subject mentioned.

207